DATE DUE			

THE POVERTY OF PREDICTION

The Poverty of Prediction

IAN MILES
Science Policy
Research Unit
University of Sussex

SAXON HOUSE | LEXINGTON BOOKS

Published by

SAXON HOUSE, D. C. Heath Ltd.
Westmead, Farnborough, Hants, England.

Jointly with

LEXINGTON BOOKS, D. C. Heath & Co.
Lexington, Mass. USA.

ISBN 0 347 01085 7

Printed in Great Britain by Robert MacLehose and Company Limited
Printers to the University of Glasgow

Contents

Preface and Acknowledgements

The prophet and the visionary could never have been replaced by the sociologist or political philosopher; nobody paid much attention to their inchoate ramblings except a few idealists and opportunists. With the advent of the computer and the statistician, however, we acquired new guides to the future. What was more, these guides could not only read the signs on the trail, but could blaze new trails with a truly modern technology, erecting signposts in an up-to-date terminology. Whereas the old-fashioned social commentator lacked a ready grasp of jargon and hid his literacy in obscure magazines and books, the hard-headed futurologist flaunts his numeracy in the mass media while reserving the detailed justification of his precisely specified plans and proposals for technical reports. Eventually social engineering becomes almost pure technology; whenever trends show the least sign of deviation from their prescribed paths, warning lights flash, circuits are operated, and the levers of social change are pulled to ensure that the future is not straying from the bounds of prediction.

Fortunately, there is no imminent danger of this future descending upon us. It has been conjured up by a process of selective extrapolation: some of the trends in modern society and some of the wilder statements of futures researchers have been taken at their face value and others have been ignored. This both dramatises the issues and displays the enormous power of selective attention where questions of the future are concerned. These trends and claims are at the heart of the question around which this book is framed. What is, and what will be, the impact of quantification in social research on the way in which images of the future are formed, both in the orthodox social sciences and in the unorthodox field of futures research?

Much of the discussion in this book is inevitably critical, encountering limitations and problems involved in addressing problems about the future in particular ways. Contrary to what this might suggest, I believe both futures research and the use of quantitative techniques in social science to be of great potential worth and importance. Accordingly I have tried to depict some of the variety and scope of this material and its possible applications. But, as the title of the book expresses, these approaches may be used in ways which impoverish our appraisal and construction of the future.

It is impossible to acknowledge more than a fraction of the people who have given me help and encouragement in preparing this work. In particular thanks must go to the STAFF (Social and Technological Alternatives for the Future) group at the Science Policy Research Unit, and especially to Chris Freeman and Marie Jahoda; to librarians Val McNaughton and Viv Johnson who displayed dedication beyond the call of duty in tracking down obscure references for me; to everyone who struggled with my handwriting, especially Hazel Robards who actually conquered it; and to my families and friends, especially Valerie and Lera. At the risk of trying their patience even further, I will follow custom and admit that the responsibility for the contents of this book is mine alone.

I would like to thank John Goldthorpe and the editors of the *Archives Européene de Sociologie* for permission to quote from the paper 'Theories of Industrial Society'; the Organisation for Economic Co-operation and Development, Paris for permission to quote from Ithiel de Sola Pool's contribution to *Perspectives of Planning,* edited by E. Jantsch; and Routledge and Kegan Paul and Basic Books Inc. for permission to quote from Karl Popper's *The Poverty of Historicism.*

The work on which this book is based was carried out while I was a Research Fellow at the Science Policy Research Unit, University of Sussex, and it was supported by a grant from the Leverhulme Foundation.

Ian Miles
June 1975

1 Prediction: an Unnatural History?

Are quantitative research methods in the social sciences bringing about a new era of social research in which accurate social prediction and successful social planning will be the rule? Or does futures research commit the error of historicism and effectively stifle debate about future possibilities radically different from those derived from extrapolating present trends?

In this chapter the paradoxical stance of futures researchers who advocate policies of piecemeal social engineering, while basing their analyses on historicist methods, is described. By disentangling Popper's views on historicism and social philosophy from those on social prediction and policy, some sense is made of the apparent paradox, and such basic questions about the contribution of social science to the study of the future as are posed above are set out. The chapter concludes with an outline of the aims and contents of this book.

Prediction in social science

The term 'prediction' is often encountered in the contemporary social science literature, especially in journals and books reporting quantitative research and analysis. For example, studies of the correlation between people's attitudes towards members of other races and their patterns of behaviour in real-life situations may lead to conclusions in which it is stated that discriminatory actions have been successfully predicted from measures of attitudes. Similarly, the discovery in a study based on statistical data drawn from various countries that a regression equation can be found which links, for example, the intensity of civil wars to the prevalence of particular socio-economic conditions, is interpreted as yielding a prediction of the former by the latter. Such examples could be multiplied indefinitely.

What is of significance here is that the use of the term 'prediction' in such studies has little in common with its everyday sense. Research of this sort is rarely concerned with the forecasting of a future event in terms of a

1

set of present conditions, although such studies do of course exist. Instead, the 'prediction' involved is usually an assessment, by statistical techniques and criteria, of systematic associations between events observed in the past. The social scientist is usually satisfied with establishing the existence of an expected relationship at a reasonable level of statistical significance in a given set of observations, and is less bothered about testing out the prognostic value of his or her findings. In contrast, the present volume is concerned with the uses of social science in prognosis and forecasting. It will involve review of both current 'movements' or orientations in social science, and of specific areas of research in which 'predictions' in the usual sense are apparent.

The causal explanation of past phenomena in terms of other past events could be seen as a stage in the movement of the social sciences along the path of scientific progress described in traditional textbooks: from observation and explanation to prediction and finally control. In this interpretation, the location by social research of systematic regularities, or of societal 'laws' whereby the consequences of a particular configuration of initial conditions can be retrospectively 'predicted' to an acceptable degree of accuracy, could be seen as opening the way for the eventual prediction of future phenomena on the basis of present events.

Social scientists are often loath to predict future developments in any degree of detail on the basis of their analyses. While much fuss is made about the importance of a given research project or the relevance of certain findings, psychologists, sociologists and other researchers in similar established academic disciplines maintain an ambivalent attitude towards anything resembling futurology. However, the demand for social prediction seems to be growing, and, whether or not this is a fad, futures research is big business, with large firms, state agencies and international organisations as its major purchasers. There have been various historically important forecasts made by social scientists, from Malthus and Marx onward, of course. In a review of the state of the art in social forecasting Duncan (1969) has provided some interesting insights into such widely circulated (and still regularly revived) forecasts made in the earlier decades of this century as the belief in declining national intelligence levels.

Proponents of quantitative methodology in social research have argued that, by adopting operational definitions which will yield numerical assessments of social phenomena that can be manipulated, statistically, social research will evolve towards the goals of prediction and control. The argument runs that, in the past, the social sciences have been overly concerned with erecting grand all-encompassing theories. These purported to explain practically everything but their concepts were so abstract and

2

loosely defined that they could in fact be used to explain and predict almost anything. Precise theories based on quantitative study will set this right. Unchallengeable social data will be gathered by sophisticated methodologists and stored in computerised data banks for the access of later researchers. Social laws and relationships between variables will be discovered by statistical analyses of such data, rather than waiting upon intuitive formulation by brilliant but often misguided individuals. Even if such analyses are somewhat more restricted in scope at present than the grand theories of the past, this may be soon overcome by the juxtaposition of 'middle range' theories to form large computer models, faithfully capturing all the significant aspects of society.

The spread of an ethos of quantification in the social sciences has taken place alongside the development of what is variously termed 'futures research', 'futures studies', and 'futurology' as a discernible field of study. Recent trends in both conventional social science and this latter field suggest that interpenetration of the two is underway, and this book sets out to examine the implications of such an interpenetration. This will be accomplished chiefly with reference to those areas of social research usually subsumed under the disciplines of social psychology, sociology and political science, where the potential contributions of social science, forecasting and planning to each other are less familiar than where research based in demography, geography or economics is concerned.

The poverty of historicism

In 1970 the sociologist John Goldthorpe drew attention to a curious paradox in the more widely publicised literature of futures research. This literature (e.g. Kahn and Wiener's *The Year 2000,* 1967) in common with the dominant American sociology of such writers as Kerr and Parsons (Kerr et al, 1962, Parsons, 1951, 1966) displayed what Goldthorpe termed a 'crypto-historicist' character. By this he meant a mode of thought which 'can be shown to rest upon historicist assumptions or claims, even though historicist arguments may not be openly advanced or may be actually disavowed' (Goldthorpe, 1970, p.1). The paradox is not merely the re-emergence of scholarly historicism some decades after Karl Popper's critique of *The Poverty of Historicism* (originally published in the 1940s, and as a book in 1957). Rather, it lies in the combination in the futures literature of historicist analysis and prediction with prescriptions for policy makers that essentially amount to the 'piecemeal social engineering' approach advocated by Popper himself. To understand this paradox it is

3

necessary to look a little more closely first at Popper's attack on historicism and advocacy of piecemeal social engineering, and then at futures research of the kind Goldthorpe has described.

Popper (1957, p.3) describes historicism as 'an approach to the social sciences which assumes that *historical prediction* is their principal aim, and which assumes that this aim is attainable by discovering the "rhythms" or the "patterns", the "laws" or the "trends" that underlie the evolution of history . . . I am convinced that such historicist doctrines of method are at bottom responsible for the unsatisfactory state of the theoretical social sciences (other than economic theory)'. It should be made clear that Popper is not arguing against all attempts at social prediction or to develop theoretical laws to explain social actions. His criticism is specifically directed against the unwarranted extrapolation of trends, and the delineation of evolutionary laws describing the succession of historical epochs, as a means of anticipating the future.

The identification of trends or sequences in history, to Popper, merely establishes an existential fact. Projecting them to given an image of the future, however, is unfounded prophecy, and involves treating such trends as if they were universal laws. The evolutionary process is a single historical statement, about whose course universal falsifiable laws cannot be constructed. 'We cannot hope to test a universal hypothesis nor to find a natural law acceptable to science if we are for ever confined to the observation of one unique process. Nor can the observation of one unique process help us to foresee its future development' (Popper, 1957, p.109). (The attack on historicism thus partly rests upon Popper's widely accepted view of scientific method, in which the test of science is seen to be the falsifiability of hypotheses rather than their verification.) Instead, evolution proceeds in accordance with all kinds of causal laws as they operate in particular instances.

Evolutionary trends (or cycles), then, are not laws from which predictions may be derived. What is required for prediction is a specification of initial conditions and a statement of an operating law, which may together yield what Popper calls a conditional prediction. Trends may properly be forecast to continue if they are 'explained trends' resulting from the action of operating laws, but they are conditional: 'their persistence depends upon the persistence of specific initial conditions' (Popper, 1957, p.128). According to Popper, historicism fails to recognise this conditional nature of trends, and accords them absolute status. If trends are seen as varying with changing social conditions, then we do not have historicism.

Popper distinguishes between prophecy, in which 'we are told about an

4

event which we can do nothing to predict' and whose 'value lies in our being warned of the predicted event so that we can side-step it or meet it prepared', and technological predictions which are 'constructive, intimating the steps open to us *if* we want to achieve certain results' (Popper, 1957, p.43). Historicists tend to make prophecies. Believing that historical change makes generalisation (other than about universal laws) and social experiments impossible, they observe the historical record in order to make long term predictions involving large scale social changes. Popper contrasts his own approach: rather than a fatalistic identification with a prophesied future, he advocates a short term, experimental approach to producing social change in desired directions.

Popper rejects the 'holistic' assumption, which he claims is associated with historicism, that a better world can only be achieved by a 'complete' reconstruction of society. One rationale for this is his stance of indeterminism where questions of human action are concerned. Not only are our scientific laws forever unverifiable and always tentative and open to refutation, but social reality is also very complex and only partly understood. Plans and policies thus inevitably have unintended consequences, and the greater the change that they set out to institute, the more numerous and significant such consequences will be. The greater the change, futhermore, the more difficult it is to link its effects to particular causes and thus learn from experience, and the more humanly difficult it is to be critical. Popper argues that large scale social change actually demands totalitarian suppression of the justified criticism needed for rational social change. (This sounds remarkably like a statement of an operating law which would be open to empirical analysis, although Popper does not advance it as a tentative assertion.)

On this critique of holistic social experiments, Popper builds his case for piecemeal social engineering. What is needed is a social technology which could monitor the unintended consequences of policy and administration. Rather than prophesying an idealised future, we should concentrate on opening our institutions to feedback about the effects of attempts to achieve social goals and about changes in such goals. New ideas of social organisation need careful experimental testing from which mistakes may be learned. The principal of scientific falsification should be built into the social order and this requires a realistic, open society.

The paradox revealed in Goldthorpe's paper, then, is the juxtaposition of Popperian tactics of piecemeal social engineering with historicist predictions of the future by theorists of industrial society and futurologists. One ironic aspect of this is that while Popper's critique of historicism was explicitly directed against the use of Marxist conceptions of social change, the crypto-historicists are often using their forecasts as a weapon against Marxism (e.g. Rostow's *The Stages of Economic Growth*, 1960, is subtitled 'A Non-Communist Manifesto'). In effect they are advocating a historicism of affluence: civilisation does proceed in predictable stages, but the Marxist analysis is wrong. Prosperity rather than oppression has been brought about by industrial capitalism, and the history of society culminates in consensus rather than beginning afresh in revolution.

Goldthorpe sees the re-emergence of historicism as pivoting around the idea of 'industrial society', which is transformed in futurological (and increasingly in sociological) thought to the 'post-industrial society'. The cruder perspectives developed around this idea essentially assert that economic development and industrialisation proceed in basically similar ways everywhere; and that social and political institutions, structures and values are determined by these factors and thus also evolve according to this 'logic'. This should eventually lead to a convergence of industrial societies to a particular ideal type, which bears a remarkable similarity to 'the "managed" and "modernised", "open" and "affluent" capitalist society of the western world' (Goldthorpe, 1970, p.4).

Goldthorpe goes on to demonstrate that even the more sophisticated theorists of industrial society, such as Kerr and Parsons, present historicist analyses depsite their claims to the contrary. Extrapolation, description of evolutionary sequences, and a slightly diluted version of the convergence thesis are employed to assess the present state of society against a future ideal. Thus, different modes of social organisation are placed on evolutionary scales, with Soviet society proving to be inferior to that of the USA, by a 'value-free' scientific analysis. In fact the values underlying this analysis are those of economic efficiency; the policies it justifies are those of piecemeal reform. These theorists attempt, but fail to meet Popper's arguments against historicism by their reference to a vague 'logic of industrialisation', an existential but unexplained and unconditional set of 'stages of growth' or trends in 'structural-functional adaptations' which lack statements of operating laws.

According to Goldthorpe's account, despite initial statements to the contrary, the industrial society theorists do not accept the real possibility of multilinear social evolution. Thus while Kerr admits to diversity within the process of industrialisation, closer inspection reveals this diversity to be restricted to the relatively early stages of this process. With later industrial development different cultures become progressively more similar. 'All societies, whatever the path by which they entered the industrial world, will tend to approximate, even if asymptotically, the ideal form' (Goldthorpe, 1970, p.6). As with the historicist theories dismissed by Popper, these modern writers clearly ascribe virtue to the future society, which is open, diverse, tolerant and in a high state of evolution; their work is 'little less politically committed than were the historicist doctrines of the nineteenth century' (Goldthorpe, 1970, p.14).

Two further aspects of theories of industrial society are worth noting. One is the technocratic form assumed by crypto-historicism: 'insofar as the new theories of industrial society seek to identify a particular group or stratum as the key social agency of the future development of industrialism, it is invariably the scientists, technologists and managers who are picked out'; and 'the ultimate goal of industrial societies is taken as given: to maintain economic advance on the basis of a dynamic science and technology, while adjusting the existing social system *ad hoc,* as the requirements and consequences of this advance unfold, and sufficiently to contain social dissensus and conflict to a manageable level' (Goldthorpe, 1970, pp.13–14). Thus future society, the ideal against which the present may be judged, will be run by technicians on the basis of technical rationality. The second feature is its ethnocentrism: Western democratic capitalism is viewed as the closest approximation to an ideal industrial society, and the possibility of different cultures or different social contingencies being able to produce post-industrial societies differing substantially in their structural and cultural forms is not taken seriously. This is associated with a tendency 'to dismiss aspirations and programmes which stem from different perspectives solely on the grounds that they are incompatible with the way in which history, or social evolution is destined to go' (Goldthorpe, 1970, p.16). Thus historicist analysis obscures conceptions of alternative futures 'which, if more widely propagated and recognised, could significantly extend the range of effective socio-political choice' (Goldthorpe, 1970, p.16).

As Goldthorpe goes on to demonstrate, while many of the European founding fathers of modern futures studies had set out to provide anti-historicist visions of alternative futures (e.g. the 'futuribles' of de Jouvenel, 1967), the widely circulated work of such writers as Herman Kahn and Daniel Bell has absorbed the historicist essence of the industrial society theorists. Thus a great deal of current futures research consists of treating trends as universal laws, of having social predictions solely contingent upon technological and economic forecasting, of technological 'fixing' and technocratic planning, of prescriptions of piecemeal reform to ensure the adaptability of the *status quo,* and of pouring scorn upon alternative conceptions of the future.

The historicism of affluence

What accounts for the revival of historicism in futures studies and for its unholy alliance with piecemeal social engineering? Historicist social prediction may have been encouraged by the very success experienced by the forecasters of technological change, for one thing. While Popper argued that knowledge of future scientific and technical discoveries was impossible, since such knowledge would make such dicoveries in the present, technological forecasting suggested that this was off the point. It might not be possible to predict the details of a future technology, but it might be realistic to forecast the operational achievements of such technologies (for example, by the technique of fitting an envelope curve to historical data about the achievements of past technologies) and to make informed guesses about the types of knowledge and skills that might achieve this performance. Lacking a blueprint of twenty-first century spacecraft the forecaster still might estimate their likely performance and thus deduce that probably only nuclear power could supply the requisite thrust.

Now the extrapolation of performance trends is still clearly historicist, but it worked in the postwar era. This means that the advantages of such technological forecasting sufficiently outweighed its disadvantages for it to become increasingly employed as a decision making tool. This does not necessarily mean that an epistemological rationale had been discovered for historicism, nor that historicist technological forecasts would necessarily prove accurate in other circumstances. One possibility is that we have here a case of what Popper (1957, p.13) calls the 'Oedipus effect' working in favour of historicism. Technological forecasts may have played the role of self-fulfilling prophecies, although even this is not necessary for their proliferation. Predictions would be welcomed by those who wished the predicted states of affairs to come about because they could employ them to actively advance their case. This is equally true for social predictions; many social forecasters cut their teeth on technological predictions and thus might have a good idea of this market.

Historicism 'worked' in another sense too. Just as it is not necessary to justify one's expectations that the sun will rise by reference to initial conditions and the operating laws of astronomy in order to predict with a fair degree of accuracy from its past regularities, so it was not always found necessary to turn technological trends and regularities into 'explained trends' by reference to conditions and laws underlying diffusion and innovation. While levels of public funding for research and development were being increased in a fairly regular manner this sort of technological prediction had a fair chance of being accurate.

8

Another feature encouraging social scientists to emulate technological forecasts was the popularity of the thesis of 'industrial society' which, as Goldthorpe pointed out, is oriented towards processes more than actions. takes technological and economic trends as the fundamental causes of social evolution, and gives little credence to the possibility of specific decisions exerting a significant effect on the direction of social change. This world view shares a superficial similarity with both the technological determinism of vulgar Marxism and with Popper's own focus on continual evolution as opposed to radical breaks and historical turning points. Relying on the persistence of technological advance and economic growth, many social scientists have assumed that social trends are linked to these and may thus be used in social prediction. In later chapters of this book such approaches to social forecasting will be looked at less in terms of their philosophical underpinnings (or lack of them) than in terms of the substance of the trends chosen for extrapolation, the problems caused by selecting only a few out of the vast range of significant trends that might be chosen for study, and the information that the study of trends can yield for the scientific study of society. In respect of this last point, it might be argued in favour of trend extrapolation that, while it is pure prophecy unless founded on some analysis of initial conditions and operating laws (in which case we have 'explained', rather than 'absolute' trends), a close look at extrapolative views of the future in the light of intuitive or theory-based reservations about the tenability of given scenarios can actually help to explicate present beliefs about initial conditions and operating laws.

As Popper points out, one justification that has been advanced for developing evolutionary laws is that the course of evolution is not unique, as he has claimed (Popper, 1957, pp.109-111). Thus some macrosociologists (such as Sorokin, whose views will be encountered in chapter 4) argue that it is possible to study the life history of civilisations, and thus develop laws of social change based on analysis of several such cases. Other theorists have argued that society may be viewed as analogous to an organism and thus laws of organismic development may be generalised to societies. Modern systems theorists (e.g. Buckley, 1967) extend this view to asserting that societies are merely one class of system, and that all systems may be analysed in similar terms. Popper argues that such analogy gives no basis for prediction, given the lack of linkage of predictions to what are often widely varying initial conditions; at best it can tend to a retrospective classification of types of evolutionary process.

In chapter 7 it will be shown that many theories of political development purporting to forecast the future political evolution of developing countries do fall foul of such historicism. Although the authors of much quantitative social research carried out on cross-national data adopt the position that they are in effect dealing with a fairly large number of independent cases of evolution, defined by different national societies, the initial conditions are rarely spelled out; instead of operating laws, universal laws are assumed. Yet the social policies such theorists advance are again those of piecemeal reform.

The historicist forecasts the distant future; Popper, the indeterminist, believes that with only partial knowledge of existing social conditions and tentative knowledge of social laws, short term predictions with prospects of rapid falsifiability are the best that can be hoped for. However, some commentators have recently suggested that we may have much more confidence in the possibility of valid long term social prediction. (This itself may contribute to crypto-historicism, since the distinction between universal historical laws and operating laws is not always clearly made.)

For example, these observers have argued that we are on the verge of a quantum jump forward in sociological understanding. This might be expected, among other things, to reduce the number and intensity of unintended effects of social action and to improve the prospects for long term planning. Among factors contributing to such a leap in understanding are often cited the development of social indicators, the application of computers in social science, and the evolution of a new form of generalist in the social sciences.

One such commentator is the political scientist Ithiel de Sola Pool, who makes explicit many assumptions promulgated among futures researchers in his contribution to the Bellagio symposium on long range planning. This conference, sponsored by the OECD, featured leading systems thinkers and futurologists whose views echo its own in many respects. The tenor of his paper may be suggested by the tone set at the beginning, where it is suggested that twenty-second century historians 'may consider that the computer virtually created what they will then call modern social science . . . The most revolutionary effects of the computer are likely to seem to them to be those in social technology . . . The details of this probable course of evolution are unforeseeable. If that were not so we would have it in our power to make them happen now. For the long-term future, the best we can infer are certain broad overdetermined trends' (Pool, 1969, p.307).

Popper (1957, p.140) argued that human rationality and goal-directedness make social behaviour actually less complicated than that of inert matter. Pool agrees that this goal-directedness is of significance, but goes on to point out that this may make social prediction difficult, particularly where unintended effects of social action are concerned. People are indeed often able to forecast the broad outcome of many causes of action, especially where a few social variables are of paramount importance. Policy makers attempt to control such dominant factors, thus making their original prediction self-fulfilling or self-defeating. But, once these have been controlled, 'many other less obvious determinants then come into their own'. Pool thus argues that 'Social evils and catastrophies are rampant. But the ones that occur are most likely to be the outcomes of subtle intentions among a large number of complex variables' and so 'only careful multivariate analysis can help gain more control over those residual fluctuations of the system' (Pool, 1969, pp.311–312).

In other words, Pool is saying that everyday forecasting of dominant social contingencies makes the social scientists' task difficult. Politicians, planners and ordinary people anticipate and manage the main consequences of social change, with unintended consequences stemming from the conjunction of a multiplicity of less obvious variables. Computers are the tool which will bring about a new era in social science in which such conjunctions can be handled. Simulation models, data banks, social indicators and associated social technologies will have 'a revolutionary effect . . . upon our ability to plan society rationally' (Pool, 1969, p.324).

In this paper Pool only dons the futurologist's mantle to predict, in a rather open-ended way, a glowing era in social science and societal management. He presents a mixture of Popperian conservativism with confidence in social technology — quite common in futures literature. Thus there is the Popperian view that social problems are unintended side-effects of policies and institutions which have evolved in an experimental, adaptive process. Rather than concentrate on changing these, then, the social scientist should be concerned with the fine tuning of an essentially adequate social order. The new era of social science means that piecemeal social experimentation can be carried out within computer simulations, within which we will be able to make increasingly accurate models of social reality and increasingly accurate predictions. Indeed, some writers appear to welcome the prospect, previously restricted to science fiction, of such computer simulations making unnecessary, and invalidating, the traditional modes of expression of political aims.

Another factor giving futures researchers high expectations for social prediction is the rise of the 'expert generalist' (Wolfson, 1972). With the Second World War, the nuclear age and the space age, traditional military expertise became obsolete. New ways of grappling with a changing international and military scene were needed urgently, and 'think-tanks' were established to apply themselves to these issues and, to a lesser extent,

11

other major problems. Such organisations — RAND being the most famous — nurtured techniques for the analysis of complex problems of any sort. Given a problem such as achieving a satisfactory level of nuclear deterrence or designing a space-age urban transportation system, these intellectual technologies were intended to establish the most efficient achievement of end objectives. As Wolfson (1972) points out, these technologies were sold as being 'value-free', that is, the values to which they were applied were those of the highest bidder, and the question of what values might be violated in the efficient means to their ends was passed over. Increasingly, organisations like RAND have become involved in studies of social policy (see, e.g., Hoos, 1972).

The expert generalist arose in such environments — the expert in analytic techniques who reveals little trace of conventional disciplinary allegiances. Such experts often regarded the existing corpus of the social sciences as passé and irrelevant. A new social science was blossoming, fertilised by the techniques and analyses of games theory, cost-benefit analysis, systematic gaming, computer simulations and policy science, and growing away from abstract terminology towards abstracted models. The expert generalist showed familiarity with the jargon and key questions in a diversity of crises and problem areas, and was regularly rubbing shoulders in the corridors of power. Such a phenomenon was bound to create the impression that social science had begun to get a firm grasp on the future — as, in some ways, it had.

As the call for social scientific involvement in forecasting gets louder, then, some social scientists seem ready to answer. As will be seen in later chapters, their answers sound the names of such techniques as 'technology assessment' and 'social indicators' as well as those of theories and concepts like 'post-industrial society' and 'political development'. This book sets out first to outline certain presuppositions of the quantitative approach to social science and of futures research techniques (chapters 2 and 3), to investigate the utility of social indicators to the monitoring and forecasting of social change (chapters 4 and 5), and then to appraise two areas of research in which concepts of the social future have played a prominent role (chapters 6 and 7). These issues will be treated from the perspective of the quantitative social scientist, and so, while little recourse will be made to Popper's arguments about historicism, they should be borne in mind in the coming chapters. One question, however, is outstanding from the previous discussion. Accepting the cogency of Popper's critique of historicism, what is implied for social intervention? In thinking about the future, are we necessarily limited to proposing piecemeal reform if our speculations about planned social change are to remain scientifically respectable?

Social design and engineering

Popper's arguments for piecemeal social engineering were based partly on his indeterminism. Only with cautious changes can the effects of policy be monitored and the cause of unintended consequences be rapidly apprehended and responded to. A fully planned society is a dangerous dream: who can plan the planners, know enough to prevent unintended consequences, or create a society which matches a blueprint without ever deviating?

Large scale planning creates opposition; furthermore, in suppressing this opposition, genuine criticisms of the effects of planning will be curtailed. As side-effects proliferate, the planners will need to institute patching-up operations with less and less valid feedback. 'Utopian' planning thus leads to totalitarianism.

It is widely recognised that Popper's critique of historicism and his advocacy of piecemeal social engineering were both directed against Marxism. As Michael Freeman (1975) points out, Popper links historicism to 'utopian' large scale planning through 'holism' which he views as a 'prescientific' attempt to study the totality of a social system. 'Holistic or utopian social engineering . . . aims at remodelling the 'whole of society' in accordance with a definite plan or viewpoint' (Popper, 1957, p.67). Marx is designated as a historicist, utopian and holist in Popper's writings.

Popper set out to relieve the fatalistic attitude towards a 'historically determined' Marxist future, and to undermine activism based on identification with such a future, by attacking historicism and the holism and utopianism he saw to be associated with it. In contrast the futurologists of whom Goldthorpe writes welcome a historically determined future, for they see trends as leading to an idealised Western post-industrial society, rather than to a revolution of the proletariat. They foresee a coming social order in which social contradictions are transcended and social problems solved by technocratic decision making based on a new era of social science. This is used to justify piecemeal social engineering itself. Historicism, masked as value-free science, now legitimises a particular political strategy. Goldthorpe (1970, p.20—23) points to three features of futurological research which show the characteristics of technocratic historicism. These are: a commitment to continuing economic growth, which is seen to set imperatives for the other features of society while itself acting as an unchallengeable imminent feature of human evolution; a concern with anticipating social problems, thus ensuring societal stability; and a vision of future society as historically transcending capitalism and totalitarianism.

13

A further irony in all this is that recent thought about Marx strongly attacks the Popperian view of his work as historicist. This attack has often, but not always, been guided by the discovery of Marx's early writings, and his *Grundrisse*. Marx's thought has been interpreted as itself a reaction to nineteenth century historicism, an attempt to provide the concepts for redirecting the historical process according to human needs. (For the continuity of Marx's thought, and the depiction of multilinear evolution in his writings, see, for example, Easton and Guddat, 1967, Garaudy, 1967, Nicolaus, 1972 and Sachs, 1970.) Marx himself wrote of initial conditions and operating laws, while recognising that many lawlike relationships are manifest only in particular historic contexts. Even official Russian Marxism, by no means open to all Marxian perspectives on the future, reveals this. In a volume critical of Western futures studies, *The Future of Society*, it is stated that 'Marxism put an end to the absolutisation of trends and laws by showing they are historically determined' (Gott, 1973, p.94). In a body of work as extensive as Marx's, however, it is possible to find writings that echo technological determinism — for example, his predictions of the impact of the railroad on India (cited by Montgomery, 1974, p.58).

Unlike Marx, Popper sees our choice as being either utopian or piecemeal social engineering, and proceeds to characterise large scale social change in terms so extreme that if his analysis were to be accepted there would be no choice. Michael Freeman (1975) has made some apt comments on Popper's position, which he sees as exhibiting three crucial flaws. One of these is the Manichean tendency to oppose exaggerated opposites as if they exhaust the range of choice: reason and violence, 'total' planning and piecemeal reform, liberalism and totalitarianism, and the open society and its enemies. An important feature of this excessive conceptual polarisation is his lumping together such empirically and conceptually distinct attitudes as historicism, holism, utopianism, and totalitarianism, whose common attribute seems to be Popper's rejection of them. Second, Popper is himself in some ways utopian, for example in the power he ascribes to rational argument in politics, and his populism. Third, he does not apply his own tenets of tentative and critical thinking to his own, liberal, standpoint. In particular this latter failing applies in the positive assertions used to damn 'utopian' planning — that it necessarily violates scientific laws, that it leads to totalitarianism, etc. — and in the lack of analysis of the cost of piecemeal social engineering. In effect, Popper makes an *a priori* assumption as to the relative costs and benefits of reform and revolution, without relating them to any initial conditions; he assumes a lawlike relationship between large scale planning and totalitarianism without attempting to falsify it.

14

Freeman also demonstrates that, even in Popper's own interpretation, Marx can hardly be said to be a holist who aimed at constructing a new society in every detail according to a plan. Marx 'wished "to radically transfigure the whole social world" in the weak sense of "whole", that is to say, in the sense of changing certain standard features deemed to be of critical importance for the distribution of power and life-chances in society' (Freeman, 1975, p.24). This is very different from those comtemporary futures researchers who believe that they are achieving a worthy 'holism' by initiating computer models of a society (or of the world) in which there are concessions to economic, social, demographic, ecological and whatever other 'sub-systems'!

As such, Popper's critique of historicism loses none of its force; as such it is relevant to much contemporary futures research. As an argument against large scale social planning (or every example of forecasting based on Marxist theory) it collapses. The paradoxical juxtaposition of historicism and piecemeal social engineering in Goldthorpe's futurologists is no contradiction, then. In Popper's case the weakness of historicism is used as a weapon against socialist thought, whereas for the theorists of industrial society the apparent strength of a historicist perspective is used for this purpose. In one case the vision of the future is reduced to an unforeseeable blur of unintended effects; in the other the future is merely a glossy and rationalised version of the present.

Prediction and futures studies

In the following chapters an attempt is made to study the contributions that may be made to our understanding of the future — that is, our awareness of how present choices relate to alternative futures — by social science. Of particular interest will be the contributions of the quantitative research methods which, as described above, are often seen as the key to the future of the social sciences. In this the aim of this book is somewhat different from that of other volumes which have set out to detail the contributions particular disciplines may make to futures studies (e.g. Freeman, Jahoda and Miles, 1975; Young, 1968). Instead, it seeks to address the question of how far the use of quantitative methods in social research could, and how far it does, escape Goldthorpe's strictures of historicism, and what this means in terms of images of the future.

A word on terminology: I do not wish to join the tedious debate about whether we should talk about forecasting, futurology, futuristics, prediction, prognostics or any one of countless other terms. The term 'prediction' will be chiefly used to refer to studies of the future in which a deterministic orientation is used to project a single image of the future. As will be seen in chapter 3, my use of the term 'social forecasting' is wider than Goldthorpe's (1970, p.24). I will use this term to refer to futures research which focuses on social dimensions of the future, whether it is concerned with exploratory sounding out of likely futures or with the attempt to design alternative futures, and submit such designs to careful appraisal.

In chapter 2, some basic concepts underlying empirical and quantitative approaches in the social sciences are laid out. The concepts of operational measurement, validity, reliability and aggregation recur throughout the book, and thus need some discussion from the viewpoint of futures research. Problems raised by the application of social indicators in forecasting mean that the assumptions involved in social measurement should be spelled out along with the more practical matters of data quality, its availability, and the tangential relevance of much established social information to issues of the future.

Chapter 3 takes up the issue of the quality and relevance of futures research for addressing the problems of formalising and appraising alternative social futures. A classification system for distinguishing between different techniques of forecasting is outlined and criteria proposed for assessing the value of a forecast. In a brief survey of the futures field the material is used to evaluate trends, tendencies and conflicts in futures studies.

In chapter 4 some of the classic sociological approaches to the study of social change are first set out. The clashes between perspectives based on evolutionary, deterministic, equilibrium, and conflict approaches to understanding social change are seen to be relevant to the stances taken by futures researchers, who draw from such paradigms even if only implicity. The work of William F. Ogburn, an early pioneer of both social forecasting and social indicators research, is described in some detail, since it proves illuminating of current thought and practice in these closely related fields. The chapter concludes with a description of the recent 'social indicators movement', its aims and its promises for futures studies.

Chapter 5 takes up a more critical perspective on the scope and underlying assumptions of social indicators research. Specific criticisms are assessed, alternative directions for research appraised, and the implications of these points for futures studies detailed.

Chapter 6 reviews the first of two specific content areas of social science, as contrasted with the previous emphasis on methodologies and techniques. The notion of 'post-industrial society' has been widely diffused in futures research literature as well as in social thought more generally. Here two particular aspects of the concept are examined in the light of theory and research. First, the work of Daniel Bell and writers of a similar persuasion, directed towards the decision making structure of future society and the role to be played by a 'knowledge élite' is considered. Second, a variety of speculations on the values of the mass public and of specific groups such as business élites will be contrasted with each other and with what empirical material is available.

A second body of research is the topic of chapter 7. Recent research in comparative political science and macrosociology, which is often imbued with a forecasting emphasis, is here reviewed. Two particular areas where study has been concentrated, the study of 'political development', and research into the circumstances of civil strife, are taken as examples of this literature, and the sorts of opportunities and problems encountered in applying this work in futures studies are described.

Chapter 8 concludes the book by summarising the previous chapters, and by outlining some directions which futures research could take if it were to be enriched by the social sciences and thereby itself enrich our views of alternative futures. Social research might profitably be directed towards helping futures studies to find the most effective way of broadening their base by encouraging wider participation in designing these futures.

2 Objectivity, Inference, and Measurement in Social Science

Forecasting cannot be a normal science, since its subject matter — the future — is not available for inspection, and falsification of any statements to be made about the future is impossible in the short term. On the other hand, forecasts are open to empirical critique as the essential assumption shared by forecasts is that continuity exists between the past and the future. The information which is employed in a forecast, deriving from history either through informal experience and intuition or through scientific principles of collections and interpretation, may itself be challenged.

This chapter sets out the issues of measurement and inference encountered by social scientists. The questions raised for social forecasting are: How valid are our inferences about past states of affairs? How reasonable are our generalisations from past to future circumstances? How far are our views of the future constrained by incomplete knowledge of social phenomena?

Operationalism and the concept of validity

In order to assess the claims and counterclaims concerning the practicability and desirability of applying empirical research methods to social forecasting, it is necessary to consider briefly the bases of empirical social research. By empirical research is meant research that employs data, whether for purposes of description, simple prediction, or understanding of the causal patterns underlying social phenomena. Ideally, the rules governing the collection and interpretation of data will have been specified by the researcher, so that other workers may compare their findings and conclusions with it.

Operationalism is the approach whereby the constructs to be considered in a research project are defined in terms of the techniques of measurement employed. It is clearly impossible to precisely replicate all the conditions of measurement of a construct from one occasion to another since no two moments are identical. In social research, the same observer cannot be present in several places at one time; an interview schedule requires translation to be meaningful to speakers of different languages; and the particular setting in which an experimental programme or condition is enacted will never be repeated. Social researchers attempt to remove any systematic effects of such variations by, for example, employing several observers in an effort to assess and remove the contamination of individual idiosyncrasies of judgement, developing methods of ensuring comparability of interviews in different languages by such approaches as back-translation, and using a standardised experimental setting. The extent to which research results are affected by variations related to factors extraneous to the research design is a crucial question in the process of inference from data to structured conclusions, and will be considered later.

Despite the impossibility of complete replication of the historical circumstances surrounding the making of a measurement, operational definition makes possible the replication of what are believed to be the significant features of measurements and interventions under varying conditions. This allows for statements about trends, about the relative prevalence of phenomena, and the association of phenomena. However, the phenomena concerned are those indexed by the measurement procedures, no more or less. Say that people in one community are more likely to answer a question in an interview by stating that they feel themselves to be members of the working class, than are people in a second community. Does this mean that the former community is really composed of more members of the working class, or that it exhibits a higher degree of class polarisation? Does a change in the level of a country's GNP represent a change in national wealth or welfare? Such questions raise the problem of validity.

Broadly speaking, validity refers to the degree to which a measure (or a measured relationship between variables) actually sheds light on the construct (or the relationship between constructs), which it refers to by operational definition. Validity is a fuzzy notion in some ways — it is asking how much is 'really' revealed by a specific set of observations — and is usually broken down into several types in the psychological and sociological literature (e.g. Campbell and Stanley, 1966).

Internal validity refers to the degree to which the measurements made in a particular instance may be used with confidence as statements of the actual situation. Two issues are involved here: first, whether the measures employed are appropriate operationalisations of the constructs with which the research is concerned; second, if this is so, whether the measured relationships between the variables considered are appropriate data for adjudging the relationship between these underlying constructs.

20

Traditionally, the first issue has been addressed by attempting to develop consensus among the scientific community that an operationalisation is reasonable, that an 'epistemic correlation' (Northrop, 1947) exists between a measured variable and a theoretical construct. This often involves 'face validation' — the construction of a measure that overtly relates to the construct, as in a measure of racial prejudice based on questions concerning one's attitudes to members of different races. Campbell and Fiske (1959) have elaborated the principles of convergent and discriminant validation, based respectively on the notions that alternative measures of the same or similar theoretical constructs should display high empirical correlations (so that a measure that behaves anomalously when compared to other measures is likely to be invalid), and that measures of conceptually distinct constructs should not display such correlations (so that a measure of one property that is found to be highly related to measures of a different property may possibly be more validly considered a measure of the latter than of the former). A related notion is 'construct validation', in which the validity of a measure is assessed by the degree to which it is empirically related to other measures in a predicted way, i.e. in a manner parallel to the relationship hypothesised among underlying constructs.

The second issue at stake when internal validity is considered is the question of comparisons — whether a true difference exists when two measurements have been made, and if so, what its causal significance is, e.g. whether an experimental treatment or unplanned phenomenon has actually had an influence, whether two groups differ, and whether a relationship exists between two constructs. Two types of analysis are relevant to this form of validation. One involves statistical analysis, i.e. the use of measures of significance which typically take into account the level and distribution of scores on a measure under different conditions or in relation to scores on other measures, to give an estimate of the likelihood of a particular difference between conditions or degree of relationship between measures having occurred by chance alone. The second involves consideration of extraneous phenomena: features of the research design employed must be scrutinised to see how much confidence may be placed in the presumption that one variable did or did not have an effect on another. Different research designs differ widely in the degree to which they control various types of extraneous effects. Rather than consider the merits of different designs — such as experimental and correlational approaches — we shall concentrate in this chapter on the validity of indices. Questions of design will be raised with respect to particular studies and research traditions, reviewed in later chapters; Campbell and Stanley (1966) provide a useful overview.

External validity refers to the generalisability of findings established in a piece of research to populations, settings and conditions other than those in which the research was originally carried out. As before, the type of research design used will be crucial to the generalisability of any effects established. Most research involves some form of sampling from a large population, whether this be the population of schoolchildren, of communes or of countries. Two matters must be considered: the degree to which any relationship or lack of relationship established between variables is contingent upon characteristics of the sample which are not shared by the entire population, and the degree to which sub-groups discriminated for purposes of research are comparable on dimensions other than those in which variation or manipulation is sought as part of the theoretical hypothesis.

Forecasting techniques involve the application of generalisations in an attempt to map out the future, and they thus rely on the external validity of the empirical research used as their data inputs. In turn, this external validity is itself dependent on the internal validity of the research, which sets limits on the confidence one may have in the structure of the data reported. A forecast will typically be based on two assumptions; that particular relationships between variables can be inferred from a historical sample or samples, and that these samples are sufficiently representative of future populations for the same relationships to be projected into the future. These assumptions will be returned to in later chapters dealing more directly with forecasting.

The concept of reliability, and the aggregation of data

Reliability is a narrower notion than validity, referring to the stability, consistency, objectivity and accuracy of operational measures, rather than to questions of their deeper significance. If a measure is reliable, then the same results should be obtained by different users applying it to the same observations, or by its repeated application to supposedly unchanging material. To the extent that a measure is unreliable, such results will vary. In practice most measures fall between the extremes of complete reliability or unreliability; some 'measurement error' is said to be associated with them. The greater the error in measures, the harder it becomes to establish validity of research. It is difficult to say how far the absence or weakness of a hypothesised relationship, for example, is due to the imprecision of the measures employed.

Different types of measure demand different approaches to the resolution of reliability problems, the common principle being the calculation of a reliability coefficient. In the case of measures that are based on human judgements – for example, expert observers coding the recorded foreign policy behaviour of nations into several categories – this coefficient will index the degree to which different observers, following the same operational instructions, agree. (It is also possible to estimate individual observers' self-consistency by making them code the same records at different times.) Where a characteristic is believed to be a stable feature of a person or other unit of observation, the reliability of a measure may be estimated by a test–retest procedure in which a reliability coefficient is calculated by correlating measures made on the same sample at two points in time. However, the assumption of stability may often be questionable where political, social and psychological variables are considered.

A further approach to increasing reliability consists in the formation of a measure out of a number of discrete observations. This aggregation of observations is, perhaps, best known from its applications in attitude measurement, where attitude scales frequently consist of a large number of questions concerned with the same basic issue. The principle involved is simply that where measurement errors are random, increasing the number of observations included in an aggregate index should increase its approximation to accuracy. Random errors will tend to balance out as the weight given to each observation is diminished. Reliability coefficients may then be calculated in several ways, e.g. by correlating scores obtained from different random samples of the observations making up the measure to demonstrate the extent to which these sub-samples give similar results. As in the other procedures for testing reliability, low values of the reliability coefficient indicate a lack of precision in measurement, and suggest a need for caution in interpretation and improvement in design. The categories and definitions given to observers may be made more detailed, the instructions given to field workers or people completing tests made clearer, or the number of items included in a measure selectively increased, discarding inconsistent items.

The aggregation of observations to form a single composite measure may be carried out for reasons other than that of increasing reliability. For one thing, a summary measure may be more easily grasped than a larger number of indices. Another reason may be to obtain a measure with 'content validity', one which samples a wider range of the properties of a theoretical construct than a single item of observation might provide. For example, the construct 'parliamentary democracy' might be presumed to consist of a host of properties: the validity of a measure based solely on observations of press freedom, voting turnout, party system or mode of selection of government executive, for example, would be lower than a measure based on some combination of all these, and other properties. Likewise racial prejudice might be better indexed by observations of attitudes to members of other races in a whole range of different circumstances than by a single observation. The formation of composite indices by aggregation of separate observations will be returned to in a later discussion of social indicators — at this point it is fitting to note that, where an attempt is being made to operationalise a complex construct, such indices may well actually lose reliability as observations of further aspects of the construct are incorporated. This is because many everyday language terms — such as 'democracy', 'quality of life', 'modern institutions', 'alienation', 'civil unrest' — actually refer to multidimensional constructs, which are, as it were, coalescences of numerous properties and phenomena that have no direct intrinsic causal connections with each other (although their co-occurrence is theorectically meaningful). The reliability of a measure will only be necessarily increased by further aggregation if the new items of observation included relate to the same unidimensional theoretical construct.

Aggregated indices often present other problems concerning validity, as we shall see when examples of such measures are encountered in later chapters. Essentially, two issues are involved: first, the component measures need themselves to be of demonstrable validity; second, decisions are necessary as to how different components are to be weighted in the formation of the composite index. Sometimes these are made with consideration for statistical aspects of reliability only, and an error-minimising approach involving, for example, principle components analysis, is used. Sometimes a theoretical or evaluative criterion is employed, in which the component measures are weighted according to their 'importance'. Discussion of the ways in which social indicators researchers have attempted to resolve the aggregation problems in deriving quality of life indices will be taken up later.

To avoid confusion, it will be useful to discuss a second use of the term 'aggregation'. This relates to the pooling of data from a variety of distinct samples to provide a single measure — reflecting the overall status, on the variable concerned, of the population from which these are drawn. Thus measures of national per capita food consumption, or the average level of reported satisfaction in a community, represent aggregated measures, which may be disaggregated to provide data about the characteristics of particular categories of the population — for example, the consumption of food per capita in particular regions of the country, or among different age, sex or income groups. The level of aggregation to be employed depends upon the research problem involved. Relationships established between variables at one level of aggregation cannot be blithely assumed to hold at another level. For example, to establish that areas with a higher per capita income are characterised by a higher level of some other variable does not mean that richer individuals within an area are necessarily characterised by that variable to a greater extent than poorer people.

Is operationalism objective?

If a forecast is to be more than speculation, it must be grounded in valid research. This applies as much to research in which attempts are made to construct consistent designs for ideal societies, as to less adventurous attempts to extrapolate to 'most likely' futures. Equally it applies to studies in which alternative futures are developed from different sets of assumptions and premises, or are forecast as the consequences of different policies and decisions.

Without operational definitions, both theoretical propositions and descriptions (such as the identification of a trend without any attempt at explanation) remain untestable, and the validity of such statements cannot be ascertained. The value of a forecast is enhanced by its use of operational terms — the use of everyday language terms which remain untied to explicit empirical referents may merely provide a connotative sense of a given future, from which different audiences may draw their own, widely differing, meanings.

However, there have been many critics of social science operationalism, and a variety of doubts raised about its adequacy, which thus indirectly cast doubt on the possibility of providing social forecasting with any valid basis. Operationalism has been accused of relying upon metatheoretical or even metaphysical notions of appropriateness, in the relating of measures to theoretical constructs. These are allegedly shared by a scientific community, but their origin and worth is uncertain, since 'epistemic correlations' are inherently unobservable. Measures may become established, although the norms of the scientific community itself may be in flux, or they may be accepted without question by inexpert users who in fact possess different norms. Likewise the availability of operational measures, nested in a web of empirical research and with evidence available concerning various aspects of their validity and reliability, may discourage alternative approaches to measurement, providing a premature

25

sense of closure. This becomes particularly important when measures are available for only some of the components of a multifaceted everyday construct, for social scientists and those using their research have often shown a singular lack of caution in identifying measures with constructs — e.g. 'intelligence is nothing but a score on an IQ test'! However, it must be conceded that both laymen and professionals are also often angered by the social scientist who proposes cumbersome new terminology, such as the psychologist Cattel's long list of personality characteristics with names like threctia, desurgency, sizothymia, etc.

Before addressing these points it is as well to rebut one charge that has sometimes been made — that operationalism is necessarily tied to a position of crude empiricism, in which theories are somehow to be deduced from a gathering of pure facts. This is simply untrue. Operationalisations represent measures of theoretical constructs whose adequacy is justified by metatheoretical assumptions and empirical tests, and without which no generalisations are possible. Without some theoretical guidelines, there would be no basis for selection out of the infinite universe of possible observations. Nor is it the case that operationalisation precludes the use of theories involving intervening variables for which no measures are available — it is simply that hypotheses to be tested can only be expressed in terms of operational variables, so that these tests may be only indirectly related to the whole of the guiding theory (Northrop, 1947). Much social research has involved the testing of hypotheses based on theories from which but few variables are accessible to ready measurement. The research is not thereby less valuable or relevant to practical matters. It is certainly not being argued that forecasting should proceed only by use of constructs that are directly tied to measures. While the elaboration of useful theories of many social phenomena waits upon the development of indicators of significant theoretical constructs, the lead time involved in their development situates a social forecasting based on such social science in the distant future!

This 'logical' critique disposed of, what of the practical criticisms of operationalism? Essentially the arguments presented are that it is difficult to establish finally the validity of a measure, since some of the assumptions involved in judging validity are unstated, variable, and themselves untestable; and that the consequences of employing particular measures may be to lend them a spurious validity in their application to unwarranted constructs or situations, or to hinder the development of competing theoretical constructs and associated measures. We shall consider these to form two qestions: is operationalism objective, and is it neutral?

In respect of varying assumptions, the case of face validity presents a clear example. The appropriateness of a measure is judged by the degree to which it overtly relates to the theoretical construct concerned. However, this 'overt' relationship itself may depend on underlying models or paradigms of social reality. Take, for example, the construct 'poverty' — different researchers have attempted to operationalise this in terms of the relationship of the income of groups or individuals to a cost-of-living measure (itself based upon value judgements about what constitutes necessities and luxuries) to an official standard minimum income as set out in social security levels, or to the average income of the population. Such divergences serve to indicate that the construct concerned is multidimensional, or that in fact quite distinct theoretical notions have been given the same name. A second example might be the construct 'achievement motivation' — one researcher may measure this by means of pencil and paper tests, one by looking at the degree to which actual achievement matches that predicted from knowledge of individual abilities. Here researchers may agree concerning the nature of the underlying construct, but disagree on its manifestation in real situations where different external factors are present.

The reverse situation may also apply — researchers may disagree about the construct to which a given measure is most appropriate. Thus, suicide statistics have been employed as indices of social integration deriving from the nature of the social structure, and also of levels of anxiety deriving from genetic and psychological factors (Durkheim, 1897, Lynn, 1971). To take another example, in the study of civil strife, different researchers have employed the levels of literacy in a country as indexing in one case the strength of factors producing 'social wants' (which, if unmet, produce feelings of frustration and deprivation), and in another, as contributing to the satisfaction of needs and thus reducing relative deprivation (see Burrowes, 1972). In these cases, the theoretical construct itself proves difficult to measure — anxiety and frustration, for example, being located in individuals and thus requiring costly survey studies to index directly — so highly indirect operationalisations are employed, and disagreements concerning the linkages of unmeasured variables are in evidence.

Face validation is unlikely to prove acceptable unless there is considerable agreement on theory and models in a particular area. Occasionally an indicator may define a concept, as in cases where a measure itself attains the status of an everyday term and thus its use involves no act of inference, or is believed to be sufficiently error-free and direct for no cross-checks with alternative statistics to be necessary (e.g. GNP, life expectancy), but more often a position of multiple operationalism will be necessary (Campbell, 1969, Etzioni and Lehman, 1969). In this perspective, it is accepted that measures are likely to be contaminated with errors of instrumentation or conceptualisation, and thus a theoretical construct should ideally be measured in several ways. This allows for convergent and discriminant validation and the construction of broad, internally consistent, and reliable aggregated indices.

Further analysis of the operationalist position may be found in many discussions of social science methodology. The volumes by Kerlinger (1964) and Blalock and Blalock (1968) represent respectively, introductory and more advanced appraisals of these issues, while Hindess (1973) and Triesman (1974) have addressed themselves to answering the ethnomethodologist's critique of operational measures. Broadly, these authors agree with the conclusions implicit in the above discussion: in principle operational measurement need not impose inevitable distortions on the data of the real world, and in practice its use is essential to the (in)validation of research and theory.

However, forecasters are faced with problems which may lead them to question the relevance of operationalism to their enterprise. One particular problem is that the validation of a measure in one context does not necessarily imply that it will remain valid in other contexts. This applies whether these 'contexts' be futures of the same population or nation, or different cultures, at any historical or future period, to the one originally studied. This is a problem that has been faced in comparative (cross-national and cross-cultural) social research — a body of research in which many questions raised in forecasting recur. Przeworski and Teune (1970) characterise it as one of possible 'system interference'. This is said to occur when the validity of inference from measures to constructs is different in the different contexts of comparative research. An obvious manifestation of this would be the invalidity of tests developed for members of one language group applied without translation to members of a different group; a less trivial example is the variation of indicators of social status across times and cultures. Thus, just as the increasing affluence of Western societies has diminished the utility of measures of material possessions (such as car ownership) as indices of high social status, so some present-day criteria are likely to be inapplicable in future societies (where, for example, private car ownership may be more nearly universal or totally non-existent).

Except in cases of simple extrapolation, and even then to the extent that extrapolation of trends is not pure historicism, but instead relies upon implicit assumptions about the stability of processes generating trends, forecasting depends on models of social reality. These models may be 'calibrated' in terms of a given set of conditions — for example, those of a given present society, or a projected utopian community — and conclusions derived about future contingencies resulting from the interaction of variables under these conditions. Existing or idealised data concerning observables, and theory concerning the relationships between theoretical constructs are thus used to forecast the data that would be provided by observations of future states of the society. In providing an elaborated image of the future, theoretical constructs and causal connections are thus essential. However, the possibility of system interference raises the question of whether a future can realistically be specified in terms of observables, if 'epistemic correlations' are potentially unstable, deviating from the high values ascribed to indicators whose current validity has been established.

In comparative social research, Przeworski and Teune argue that equivalent indicators may be established in different contexts under conditions of system interference. This involves testing measures common to different contexts to check if they retain similar empirical relationships, such as patterns of intercorrelations, and by adjusting them to display similar properties by partialling out those contextual factors thought to be the main causes of system interference. Alternatively indicators may be developed which are specific to different systems, but which exhibit the same reliability, structure of differential and convergent validity (with respect to underlying dimensions if multidimensional constructs are involved), and construct validity (in terms of showing the same empirical relationships with other variables where these are theoretically predicted).

These procedures for establishing equivalence clearly cannot be applied in forecasting. The appropriateness of a measure or set of measures in a future context cannot be tested on data from the future, since they do not exist. In forecasting it is common to seek to reason from a theoretical construct to operational variables; thus if past experience or theory predicts that increasing educational levels in a population will increase political participation, the forecaster will be concerned with what actual behaviours correspond to this increasing political participation. The problem of equivalence remains the same, although in conventional research the data are given and inferences made concerning the properties of the theorectical construct, while in forecasting this procedure is reversed.

For forecasting purposes it is thus necessary to make assumptions justifying the use of indices. It may be assumed that the validity of a measure is invariant for practical purposes (e.g. that frustration will always be expressed by aggressive acts such as rioting, assaults, vandalism etc.), that the contextual features influencing this validity are known and are taken to be stable in the forecast (e.g. that frustration will always be expressed by such aggressive acts in post-agrarian urbanised societies which are taken as given in a forecast), or that the effects of contextual variations on the validity of different indices may themselves be forecast (e.g. that in one type of future society frustration will be expressed by extrapunitive agression, and in another type by harming oneself).

These assumptions may be subject to some degree of empirical test by using existing data. If the indices retain their validity in a range of different contexts in which these specified features are stable and common, then at least the assumption has not been falsified by history. For example, if in known cases of parliamentary democracies, party membership is associated with other indices of political participation, and displays construct validity in terms of exhibiting the expected relationships with other variables such as educational level, etc., then there is more reason for confidence in employing it in forecasts of future political participation in parliamentary democracies than if it showed lack of equivalence in such tests. Even if there is no theoretical rationale on which to base specification of the relevant contextual features, it may be possible to provide support for the idea of stability simply by ascertaining that an indicator remains valid in a wide sample of different contexts.

If an assumption of the second type is to be made, it is necessary to use a more elaborate model in which variables reflecting the contextual features play an active role, and again this model may be tested against available data. For example, if it is forecast that the type of political system will change away from being a parliamentary democracy, but that educational level will continue to influence people's degree of political participation, then it is feasible to test assumptions concerning the appropriate operationalisation of 'political participation' under different types of political system existing in the present world. Hypotheses concerning variations in the relationship of the 'participation' construct to actual behaviour, as features of the political system vary, may be tested.

A question remains for forecasters: What if the contextual forecast is so unprecedented that it seems that no historical contexts may be used as such tests of operationalisation? Such is often the case in utopian images of future society, as well as in the more deterministic pictures of some futurologists who anticipate futures ranging from global collapse and thermonuclear war to vastly wealthy 'world societies'. Indeed, if forecasting is to be a liberating area of thought, it must consider futures freed from 'the dead hand of the past'. This applies equally to the problems of constructing indicators and broad theories.

It was argued above that forecasting without the involvement of empirically testable models is speculation; its acceptance as a basis for action can only be based on ideological motives. (This is not to deny that the acceptance of empirically grounded models may equally be based on such motives). Whether derived from experience or from rationalisation, social forecasts incorporate notions of human conduct that require justification. When unprecedented futures are considered, this justification may come from scientific theory, while when only quantitatively different futures are projected, it may be more admissible to rely on empirically established but theoretically equivocal findings. In Popperian terms, the ultimate test of a scientific theory is its falsifiability; thus even forecasting human behaviour in novel circumstances (and it is impossible to imagine a totally novel environment) must employ empirical evidence at some stage.

This issue of equivalence has been raised here with respect to the validation of measures, but it applies with equal force to the generalisation of 'causal' relationships from one context to another. Thus it may be argued that it is meaningless to attempt to forecast the responses of people to particular stimuli when the social order has undergone significant transformation; for example the question of whether or not possessive and selfish feelings or interest groups would arise in a utopian equal society. Research concerning the experience of small communities who have tried to organise themselves on such lines could be suggested as one avenue for exploring the tenability of alternative concepts of human nature in such situations. However, it might be argued that the findings of such research are invalidated by our inability to control the wider environment in which such communities have to be established until the dawning of a new world order.

Just as there can be no final 'objective' surety of validity, only some degree of consensus about the appropriateness of carrying out operations, making inferences, and trusting the reports of other observers, so such questions may never be resolved. Clearly, it would be possible, in the example above, to construct weaker and stronger approximations, out of historical experience, to the ideal situation, but objections to the appropriateness of generalisations may be multiplied indefinitely. Increasingly detailed data and greater sizes of sample become necessary to answer each objection. Given the current state of social research, the boundaries of empirical knowledge will be reached sooner rather than later. This means that the values of a forecaster, and a philosophy and ideology of the nature of man and society must inevitably determine much of his or her work. Empirical research may well serve to refine beliefs, make simplifications untenable, and clarify possibilities, and as such it is indispensable. To portray it as rapidly allowing us to predict previously unknown aspects of the future is premature, not to say abortive.

Is operationalism neutral?

The discussion above, concerning the objectivity of the operational approach to social research points to two conclusions. First, operationalism is not antithetical to the development of theories incorporating unmeasured concepts. Second, operational validity is at most a matter of degree, so there will generally be several fairly obvious grounds on which the assumptions and interpretations of any research may be challenged. These conclusions may be recast as follows: operationalism does not imply a purely empiricist approach to social science, in which a comprehension of the future will emerge simply from a collection of enough data about the present; indeed, the impossibility of achieving final verification of a model, as Popper argues, suggests that the acceptance of particular measures and models for forecasting will depend on, among other things, the norms of a scientific sub-culture, ideology, and personal values.

It is scarcely necessary to engage in the construction of measures and the plotting of trends to accept that, in general, the social sciences as practised in the West have increasingly been carried out with the aid of operationalisation. Likewise, the recent thrusts of the 'systems approach' to planning call for, and have led to, the development of measures of the system which is to be planned for, both in order to provide preliminary information and to monitor the effects of programmes for change. Powerful forces, ranging from the professionalisation of social scientists and the development of electronic computers to the political interests involved in the 'social indicators movement' would seem to be at work in producing this trend. Some counterforces are in operation, as witnessed by increasing public reluctance to co-operate in survey research, concern about misuse of data banks, and a disavowal of the research techniques as well as the theoretical substance of mainstream social science by many young radical critics within the social sciences, for example. But, given that the main trends may be expected to continue, and that, in terms of allowing forecasters some degree of validity in developing theoretical and empirical bases for forecasting, operational thinking appears to offer many benefits, the question may be again raised: is operationalism neutral?

This question is impelled by the following considerations. The choice of constructs is a matter of values and goals, whether these constructs are invoked to deal with a scientific problem or for purposes of social administration. Those measures in existence at any one time, therefore, reflect the amount of attention paid to specific constructs, modified by the resources available to those involved in the research or administration. Furthermore, some constructs are more difficult to measure than others (e.g. the incidence of unhappy marriages compared to that of divorces), more controversy is involved in the measurement of certain attributes (e.g. the debate over verbal reports of attitudes), and some phenomena may be deliberately concealed (e.g. expenditures on secret or illegal activities).

Given that the development and validation of new measures, as well as the collection of relevant data derived from them is a resource-consuming activity, it is to be expected that data and measures will often be 'recycled' and used for purposes other than that for which they were originally prepared. In itself this is healthy, since reinterpretation and replication of observations are important and much neglected activities. However, these measures will often be only partly valid in terms of the constructs that are at issue in the present case. This is particularly evident in many recent discussions of the 'quality of life' in a community, and in attempts to monitor the performance of institutions such as schools. Typically the procedure that has been followed in such discussions has been to take existing measures — such as health and crime levels, or verbal achievement test scores — as suitable tools to answer questions about trends, differences between places, or the probable effects of policies. In particular, quantification in social policy areas has tended to stress those aspects of society that have proved problematic in the past, and to ignore its more subjective aspects.

Both the indices and the data that are available at any one time, then, will reflect the concerns of historic interests in social research. It is not being argued that researchers and archivists are forever bound by what has already been done. Before the advent of data banks and compilations of source material, attitude survey researchers for example, often found it more convenient to construct original measures rather than employ those used previously. In consequence, there is a proliferation of measures of certain constructs, some of very dubious reliability, which has hindered the making of comparisons. Nor have compilers of official statistics always attended to each other's activities. The social indicators employed in different countries vary widely, again making comparisons difficult — for example, Van Dusen (1974) points out that it is difficult to compare data on housing crowdedness indexed by persons per room with that indexed in terms of square metres per person. Finally, of course, political expediency has often been known to dictate changes in the operational definition of such salient constructs as cost of living! This sort of index change is usually accomplished by a simple manipulation of presentation format, possibly coupled with concealment of previously accessible data, rather than by any innovations in measurement procedure.

The problem of the slow evolution of indices is worth following, especially as it may prove on inspection to be more of a burden to applied social research — including forecasting and planning — than to research in which demands for quick answers are of less importance than are those for methodological sophistication and theoretical one-upmanship. One effect is likely to be that the constructs for which measures are most readily available are biased towards issues that have arisen in the past, while constructs reflecting emergent issues may not be available. The discovery of the 'environmental crisis' in the mid-1960s may have partly been stimulated by the ongoing development of indices of environmental quality, but it certainly highlighted the lack of necessary data and constructs in those fields of social science impinging upon environmental questions. Likewise, the study of political development in the Third World has been hindered by a shortage of suitable conceptual tools and the attempts of researchers to rely on constructs stemming from earlier research traditions (see Almond, 1970, chapter 10, and chapter 7 of this book). Another example is provided by an exercise in manpower forecasting. Bezdek and Getzel (1973) found existing official job classification schemes inadequate for forecasting future job content and skill requirements. It proved necessary to recode data in terms of new indices for the purposes of their model.

A second bias in the availability of indicators derives from the interests that have been involved in defining problems for the applied social scientist to research. Shapiro and Neubauer (1973) employ the term 'meta-advocacy' to describe the implicit evaluative suppositions involved in stating problems. Meta-advocacy specifies the sorts of constructs and measures that would be needed in order to research, locate, and advocate solutions. Thus policy-relevant research into the characteristics of schooling that are associated with income in later life may produce conclusions suggesting that particular changes in the provision of educational facilities to different groups in society would increase equality of opportunity. At the meta-advocacy level such research specifies individual achievement as the problem rather than questioning the perpetuation of income inequalities, and affirms the tying of rewards to ability rather than to needs. The data developed will reflect these concerns and, even if only weak relationships are found (e.g. Jencks, 1972, found schooling could only account for 12 per cent of income variance), will carry the stamp of scientific legitimacy which statements based upon other diagnoses of the problem may lack.

Many of the most used measures in the social sciences have clearly stemmed from particular concerns and definitions of problems. Ability tests in education, for example, originated with the desire to select and stratify pupils in order to achieve greater efficiency, with little concern for the impacts of this procedure on self-evaluation, democratic values, etc. Such tests have also been instruments of racism for many decades, yielding 'objective' evidence on the natural inferiority of underprivileged groups which lends itself to the argument that their innate qualities, rather than social organisation, are responsible for their low social positions. In survey research, more information is collected concerning people's attitudes to transient issues and figures than to pervasive matters of political or social structure. Constructs are often redefined in the course of operationalisation; see for example, the transmutation of alienation into a psychological state by survey-wielding sociologists (described by Schact, 1971).

While 'critical' social research certainly does exist, and its very presence is used as a basis for attacking the social sciences by those who gain from maintaining the *status quo,* it is surely unnecessary to elaborate the point that research, especially large scale research, requires funding. Research sponsors are thus in a position to influence the development of measures. In the USA, for example, a government office reviews all questionnaires and survey measures used in federally supported research. (This is pointed out by Hoos, 1974, in a paper rich in examples of official distortion of statistics and the reliance of bureaucracy on the measures and definitions of areas of social concern by those private corporations most heavily invested in such areas.)

One broad effect of this historical development of measures has been the proliferation of economic statistics. Such indicators have been devised as aids to economic planning by the state, and as sources of information for corporations seeking a basis for decision making. While there has been a long term trend of increasing government publication of economic, trade and census statistics in most countries (Flanigan and Fogelman, 1967), the Great Depression and the Second World War stimulated the development of econometric data. The need to understand the causes of the depression created a demand for national economic accounting which was also explicit in Keynesian policy. The war added to these motives with the attempts of nations to regulate their output, control inflation, and, finally, reconstruct their economies. Out of these accounting efforts arose the GNP measure.

Gross (1966, pp.162–71) has reviewed these developments, pointing to two associated problems. The first is Morgenstern's (1963) point that economic statistics are often laden with large error components – often because they are by-products of activities other than economic accounting and are thus of low validity in measuring economic constructs with different definitions. The second is 'economic philistinism': the evaluation of performance only in terms of monetary values and the neglect of subjective, 'soft' information about factors that, while socially valued, lack clear ties to an economic metric.

The social indicators movement has been proclaimed as a selfconscious effort to overcome many of the difficulties cited above. Proponents of social accounting have argued that, given a specification of national goals or values, operational measures can be created appropriate to the assessment of progress in terms of such constructs, and thereby a system of measures will be established free of the biases of convenience and vested interests. How far this is a likely result of the social indicators movement will be assessed later. For the present it is sufficient to note that major reviews and compilations of social indicators have both been driven to employ, and to express regret at the limitations of, data gathered for a variety of purposes. These data deviate to varying extents from the requirements of valid measurement both in terms of completeness and focus, and from the aim of comprehensive accounting in terms of the virtual absence of measures of key variables (e.g. Sheldon and Moore, 1968; Biderman, 1966).

It is of interest to note that the contemporary social indicators movement was prefigured in many important respects in the work of certain American sociologists during the early years of the depression. In the work of William Ogburn and his collaborators (Ogburn, 1929–35; Report of the President's Research Committee on Social Trends, 1933) attempts were made to assess the state of the nation and its likely prospects. These researchers were concerned with monitoring changes in areas like population, the family, labour, and so on. Ogburn called for greater government assistance to the social sciences; their techniques could, if improved, aid planning and forecasting considerably. However, with the possible exception of rural sociology and the previously mentioned rise of econometrics, interest in social accounting dramatically withered in the USA following the Second World War.

Two recent analysts of contemporary sociology, Friedrichs (1970) and Gouldner (1970) have argued that, in at least this branch of social science the postwar period marked the rise of a 'value-free', scientistic ideology. (Similar critiques of other branches of social science have been prominent in recent years. See, for example, Armistead, 1974; Blackburn, 1972a; Brown, 1973; Colfax and Roach, 1971, McCoy and Playford, 1967; Weisskopf, 1971.) Thus the interests of researchers largely turned away from attempts to stimulate social change, and towards trivial problems of theory and methodology. To what extent this reflected professionalisation and financing, or was a pragmatic response to the pressures of the Cold War is a hotly debated matter, but both authors agree that the focal subject matter of American sociology (which has exercised a major influence on all English-language social science) has been selected according to conservative principles. (Nisbet, 1966, goes one step further: he argues that the sociological tradition has always been conservative.)

One feature of the sociological scene of the 1960s was the emergence of the thesis of 'the end of ideology'. (See Bell's 1960 book of that title; Lipset, 1963; and the volume edited by Waxman, 1968.) Baldly put, this thesis treated recent developments in industrial society — such as working class affluence, the welfare state, wider education — as symptomatic of a convergence between socialist thought and capitalist practice. These theories of society reflected the dormancy of the extremes of political opinion in the Cold War era, and articulated the view that value-free social science could now flourish. Friedrichs and Gouldner make clear the inadequacies of these perspectives on society and on social theory. Both authors agree that the conflicts of the 1960s have sundered the sociological paradigm of well-integrated social systems, and brought about renewed emphasis on conflict, deprivation and stressful change. Nevertheless, their arguments would make it probable that both the development of measures, and the socialisation of those social scientists who are in positions to make direct development of new official statistics, will reflect this toppled paradigm. In other words, we may lack the necessary data to validate radical perspectives on problems of social change, and forecasting will consequently be impoverished as to theory or data or both.

The foregoing discussion has necessarily been rather abstract. The questions raised in this chapter bear heavily on the assessment of the contribution that empirical social research may make to forecasting. In following chapters, we shall examine first, the procedures employed and advocated in the literature of futures research, and then the role that has been played by the social sciences in such research. The significance of questions of inference and objectivity will be apparent in the concrete examples of research cited, and light will thereby be cast on its potentials and limitations.

3 Futures Research: Techniques and Values

Futures research has enjoyed a vogue in recent years, in which a bewildering array of methodologies and experts have been presented to the public. Just as the empirical bases of forecasts were shown to require critique in the preceding chapter, the assumptions underlying forecasting techniques need to be scrutinised.

This chapter is concerned with the classification of forecasting techniques in terms of their premises, which are inevitably value-laden, and with depicting criteria whereby futures studies may be assessed. It also charts the recent development of futures research, from its origins in military and economic planning to the creation of technology assessment. The reasons for the success of forecasting techniques may lie as much in this history as in their predictive accuracy.

The techniques of futures studies

Serious social forecasting requires both theory and data about social processes, and specific techniques for projecting futures from this basis. In the previous chapter the range of theoretical constructs and measures concerning social change was seen to be restricted by the historical representation of interests in social research. In this chapter the range and application of techniques of forecasting will be considered. There has been surprisingly little attention given by futures researchers to the recent history of forecasting, although discussions of the origins of 'futurology' in antiquity abound, as if in an attempt to legitimise a 'disreputable' field of study by ascribing it to a venerable tradition. (Even terms like 'canonical variation' and 'Delphi' seem to bear witness to this.) Part of the explanation for the lack of repute of futures studies, by and large, as well as for the general overlooking of the context of their contemporary growth, may lie in the nurture of many current practices and practitioners within the military—industrial complex.

This origin is well illustrated by the first generation of American futurologists, among whom were men like Herman Kahn and Clark Abt, often situated in institutes like RAND, prominent in forecasting developments of strategic technology, war gaming, and studies of potential international conflict and domestic unrest in various countries. It is still routine for forecasting techniques such as Delphi, trend extrapolation and morphological analysis to be illustrated in reviews of futures studies with examples of military and aerospace research.

This is not to argue that futuristic thinking was born in the Cold War Pentagon or even in the wartime British Operational Research groups. Perkin (1975) traces the rise of holistic forecasts of entire future societies to the early Enlightenment, with its developing notion of 'progress', and microforecasting in demography, economics and sociology to the eighteenth century reaction to the naive optimism of much holistic speculation. From their beginnings the social sciences were involved in the attempt to predict the future and construct desirable futures (e.g. positivistic sociology in the early nineteenth century) – efforts which have hardly gone unnoticed (e.g. the impact of Marx's work). However, several factors have combined to mute this tradition.

First, there is general division of futures-oriented research into disciplinary segments, so that population forecasts, economic forecasts, and social forecasts were generally carried out independently. Indeed, they are often restricted now to forecasting even more specialised details of processes within these three categories. Second, social researchers have generally failed to apply forecasting methods other than those based on the extremes of extrapolation of trends and prediction from controversial 'grand' theories of historical evolution. A third factor has been the recent predominance of the 'value-free' stance in the social sciences and an associated focus upon stasis and equilibrium rather than progress and change.

Thus, by the late 1960s, Winthrop was bemoaning the absence of professional sociologists from futures research, pointing out that both in the development of techniques and in the acts of forecasting and utopian thinking, 'economists, political scientists, psychologists, computer technologists and interdisciplinary professionals like operations research analysts are now making such projections for business, government and military leaders' (Winthrop, 1968, p.142). In fact, his review of futures research suggests that the role of both psychologists and political scientists in futures research is also strictly limited. The most prominent social scientists in this area derive not from traditional disciplines, but from management science and systems research, as noted in chapter 1.

Whether or not this is regarded as an abdication of responsibility by social scientists, the fact remains that, despite a worthy tradition of concern with the future, the dominant techniques employed in contemporary large scale forecasting research originated in attempts to cope with military and technological planning. By 'large scale' here is meant what Perkin (1975) refers to as 'macroforecasting': the attempt to present a wide panorama of developments in future society extending well beyond one single issue of concern. How far are these techniques, developed for situations where there are notionally few and clear goals to be achieved, applicable to the forecasting of complex social reality? Indeed, how far do such techniques yield 'valid' results in military and technological forecasting? The fact that such a technique has been widely adopted is no guarantee of its accurate insight into an uncertain future. The question of what 'validity' might mean for a forecast will be taken up shortly; for now it suffices to remark that advantages may accrue to users of forecasts independently of whatever truth value they might possess. Thus, for example, Malthusian doctrines proved a useful argument for nineteenth century gentlefolk seeking to prevent their compassionate contemporaries making social provisions for the poor; see also the use of pessimistic forecasts of world food supplies in attacks on aid to Third World countries.

The wide range of application of futures research techniques — in forecasting industrial marketing, administrative and scientific development — argues against their being solely appropriate to combat, defence and strategic technological issues. They may nevertheless have been generally adapted so as to apply to particular types of problems (e.g. those in which competitive advantage or profit is the predominant goal) or to serve particular types of interests (e.g. decision makers seeking approval of their plans).

There have been several valuable discussions of forecasting techniques. Jantsch (1967) exhaustively reviewed technological forecasting, drawing the distinction between exploratory and normative techniques that has been applied by many subsequent authors. The volume edited by Encel, Marstrand and Page (1975) provides extensive critiques of forecasting methodologies, and Mitroff and Turoff (1973) consider different epistemological bases for futures studies. Among other surveys of the field may be mentioned the May 1967 edition of *Science Journal,* devoted to futures studies, the general review of de Houghton et al (1971), and the technological forecasting collection of papers edited by Bright and Schoeman (1973). Although Jantsch distinguishes a large number of different techniques (and he is by no means exhaustive, since methodologies have continued to proliferate), most of these are variations on a few basic approaches, and many may be better viewed as aids to thinking and decision making rather than as forecasting tools. Again, it should be noted that many of these techniques do not appear to have found application to social forecasting at present.

A classification of forecasting techniques

Rather than describe each of a large number of techniques which are treated adequately in the sources mentioned above, I shall describe some conceptual bases for distinguishing among techniques. Five dimensions are discriminated in the following discussion. These suggest questions that may be posed concerning the stance taken by futures studies. The poles of each dimension represent extreme foci of different methods, and few studies adopt the polar extremes. These are distinctions between techniques; thus they do not exhaust the range of distinctions that may be drawn among different futures studies, which may differ in terms of, for example, timespan, geographic or cultural focus, scope (holistic versus microforecasts), etc. The five dimensions are:

1 *Normative versus exploratory* This dimension also encompasses the distinction between techniques that assume the future is malleable and those that view it as purely deterministic. Normative forecasting techniques are those that construct future alternatives in terms of specific goals and values, and illuminate the choices and actions required to actualise these futures. Exploratory forecasting techniques are those that attempt to determine the most likely future, and are thus most closely tied to the notion of prediction.
2 *Empiricist versus theoretical* This dimension expresses the distinction between techniques that derive forecasts from a combination of data and logical criteria, as against those that rely on formal and often complicated models of the phenomena concerned.
3 *Judgemental versus deductive* Some techniques rely heavily on the intuition and observation of experts and decision makers, while others employ information drawn directly from the area involved in the forecast.
4 *Quantitative versus qualitative* Forecasts may attempt to indicate the precise degree to which particular characteristics obtain in alternative futures, or they may simply suggest that relative increases and decreases exist and only loosely define many of the variables concerned. Some forms of quantitative technique attempt to reduce all the variation between alternative futures to a common metric, such as their profitability or social value, while qualitative techniques are much less specific.

5 *Consensual versus dissensual* Finally, some techniques strive to ignore or integrate divergent perspectives and produce a definitive conclusion, while others attempt to maintain variety, opposition and conflict without imposing an inadequate 'synthesis'.

Our ability to discriminate five dimensions suggests that the development of techniques has not been as restricted by the origins of modern futures research as might have been assumed. However, the distribution of research has not been uniform among this range of diverse techniques by any means. Dissensual techniques have only been rarely employed (see Mitroff and Turoff, 1973, who refer to 'Hegelian' approaches to forecasting), and some areas of research rely preponderantly on a single approach — e.g. population forecasting as carried out by government agencies largely uses exploratory, empiricist, deductive, quantitative and consensual techniques (such as trend extrapolation and components projection, as described by Brass, 1975; Glass, 1975). Other techniques, such as the conventional form of Delphi (exploratory, empiricist, judgemental, semi-quantitative, consensual) have been the subject of much attention. Delphi, for example, has found much uncritical application in forecasting developments in technology and science, although considerable scepticism has been expressed concerning its efficacy (e.g. Pill, 1971; Sackman, 1974). It has more dubiously been applied to the prediction of social and cultural changes, in respect of which the location of expert judges is a highly contentious matter.

The type of problem with which the forecaster is faced determines the type of technique most suitable for analysis, and, since the definition of problems involves value judgements, this will inevitably be the case with the choice of technique. The basic distinction between forecasts whose orientation is mainly normative and those which are mainly of exploratory nature requires clear value judgements. Exploratory forecasts may be thought of as providing advance warnings concerning future developments which may help those concerned to grasp opportunities or cope with the future. Normative forecasts, in contrast, are statements of points of influence and alternative policies which may be acted on so as to shape futures in desired directions. This is reminiscent of Popper's distinction between prophecy and technological prediction. The type or mixture of techniques chosen will depend on several factors: the believed capability of those to whom a forecast is directed to determine different aspects of the future (e.g. an industry may be seen as capable of developing particular commodities to meet a demand, but not of moulding the social forces creating the demand); their will to play an active role in planning various aspects of the future (e.g. until recently many governments were anxious not to be seen to be pursuing population policies, and so adopted passive roles in respect of demographic projections); the degree to which unpredictable factors may have intervened in this area, or to which there is controversy concerning the underlying causes of a phenomenon (e.g. the problems of role definitions faced by institutions concerned with cultural affairs, such as Britain's Arts Council); and the degree to which there is consensus, at least among those with effective power, concerning the desirability of alternative goals (e.g. the use of exploratory and normative approaches respectively by manufacturing/commercial and consumer interests in the study of futures in areas like transportation, environmental protection and communications).

Exploratory techniques tend to take for granted certain conditions that are questioned in normative techniques. For example, the extrapolation of a trend (e.g. admissions to particular institutions) or solicitation of expert judgement on rates of future progress (e.g. in an area of technical capability to achieve particular aims) assume the maintenance of whatever dynamic is creating the trend or progress — an unchanging social evaluation of the phenomena concerned. Thus early forecasts of the progress of the US space programme were accurate — until the political will to push it ahead began to weaken. Even exploratory forecasts which contain a greater theoretical component, such as the fitting of more sophisticated curves like the logistic, which is applied to trends which have clear logical or theoretical ceilings to their growth (such as the proportion of a population adopting an innovation), or the development of mathematical models which take into account public values (e.g. demographic—economic simulations that take into account economic determinants of desired family size), accept as fundamental the existence of relationships that may derive from a particular social matrix of pressures and policies. They thus often have a historicist character; but some exploratory forecasts are used within a framework in which the effects of different initial conditions (e.g. policies) are assessed.

In contrast normative forecasting techniques tend to focus more on constraints than on constants. Rather than, for example, attempting to predict the rate of diffusion of an innovation, or of change in some other social variable, these techniques are concerned with developing notions of what goals might be aimed for (in terms of ideal rates of change or levels of particular indices) and what efforts would be needed to achieve them. In fields such as economic planning, a 'normative' forecast will often be made following an exploratory forecast which suggests that, without intervention, some critical limit will be passed (e.g. that the unemployment level will be above 5 per cent). Normative forecasts adopt an approach of conditional prediction, 'if A happens then B will probably follow', but take as a starting point for analysis a statement of what 'B' is desirable and then attempt to find an 'A' that will maximise the likelihood of obtaining this future at least cost, environmental disruption, etc. Exploratory forecasting techniques may use either straightforward prediction, or conditional prediction in which analysis starts with a statement of what 'A' or range of 'A's' is feasible and probable. This distinction is important, since in Ozbekhan's (1968) terminology, in much futures literature, 'can' implies 'ought'. He argues that the effects of alternative developments – technological innovations, policies – are projected into the future to determine what might happen, while there is little attention paid to developing images of a desirable future which policies and technologies may be designed to create. Jantsch emphasises that normative forecasts are forecasts rather than simply plans. This is based on the necessity, when establishing future goals, of making forecasts of future needs rather than striving to meet the present level of needs at a future date. For example, if the population is expanding or contracting, it is clearly inappropriate to use the present levels of homelessness or malnutrition as guidelines by which to set future goals for housing or food production; instead some forecast of future levels of these needs is required. In practice, then, normative forecasts will rarely be 'holistic'; they will be supported by certain exploratory projections.

The distinction between empiricist and theoretical forecasting techniques can readily be illustrated by contrasting, on the one hand, techniques involving extrapolation of trends to obtain a view of the future or use of expert judgement to determine the probability of events occurring, with little concern about the social forces bringing this future into being, and on the other hand techniques which rely on explicit assumptions about relationships between different variables, such as computer simulations or forecasts based on theories stemming from sources as varied as Marxism, humanistic psychology, and games theory. Some techniques occupy intermediate positions on this dimension. Thus the application of logistic curves to trends usually involves a model of the underlying growth process in which an analogy is drawn with biological growth, and the development of cross-impact matrices and relevance trees by experts in a sense involves partial explication and formalisation of the implicit models on which expert judgements in techniques such as Delphi are based. What balance of theory and data is involved in a forecasting technique may or may not correspond to the development of research in the problem area. While no forecast can be entirely theory- and value-free, for reasons stated above (including the selection and interpretation of content areas and appropriate indices, and assumptions concerning the lack of influence of exogenous variables), much work has been presented without any spelling out of its underlying rationale, as if the forecast springs directly from neutral data once the assumption of historical continuity is invoked. At the opposite extreme, there has been a welter of 'forecasting' exercises using computer models of various systems in which the data used bear little resemblance to any real-world situation.

This issue also persists in the distinction between judgemental and deductive techniques. Computer simulations such as those just discussed often employ 'common-sense' or received notions of the incidence and relationships of phenomena, without subjecting them to empirical validation. (These tend to reflect a piecemeal set of assumptions rather than components of an integrated social theory.) Deductive techniques are those in which an attempt is made to derive or validate assumptions of the incidence and causality of phenomena from real situations. Judgemental techniques may involve just as much detail and formality as deductive techniques, but the measures then operationalised refer to the judgements of people believed to have knowledge of a situation rather than more directly to the aspects of the situation involved. Studies involving gaming, where human actors are involved in playing out roles in a simulated future, are judgemental in this sense, although the construction of the simulation ('the rules of the game') may be based on deductive technique, and the results of such studies may themselves be employed in theory construction to provide basic assumptions for other studies. One of the major thrusts of the systems approach to planning and forecasting has been an emphasis on operational measures of the performance of systems, but the time, resource and political costs of collecting such information still regularly make a case for mainly judgemental approaches. Helmer (1966) has argued the case for the use of expert judgement in situations where accepted theory fails to provide a clear action directive. He suggests, on the basis of Delphi studies, that an expert's own evaluation of his competence in an area is a useful guide to the quality of his judgements in that area. On the whole Helmer claims that there are large reservoirs of untapped expertise in the social sciences, but is unable to offer any adequate guidelines for choosing judges.

Some overlap of concern is again apparent in the distinction drawn between quantitative and qualitative techniques. Judgemental forecasts are often qualitive, concluding that a vaguely described but phenomenologically significant trend will continue, but they may also involve quantification: specific rates or dates may be proposed, probabilities may be attached to discrete judgements and the overall likelihood of composite scenarios calculated, etc. In current practice, deductive techniques are often used in conjunction with a high degree of quantification, but it is by no means uncommon for social research to conclude that a specific direction of effect occurs when one variable influences another, without achieving precision about the degree of this effect. Such findings may be employed in qualitative forecasting. Often it is useful to know that some phenomenon is likely to increase or decrease in frequency, without specifying the exact extent of this change; or to know that different policies are complementary rather than acting in different directions, without being able to ascertain immediately the strength of their effects. The demands of policy makers for quantitative forecasts whereby the 'effectiveness' of alternative policies can be compared has, however, led to the development of quantitative forecasting methodologies such as cost-benefit analysis in which an attempt is made to quantify all the forecast features of a scenario in terms of a single measure (money) – a move resisted by forecasters concerned with more intangible variables which seem to be best depicted in qualitative description. Other forecasters associated with the social indicators movement have argued against employing purely economic criteria, and have been enthusiastic about the prospects of quantitative forecasts over a wide range of societal variables (e.g. Gross, 1969; Bauer, 1966). Their general hope has been to develop social accounting systems which would allow for social fore- casting to develop along the lines of econometric forecasts. The distinction between quantitative and qualitative techniques, finally, is more than a distinction between the types of data available in dealing with specific issues, although a poorly developed data base may be of little use for quantitative techniques. It involves the difference between strong and weak assumptions about the continuity of historically observed relation- ships – system equivalence again – the former enabling the application of complex mathematical manipulations to one's information in which phenomena and relationships must be specified in exact detail, and the latter only involving a loose collation of inferences.

The distinction between consensual and dissensual forecasting tech- niques is one that is rarely required in practice, since the vast majority of futures studies involve consensual methods. The distinction is, however, perhaps indicative both of the traditional paradigms and of fairly recent changes in climate in the social sciences and planning. The social sciences, as described in the previous chapter, have been attacked as focusing too much on equilibrium and too little on conflict; planning has been accused of lacking in participation and openness to a diversity of publics.

Consensual and deductive approaches to forecasting are most readily exemplified where the technique used is overtly judgemental. In such cases forecasters frequently rely on averaging diverse opinions or on reiteration of judgement after feedback of the spectrum of results to achieve convergence of opinions (as in Delphi). However, the reasons for diverging opinions in forecasts can be crucially important, suggesting that erroneous or overlooked information is available to some individuals — factors that should surely be taken into account. Dissensual techniques, in contrast, attempt to identify the values, assumptions and information which lead to polarised judgements. By witnessing the conflict of forecasts, the forecaster or public may be in a more informed position to choose between alternative goals and strategies. Forecasts with a large deductive component in this technique may also be carried out either by consensual or dissensual methods, since the selection of constructs, validation of indices and credibility of alternative accounts of causal relationships themselves rely on assumptions that are open to dispute. Insofar as they have been deliberately employed, however, dissensual techniques seem to have been directed more towards revealing policy alternatives aiming to prevent false assumptions of consensus and to achieve synthesis in debate, than towards developing elaborate forecasts.

The 'validity' of forecasts

These five dimensions neither exhaust the possible contrasts that may be drawn between techniques, nor is their presentation meant to imply that most forecasting studies employ pure polar types of techniques. However, the main divergences that are of substantive interest are captured in these distinctions, and though it is possible to point to additional dimensions (e.g. techniques in which all relationships and events are taken to be completely determinate by known and predictable factors, as against those in which random and chance events may intervene), these are of less significance to the actual practice and output of forecasting. (See Bell et al, 1971, for a discussion of further issues of technique and underlying assumptions in the study of the social future.) Nor is it imagined here that, for example, it is really possible to be exploratory without using values, or empiricist without using theory, in choosing what and how to forecast. These distinctions reflect the degree of emphasis and affirmation of values and theories given in various techniques.

The description of these five dimensions of forecasting technique enables us to evaluate broad methodological approaches to the future rather than exhaustively review each of a large number of approaches. Likewise we avoid categorising techniques by their immediate ancestry, which would mean ignoring substantial differences in orientation. For example, Delphi techniques include not only the traditional empiricist exploratory and consensual Delphi, but a dissensual approach known as the policy Delphi and a normative technique called the goals Delphi. Delphi methods may be used in cross-impact matrices to evolve a more theoretical basis for forecasts. Likewise, simulation models may be employed in exploratory or in normative models (linear programming being a familiar form of the latter), and have been linked on-line to human actors and judges in some studies.

Broad considerations of validity and value apply to these dimensions of techniques, and it will be useful to discuss these here rather than when dealing with content areas of forecasting. Among many relevant enquiries concerning forecast 'validity', the following discussion is particularly indebted to those of Amara and Salancik (1972), Encel, Marstrand and Page (1975, especially part 3.8) and Martino (1973). As these reviews make clear, the problem of assessing forecasts is more than simply estimating 'correctness' or 'accuracy'.

The 'validity' of a forecast, in the sense of its having provided a substantially correct image of a future, cannot be ascertained until the eventual future has been realised, which is of little use to those seeking to base current decisions on such images. Furthermore, the role of the forecast itself in influencing social choice and change is important: the 'self-defeating' forecast clearly cannot be assessed in terms of its subsequent accuracy; nor can a 'self-fulfilling' forecast be assessed in terms of the options for future development which it implicity or explicity ruled out.

Building on Mitroff and Turoff (1973), who break down the forecasting process into a number of components, it is possible to distinguish:

(a)   a world of raw data, opinions, individual and group interests;
(b)   procedures for filtering, transforming and translating this data into usable information;
(c)   a forecasting technique that derives an image or images of the future from this information;
(d)   procedures for filtering, transforming and translating these images into a forecast usable in decision making; and
(e)   a decision making stage where policies and strategies are proposed.

(To take this working description as referring to a single flow without feedback would be crude. The decisions reached in stage (e) may be input as data into stage (a), so that the forecast is reiterated in the light of the proposed policies, and the forecasting technique in stage (c) may attempt to anticipate and create policy alternatives in advance of any action by the effective decision making individuals or bodies. Also, the discovery of particularly unexpected results at any stage in the process may cause a questioning and possible reorganisation of procedures carried out at earlier stages.)

Stages (b), (c) and (d): data selection and interpretation, application of techniques, processing and interpretation of results, constitute the forecasting act proper. Concerning each stage a number of issues arise which effect the 'validity' of the forecast. A schematic presentation of these criteria for assessing forecasts is provided below.

Stage (b): External consistency — is any important information omitted whose inclusion would be likely to affect the forecast?

Adequacy — is any information included which is invalid as a measure of the constructs or relationships employed in the forecast?

Representativeness — are the constructs selected appropriate for the concerns of the audiences to which the forecast is directed? Is the whole range of concerns dealt with, or are some aspects overlooked?

Stage (c): Reproducibility — does the technique reliably provide the same results when applied to the same data base?

Internal consistency — does the technique provide logically cohesive results?

Sensitivity — to what extent does the technique 'amplify' errors in the data base?

Stage (d): Clarity — is the forecast unambiguous with respect to variables of most concern to the audience?

Closure — are uncertainties explicitly represented as probabilities?

Temporal specificity — is there an attempt to specify key variables and turning points at which intervention has most impact upon the forecast future? Is the forecast temporal or atemporal — is there presented a line of evolution from the present to the depicted future?

Comparability — are alternative futures described in common terms so that their costs and benefits may be assessed relative to each other?

These general questions often take on specific forms when addressed to forecasts exemplifying poles of the five dimensions described earlier, and some of the major issues may thus be set out. Let us take the question of external consistency in some detail. While all forecasting techniques are forced to limit the amount of data input, the ways in which this becomes manifest vary, and may be represented in a rather exaggerated fashion as follows. Exploratory approaches involve scanning for data indicative of trends or discontinuities, normative approaches for those relevant to the realisation of values. Empiricist approaches rely on available 'common-sense' information without any explicit criteria of what is and is not relevant, while theoretical approaches prejudge what are appropriate data on the basis of what may be a limited perspective. Judgemental approaches call for selection of appropriate judges, and deductive approaches for statistical propriety in what may be a very improperly controlled reality where additional variables may always be called in to account for inconsistent observations. Gathering appropriate data may simply require too much effort for most researchers to attempt (for example, it is common to find empirical relationships that have been established by cross-sectional analysis of one point in time, being employed as surrogates for longitudinal relationships indicative of the dynamic interactions of variables over time). Quantitative approaches involve precision and the exclusion of unmeasured factors, as opposed to the fuzzy material used in qualitative approaches where the drawing of boundaries may be very difficult. Both consensual and dissensual approaches rely on some definition of competing interests, each of which may propose new categories of information, although consensual techniques involve either the exclusion or the obscuring of some competing viewpoints.

Rather than exhaustively list the application of each criterion to each idealised technique in the fashion outlined above, major points of concern only will be raised in the subsequent discussion. The question of adequacy has been given some treatment in the preceding chapter, where questions of the validity of indices were taken up. Discussion of the validation of theoretical statements or relationships will be considered at more length in the analyses in later chapters of social research traditions. With respect to normative forecasting, the selection of adequate indices in terms of which goals may be expressed is crucial; the ways in which social indicators researchers have addressed themselves to such matters is reviewed in chapter 5. Clearly, basing action on a normative forecast which revolves around a construct other than that with which one is really concerned – e.g. per capita food consumption, a measure which overlooks the distribution of food in society, rather than a direct measure of the incidence of malnutrition, if one's goal is a society free from hunger – can lead to serious problems. Both quantitative and qualitative techniques require particular assessment in terms of data adequacy: the former because of the possible oversimplification of complex phenomena into a small and trivially related set of factors, and the latter because of the problems of validation imposed by their frequent resort to broad categories whose implicit definition may vary from person to person. (For example, 'development', 'Westernisation', 'the information society', 'anomie' and 'equality' are all subject to a variety of interpretations.)

Representativeness is again of particular significance when normative forecasting techniques are employed. Of concern here is to what extent the goals and values used in the forecast are truly representative of the needs of those for whom the forecast is carried out, and whether attempts have been made to ascertain the degree of match. In general it is important to understand what values are incorporated in a forecast, either directly as in normative approaches or indirectly in the selection of constructs for exploratory techniques. As was pointed out in the preceding chapter, social science constructs and measures have been criticised for often reflecting conservative and inegalitarian biases.

The criterion of reproducibility may take various forms. Thus for empiricist techniques the stability of a projection when different statistical or quasi-theoretical assumptions are employed may be inspected (e.g. the form of an extrapolated trend when different curve-fitting methods are used). Theoretical techniques may also be scrutinised for the degree of dependence of a forecast to differing degrees of stringency in theoretical assumptions (e.g. the use of more or less probabilistic statements or, as in the case of stochastic simulation models in which random factors are incorporated, whether the model, when allowed to generate change through several trials representing the same lapse of time, yields similar future courses of development). One aspect of reproducibility applying to judgemental approaches involves the degree to which different judges and groups of judges yield similar appraisals of future developments; and in dissensual techniques there is the possibility of determining whether alternative opportunities for the grouping of interests yield similar polarisations and syntheses.

The striving for internal consistency of forecasts is exemplified by the checks carried out in quantitative and trend approaches to make sure that a component of a population (for example, the number of people experiencing some change) does not have more members than the total population. Salancik (1973) provides an interesting test of internal consistency for judgemental forecasts. In a Delphi study he related judges' estimates of the data at which events would occur to these events' estimated costs, benefits and technical feasibility. Internal consistency of the group forecasts was found in that less costly, more beneficial and more feasible events were, reasonably, expected to occur earlier. Clearly this sort of test could be applied to other judgemental techniques such as the construction of probabilistic relevance trees — it must be borne in mind, however, that all it is really assessing is the logical coherence of the expert judge, which might often be more profitably exposed to critical analysis by soliciting judgements of a less global and intuitive kind.

The sensitivity of forecasting techniques is a similar criterion to that of reproducibility, but refers to the effects of measurement errors on the forecast rather than to those of varying theoretical assumptions and statistical manipulations. Certain variables may be more important than others in a given forecast, in that small changes in their values may produce large changes in the depicted future. This criterion is particularly applicable to empiricist techniques where there is reliance on evidence of recent changes in variables, especially where these employ estimates rather than fully ascertained values. That class of quantitative–theoretical techniques that involves computer simulation is also of interest here: the models employed for forecasting in such simulations have often inbuilt characteristics that mean they are exceedingly insensitive to variations in their actual data input. For example, Hugger and Maier (1973) have shown that one world model (Forrester's World 2) yields forecasts of similar structure even when major changes are made in its data, although the time spans involved change considerably. In contrast, Scolnik (1974) undertook a sensitivity analysis of another world model (Meadows's World 3, the basis of *The Limits to Growth*, 1972). He found that changes of less than 5 per cent in the data input of a number of key variables were sufficient to change the forecasts for the next few centuries from catastrophic scenarios to more optimistic ones. It is impossible to make a general statement about how sensitive a forecast should be: the basis for using this criterion depends on the trustworthiness and error margins in one's data and the costs and benefits involved in acting or not acting on the forecast. Without knowing its sensitivity, however, an assessment of its worth for decision making is difficult.

Clarity of presentation of a forecast is not merely a matter of technique: skills of presentation and popularisation are involved. Quantitative techniques pose the problem of translating statistical and formalised language and conclusions into terms comprehensible to a less specialised public, whereas qualitative techniques, as already pointed out, are potentially prone to the production of ambiguous conclusions in which

c

even the direction of change may be unclear. The closure criterion asks whether the forecast as stated expressly presents statements of uncertainties and attempts in some way to survey this magnitude, or if it avoids or is imprecise with respect to these issues. In judgemental techniques the range of agreement among judges and in deductive techniques the percentage of variance which abstracted relationships account for, are among the determinants of the confidence one may have in a future eventuality and may thus be compared with the degree of closure presented in the forecast. Whether closure is justifiable is highly relevant to the formulation of action on the basis of forecasts. The likelihood of a disaster occurring obviously needs carefully weighing up with the other factors to be considered in making a decision about proceeding with development of a technological project. In normative forecasting, the feasibilities and potential constraints on action make similar demands for closure: the degree, the speed and the certainty of attaining a desired future must all be taken into account.

The criterion of temporal specificity serves to distinguish atemporal forecasts, that simply describe a future time without any credible description of the evolution of this future out of the present, from temporal forecasts in which a route from present to future is devised. If a normative forecast is a utopian statement of an ideal future with no guidelines given as to how it may be practically achieved, then it is temporally unspecific: its use as a forecast is less than any possible value it may have as critique of the *status quo* or expression of unrealised aspirations. The same objection may be raised against some theoretical treatments of the future in the social sciences: 'ideal types' are often invoked which lack correspondence with concrete realities – their value lies in the illumination of actual structures they provide, rather than in themselves representing temporal futures. More generally, temporal specificity may be seen as an analogue of the sensitivity criterion in terms of action directives. Does the forecast include statements about what interventions may be made and which variable values require particular degrees of change, so as to influence most the course of the future? Consensual and dissensual techniques differ in terms of this feature, with the former suggesting what interventions are most generally acceptable, and the latter suggesting those which are most effective for alternative ends. A temporally unspecific forecast may be very valuable in several ways. For example, the demonstration that a novel economic order is a self-consistent possibility not only undermines historicist assumptions, but may encourage forecasters or activists to find out how this order may be achieved.

54

Finally, the comparability criterion involves the assessment of forecasts in terms of whether they use a common language in describing alternative futures. Some quantitative techniques (e.g. cost-benefit analysis) attempt to reduce alternatives to a single criterion of monetary value, but in doing so they may actually be obscuring the crucial components of evaluation — the costs and benefits of alternative futures in terms of such variables as risks of fatalities, increases in income, comfort and leisure, changes in employment and health, etc. Few forecasts have made use of comprehensive, disaggregated, comparability procedures in which the implications of alternative futures — or even of a single future as compared to the present — are described in terms of those variables of most concern to the audience in a consistent manner.

The mechanics of quantitative techniques usually admit of such detail, for example a computer simulation model will usually use the same set of variables when describing different futures, and these futures may thus be compared directly in terms of such variables. Qualitative techniques are generally less capable of yielding comparability: it may be possible to say that each of two futures, for example, exhibits more of a particular quality than does the present, but not to discriminate between them.

The performance of forecasting

Different types of forecasting problem demand different forecasting techniques, and should emphasise different aspects of 'validity' as the above discussions indicate. The values and goals of individuals, groups and organisations diverge within the wider community in which they are situated, and the constructs employed in forecasts for such actors are likely to be correspondingly weighted towards their interests. Actors lacking effective power to influence wide social trends may seek exploratory forecasts in order to cope with a future whose main characteristics are more or less to be imposed on them. If 'predictive' theory is unavailable in a particular field, then making exploratory projections may be a more worthwhile investment of resources than attempting to develop new theory. The use of authoritative judgement may likewise be more feasible than trying to derive forecasts from data which would take undue time to collect or which are questioned by such authorities. Quantitative techniques may be seen as over-precise given the state of development of social research, or as exclusive of too many unquantified issues of major concern; and dissensus may be avoided in order to prevent irreconcilable positions developing which would prevent future compromise.

How far, in fact, has forecasting been addressed to problems of different sorts, and how appropriate have the techniques employed been for dealing with them? In the remainder of this chapter these questions will be asked in a brief survey of 'mainstream' futures research; in later chapters we will consider forecasting's role in the social sciences proper.

The immediate ancestors of the modern American futures studies which have influenced such research so widely are, first, the forecasts of technological developments and international conflict prepared originally for military application, and, second, forecasting of demographic and economic change for the use of economic planners. In the initial period following the Second World War, the techniques elaborated for these purposes mainly consisted of trend extrapolation techniques for technological forecasting, gaming and scenario-building (with some use of operational research ideas in evaluation of strategies) in conflict research, and accounting in microeconomics and population forecasting. By the early 1950s these approaches were beginning to find wider application in industry, marketing and associated consultancies, while newer techniques were being diffused — notably the formalisations of game theory (for conflict research), mathematical modelling (econometrics) and morphological and decision tree analyses (normative technological forecasting). Although the roots of some techniques had existed for some time, they only began to blossom fully in this period. Technological forecasting developed rapidly in the booming aerospace industries of the late 1950s, with the novel difficulties involved in the co-ordination of logistic components of achieving such specific goals as landing a man on the moon. The systems analysis approach evolved as a way of coping with the complexity of the organisational problems there encountered. As the US administration confronted a changing world situation, 'rational' planning methods were imported into governmental defence policy making, and later into other policy fields: PPBS (program planning budget systems) and cost-benefit analyses were imposed on the Pentagon by Robert McNamara; tools evolved by economists and mathematicians began finding application in political and social planning decision making. With the changing social climate of the middle and late 1960s — student and racial unrest, Vietnam, the 'environmental crisis', separatist and anti-bureaucratic movements in Western countries — a submerged stream of futures research came to the surface. Once again macroforecasting was acceptable, perhaps because of the manifest failures of policies based upon microforecasts to satisfy changing public needs and of technological forecasts to exercise an antitechnology *Zeitgeist*.

The re-emergence of holistic forecasting drew upon researchers and techniques from many sources. Social issues became the concern of systems analysts, who often turned to tackling social problems through the construction of computer simulations. World futures were more generally approached by extrapolative techniques which would tend to focus on problems of population growth and environmental disruption, although Kahn and Wiener (1967) brought scenario-writing techniques to geopolitical issues. European scholars who had for many years been pressing the case for systematic futures studies at last found an audience. Futurology was a fad.

With the establishment of journals of futures research (e.g. *Futures, The Futurist, Technological Forecasting and Social Change),* futures studies groups and futures conferences, research techniques and interests proliferated and interbred. Systems analyses were applied to world problems, Delphi studies to cultural change, trend extrapolations to forecasting wars, and so on. Conflicts have become apparent between predictors, planners and utopians, activists and scholars (Dror, 1973; see also Amara, 1974). At a less academic and less publicly apparent level, forecasting proceeds quietly within various governmental institutions and is regarded as indispensable for policy making; intergovernmental organisations have been increasingly concerned with the related issues of social accounting and technology assessment.

Clearly forecasting techniques have been applied to a wide range of issues, and, equally, a wide span of techniques has been generated. The task of assessing even a fraction of this output would be enormous. However, it is less difficult to look at broad tendencies and emphases of futures research.

A first point is that the applicability of the currently dominant forecasting techniques to many problems appears to have been overstated. Even their apparent success in dealing with military strategic and aerospace problems has been seriously questioned. Hoos (1972) mounts a trenchant attack on the use of systems analysis and Wilson (1970) points particularly to the failures of simulation and gaming research. Such critics have cited examples of massive underestimation of costs, the development of practically functionless information systems, and major strategic failures in the application of these techniques. Wilensky (1967), writing before the criticisms were widely diffused, addressed similar issues of knowledge and policy making from a sociological standpoint, describing a variety of processes that affect the effective use of such 'intelligence' as forecasts within complex organisations. In many cases these problems relate to the multiplicity of goals in social organisations, even those popularly regarded as monolithic. Rivalry between departments, for example, may lead to the production of a forecast reflecting particular interests and stressing those factors advantageous to the department initiating it. Wilensky argues that units of organisations that can employ apparently 'hard' data showing that following their priorities rather than those of other units will be most cost-effective, are at an advantage where budgeting is concerned. (See Beneveniste, 1972, for further pespectives on such issues.) Thus contenders for resources will sometimes benefit from producing forecasts whose 'validity' is likely to be questionable in terms of most of the criteria cited earlier.

Nor did Wilensky find that the use of systematic assessment techniques was proving satisfactory in situations where a supposedly unitary goal (military victory) is, in a complex situation, translated into a large number of sub-goals. Commenting on the use of such measures of 'progress' in the Vietnam war as body counts and kill ratios, he points out their focusing of attention away from unquantified variables, such long run costs as declining levels of popular support, and aboslute outcomes, to the relative short term, qualitative performances of the combatants. In the counter-insurgency situation, these statistics can be seen as desperate substitutes for the battle line that provided a fairly obvious indicator of progress in conventional war.

It may be questioned whether such failures truly represent short-comings of forecasting techniques themselves, or a lack of resolve to develop 'valid' forecasts in the face of functional interests, political pressures, wishful thinking, etc. As has been argued, however, problem definition and selection of constructs reflect values, and thus any forecast must possess an evaluative component. While criteria for 'validity' may be applied within institutional contexts, the degree of value consensus within institutions will affect the degree to which the forecast is critiqued in terms of representativeness, external consistency and closure, for example. (This is not to mention the possible limitations of those interested in a forecast to test the reliability of information involved, which may be confidential, proprietary or deliberately and carefully distorted. This is not only a problem with military secrets: estimation of reserves of natural resources, for example, may be in the hands of those organisations who extract them, and who stand to gain or lose by forecasting shortage or abundance.) Dissensus concerning forecasts certainly does exist, and is even institutionalised with different government departments and agencies creating their own forecasts. But the resolution of such dissensus is generally conducted at a purely political level, with little exposition of underlying values and assumptions in the light of criteria such as those outlined above.

Turning to futures research in general, and its social planning applications in particular, it is relatively easy to find critical reviewers and researchers who are of the opinion that mainstream futures studies are heavily weighted towards particular values and interests. The technological determinism of much forecasting has been a particular target. This is subject to two interpretations: that technology has its own inbuilt evolutionary imperative, driving material progress along a single inevitable course, or simply that technological change is the major cause of social change. These interpretations are by no means contradictory, and many commentators have merged them into the thesis that the course of societal development is inevitably largely unidirectional, with the rate of development dependent on the rate of innovation in an ordered series of technologies. Aspects of this viewpoint and its limitations were encountered in chapter 1 and will again be raised in later discussions of social theory.

The critique of technological determinism in forecasting may be seen to be an indictment of futures research as preoccupied with exploratory methods of study. Other deterministic viewpoints (economic, sociological psychological, biological) are criticised on basically similar grounds – they fail to allow for the possibility of designing desirable futures and acting so as to attain them. Even many studies presenting 'alternative futures' are fatalistic in that the factors producing these alternatives are the starting point of analysis, rather than an image of the future.

Whereas in its original military–industrial contexts technological forecasting often had a normative stress, directing the search for new gadgetry to achieve strategic or corporate ends, when adopted in other contexts for futures research it becomes decidedly exploratory. Thus potential technologies are uncovered by organisations which regard them as desirable in terms of their own ends; these technologies enter a wider consciousness without so much being questioned concerning the 'imperatives' that have given rise to them as being viewed as givens, the assessment of whose social impact is the proper task of futures studies. The technologies are predicted with confidence; the forecaster is left with the task of anticipating their effects.

In this vein Jungk (1969), who has been long involved in futures research with the Mankind 2000 project and the Institute for the Future (founded in 1954), argues that many futures studies simply rationalise the interests which stand to gain from particular technological changes. These interests seek to make opposition appear romantic, atavistic or nihilistic by portraying particular technologies as evolutionary necessities. As an example he quotes this theme in the aircraft industry's arguments and forecasts for supersonic transport. The inclusion of social research considerations into technological forecasts he views as increasing the sophistication of manipulation rather than clarifying issues of design – a point that may readily be evaluated by looking at the treatment of values, social change and politics in anthologies of technological forecasting literature (e.g. Bright and Schoeman, 1973). Cross, Elliot and Roy (1974) have edited a selection of readings on futures research that reprints several discussions of the passive fatalism of much of this field, notably Jungk (1969), Kumar (1972) and Ozbekhan (1968). Relevant assessments of normative and exploratory approaches may also be found in Encel, Marstrand and Page (1975).

To some extent the dissatisfaction with the technological determinism of futures studies is a reflection of a more general critique of the role accorded technology in Western societies. This critique deplores the bureaucratic and centralised features of modern, industrialised societies, and the possibilities of mass destruction through military technologies. It often involves the fear of ecological imbalances resulting from unrestricted pollution, and less specific sense of a deteriorating quality of life. The impact of these concerns on forecasting activities is twofold. First, diverse scholars have forecast ecological doom and/or technocratic repression (e.g. Ellul, 1965; Heilbroner, 1974). Diverse prescriptions follow from such diagnoses: fatalistic acceptance of an erosion of freedoms, abandonment of high technology and luxurious living, some form of strict international policing authority to co-ordinate world interests, building alternative institutions into a viable counterculture, armed resistance to state repression etc. Recent critiques of the antitechnological and élitist stance of some of the more pessimistic forecasts have included Cole et al (1973) who exhaustively analyse 'systems dynamics' models of the world both in formal and ideological aspects, Golub and Townsend (1975) who provide further comment on the interests of multinational organisations in particular kinds of world stability, and Christopher Freeman (1974) who reviews Heilbroner's 'human prospect'. Second, interest has arisen in technology assessment, usually defined as the attempt to forecast the social and environmental effects of technological alternatives, as well as their purely economic consequences, in order to facilitate social choices and strategies for control.

The growth of work in this latter area is illustrated by the publication by the OECD of a volume reviewing the technology assessment (TA) literature (Hetman, 1973) just six years after their publication of a review of technological forecasting (Jantsch, 1967). The practice of TA has itself, however, been subject to criticisms of the same kind as have been levelled against other futures studies (e.g. Encel, Marstrand and Page, 1975, part 3; Wynne, 1975). Among these criticisms is the fundamental charge that TA has not been concerned with the normative design of technologies whereby desirable futures may be obtained, but with passive, exploratory forecasting of the effects of proposed innovations. Even though TA is supposed to help in decision making about such innovations, it is rare to find assessments which are not focused on a single innovation rather than a range of alternatives. The funding and practice of TA is restricted mainly to powerful and interested organisations, furthermore, and the range of effects considered is often patently inadequate (Wynne, 1973).

TA has been institutionalised in the USA by Acts requiring assessment of the environmental consequences of major projects; it is applied in the British Ministry of Technology, and has been urged upon all of us rather as 'the future' was in the late 1960s. Again, the 'technology assessors' are, in many cases, yesterday's futurologists and technology forecasters. As a step towards futures studies making explicit their value premises it is long overdue, but as these criticisms suggest, the process is far from complete in contemporary TA.

So far the problems of futures studies have been described mainly in terms of the emphasis on exploratory rather than normative forecasting techniques, and the biasing of forecasts by judicious use of data and constructs. It could also be pointed out that, where social considerations have been tacked on to what are often predominantly technological forecasts, these factors have usually been described and worked out in qualitative and judgemental fashions. One consequence of this has been that futures research is not accepted as a branch of the social sciences — at least, there are few texts on social research that mention futures studies (an exception being Easthope, 1974, who, however, believes that comparative research in sociology is inherently unscientific due to history providing insufficient cases for comparison!). The rise of social indicators research, which often has an explicit future orientation, may change this state of affairs.

Several authors have attacked the predominance of consensual techniques in futures research. The question of conflicting norms and values is one that is rarely raised in such research, unless it be for the purposes of optimising the marketing or acceptance of innovations. To some extent this may be attributed to the enormity of the issues faced by futures researchers: nuclear war, the population explosion, radical new technologies. Probably more significant is the institutional context of such research. As Beneveniste (1972, chapter 4) points out, expert advisers are prone to play down the political components of their work, concentrating on the value of systematic analysis for increasing the efficiency of achieving goals selected by policy makers. Likewise Boguslaw (1965), who identified systems analysts as being the technical group most concerned with social design, concluded that the values stressed by these 'new utopians' were efficiency values rather than normative goals, which are not seen to pose any problems of definition! Beneveniste argues that the specification of goals for forecasting and policy analysis threatens conflict unless consensus already exists within the organisation, and so dissensual aspects of future strategy and assumptions about the present are prudently minimised.

Several commentators have explicitly viewed futures research as often attempting to produce social consenus (e.g. Carey and Quirk, 1973). By forecasting better times ahead, it is argued, authorities may ease present discontent; by forecasting unpleasant contingencies if the future remains unplanned, they may legitimate proposed extensions of their power (e.g. Golub and Townsend, 1975). Of course, some futures studies do emanate from critical sources non-supportive of the present distribution of power (Amara, 1974 estimates that between 10 and 25 citizen groups are active in the futures field in the USA), the work of proponents of alternative technology could be cited (e.g. Dickson, 1974), and much Marxian writing is highly future-oriented, for example. Such work is itself partisan and presents a particular viewpoint.

There have been few studies which have deliberately set out to capture dissensus (as compared to those which create or reinforce dissensus by reaching conclusions with which others disagree). Those known to the author are Schneider (1972) and Skutsch and Schofer (1973) which are applications of Delphi method to goals definition, the Koelle (1974) study of the development of social indicators, and Mason's 'Dialectical Inquiring System' reported by Mitroff and Turoff (1973). Of these, Skutsch and Schofer and Koelle apparently failed to provide participants with information concerning the group origin of different opinions which would have allowed for conscious polarisation to take place, and their studies may be thought of as lying in a tradition of psychological research into individual determinants of future perspectives (see the bibliography of Huber, 1971, and the review in Weaver, 1969 for this tradition).

The idea of dissensual forecasting seems to amount to a formalisation of political decision making. Whether it is really feasible to translate conflicts of values into scientistic structures of rational choice is at least doubtful. However, the acceptance of dissensus as a feature of forecasting could produce a welcome opening of the forecasting process to wider participation. Futures research is carried out by experts — academics and planners — and the assessment of alternative futures has largely been a technocratic function. De Jouvenel (1967) has called for the establishment of 'surmising forums' in which alternatives might be developed and presented for democratic choice, and Mankind 2000 is currently attempting to establish resources for more widespread communication for such purposes. At present public involvement in futures studies is discouraged by institutional and informational factors, despite grass-roots campaigns and officially avowed support for increased participation in community and local planning.

In general the possibility of democratic involvement in futures studies and associated fields has been largely overlooked. Citizens could be involved in many roles: selecting relevant constructs for forecasts, developing and criticising social indicators, creating policies and goals, evaluating possible futures for reiteration of forecasts, in gaming and human simulations of futures, etc. The current involvement of the public in forecasting is systematically biased: some groups have more economic and political information and influence than others. Thus constructs are selected for policy makers by lobbying and political contacting; complaints about the functioning of the social services help define appropriate social indicators, and voluntary associations propose policies and goals and criticise party platforms and official forecasts. Futures researchers have largely ignored such issues of citizen participation, and it is appropriate that their optimistic forecasts are so often of 'efficient', technocratic societies.

4 Social Change and the Social Indicators Movement

Futures studies have rarely explicitly acknowledged sociological theories of social change, and what contact has been made is selective. This chapter sets out to review some elements of social change theories, relating these to the underlying assumptions of mainstream futures research.

A pioneer in the use of statistical material for social analysis and forecasting, William F. Ogburn, left a body of theoretical and empirical work which provides useful insights into the practice of futures research. Contemporary social indicators research can be seen to be prefigured in his work. The growth of the 'social indicators movement', is outlined briefly, in this chapter which concludes with a summary of some contributions social indicators research might be seen to make to futures studies.

Theories of social change

As remarked in chapter 2, the study of social change, especially where large scale changes in whole societies are concerned, was largely neglected in the postwar era by sociologists. It was during this period that modern futures studies evolved. Classical nineteenth-century sociology was addressed to the problems faced by Western societies in the throes of the industrial and political revolutions. Founding fathers such as Comte and Marx were concerned with uncovering the regularities underlying these massive social changes, and attacked a view of history as produced by unpredictable individual genius or metaphysical forces. In the turbulence of the early twentieth century, the phenomena of growing bureaucratisation and increasing differentiation of the occupational structure also engrossed major social theorists. Following the Second World War, international polarisation and a decline in overt domestic conflict in economically growing Western societies seem to have been involved in directing social research away from the question of large scale social change. While exceptions may be found, an academic consensus seems to have been reached that macrosocial change was no longer a problem for either social theories or modern societies and their leaders.

The resurgence of interest in such matters seems to have initially been restricted to the study of developing countries, with the theory of post-industrial social change emerging fairly recently as a tool for understanding Western social change. These approaches to the study of change will be reviewed in latter chapters; this chapter is concerned with the evolution of a methodology for studying social change (social indicators), and, immediately, with different approaches to explaining change. The degree to which these underlying conceptions of change are employed in futures studies will affect the type of forecasts produced, their compatibility with social theory and data, and the prescriptions for action that derive from them.

Various reviewers have drawn distinctions between different views of change (e.g. Allen, 1971; Appelbaum, 1970; Cohen, 1969; LaPiere, 1965; Nisbet, 1969). A primary distintion is made between theories that are 'evolutionary' and those that are not. Assumptions similar to those of evolutionary theories are most generally reflected in futures studies, although these assumptions are rarely stated or scrutinised. In statements of an evolutionary perspective by classical sociologists, it was often assumed that societies pass through a unilinear series of stages, representing progress, a civilising of human nature and society, a transition from lower to higher forms of organisation. Understanding the nature of this series would enable social prediction. Transition between stages was generally viewed as inevitable, regular and smooth, although some theorists (e.g. Marx) saw it as marked by conflict, while being no less natural and lawful. The prime mover of change was attributed by different writers to various causes lying within the society, such as the growth of knowledge, the organisation of production, or the growth of national populations. Often pure historicism reigned: social evolution was treated as a natural law.

The main classical non-evolutionary perspective is that of 'cyclical' theory: again societies are seen as passing through a series of stages, but this series represents a movement from growth through maturity to decay, following which growth begins anew. Evolutionary theorists often draw a parallel between the development of societies and that of species in biological evolution; cyclical theorists are more likely to point to the resemblance between the history of societies and the life cycle of a single organism. Since most contemporary cyclical theorists view Western society as passing through the last phase of the cycle (see Sorokin, 1950), and thus to predict disintegration followed by the emergence of a new order, their writings have little appeal to most forecasters (whose underlying commitment is to an ideal of progress). Hence Kahn and

Wiener (1967) directly employ many of Sorokin's concepts in describing their 'multifold trend' of Western society, but divest them of their cyclical underpinnings.

The techniques of futures studies (see chapter 3) are largely derived from technological forecasting. The striking centuries-long and apparently uninterrupted growth of technological capability in the West lends itself to exploratory forecasting of technological parameters. The techniques developed for this purpose are not readily compatible with cyclical notions of social change, let alone predictions of social collapse. Furthermore, while simple extrapolation of some social parameters might lead the naïve forecasters to predict that in the near future growth levels so unprecedented will obtain that some form of collapse seems inevitable, the professional is armed with logistic curves and feedback loops which can ward off such anticipations. For example, Frejka (1973) avoids the doomsday projections of population growth circulated by some commentators by introducing tendencies for the world population to reach an equilibrium state. There is, of course, a more apocalyptic fringe of the futures studies movement, to whom cyclical notions may prove congenial, but even so the notion of cultural decline rarely occupies a central place in futurological writings, and if collapse is predicted, then it is either an ultimate catastrophe (e.g. annihilation of life on earth) or a temporary setback (e.g. limited nuclear war).

Evolutionary approaches are prevalent in the current literature of social change, despite being assailed as ethnocentric or overly deterministic by many sources. These criticisms have been responded to by more sophisticated neo-evolutionists, taking into account the divergent development of societies by proposing theories of multilinear evolution. In such theories the 'prime mover' or combination of influences promoting social change are seen to have different effects when acting in different contexts (such as seventeenth-century England and twentieth-century India), and thereby promoting distinctive causes of social evolution. The modern adherents to evolutionary views are also less prepared than their forebears to see change as inevitable, although speculation about whether stages may be leapfrogged, whether evolution is reversible or whether societies may change from one evolutionary path to another is uncommon. Cyclical approaches to change are much less widely espoused at present, one cause probably being their conflict, whether apparent or real, with the fact of contemporary attainment of unprecedented levels of material growth. While the cycles depicted in such theories often referred to moral or ideological changes, social commentators have been struck by the magnitude of technological and intellectual change, and frequently see this as the major component and motor of social change. Even influential proponents of cyclical theories have appeared to modify their views so that history could be viewed as a spiralling progress (see Sklair, 1970, chapter 5).

However, one aspect of the cyclical perspective has been assimilated by social theory: the organismic metaphor for society. From this metaphor is derived the notion that societies strive to maintain equilibrium, and that social phenomena may thus be understood as serving equilibrating functions. The transmission of this metaphor may be related to the fact that Talcott Parsons, whose structural–functional theory dominated American sociology in the 1950s and 1960s, himself studied under Sorokin.

As well as viewing the pattern of social change as taking different forms, social scientists and historians have disagreed as to the factors promoting change. Some changes are viewed as stemming largely from within society itself: it creates its own dynamic and change is immanent. Sorokin (1947, 1957) studied the historical evolution of cultural systems (e.g. the Chinese, Graeco-Roman, and Western), employing quantified judgemental measures of cultural tendencies in such areas as science, the arts and law at different periods. His work should thus be of particular interest to those who employ quantitative material in the study of long term futures, but it is currently neglected. (This is probably in part due to his idiosyncractic style, cyclical theorising and moralising. The only researcher to approach Sorokin's level of detail has been Kroeber, 1944, whose mammoth effort of data collection concerning developments in philosophy, arts and sciences did not, in contrast, indicate any general laws of social change. He did, however, locate periods of 'cultural florescence'.) The perils of extrapolation from a restricted data base (e.g. predicting the growth of population for centuries hence on the basis of trends in the past fifty years) remarked on in chapter 3 might be expected to lead exploratory forecasters to make use of long historical time series. As it is, Kahn and Wiener (1967) have referred to Sorokin's work, but most social forecasting has relied upon much more restricted analyses – for example the work of Riesman (1950) on value changes in contemporary America is a clear influence on authors speculating about the post-industrial personality.

To simplify Sorokin's exceedingly elaborate description of the change process, which he sees as continual, all institutions are viewed as being able to take only a limited number of basic forms which reflect different underlying world views. As a society becomes saturated by forms of a particular type, creativity is stifled and achievement inhibited by over-organisation until social disintegration is inevitable. Sorokin (1957, pp.699–701) forecasts that the future of Western society is such disintegration. Cynical and war-mongering governments will reign, uninterested in their citizens' welfare as the standard of living falls; legal authority will become corrupt and force and fraud rule; high culture will be abased by mass media.

Most evolutionary theories are based on immanent principles of change. Marx and Engels (1849) and Marx (1867) viewed social evolution as the result of class conflict which changes the economic relationships within society as new means of production arise. Ogburn, whose work will be reviewed in more detail shortly, saw technological change as creating the necessity for social changes, with institutions adjusting to new technological capabilities after a 'cultural lag'. Durkheim (1893) saw social change as a product of increasing differentiation (division of labour) in society, itself reflecting technological change and population growth. Parsons's theory (1951, 1961) is less concerned with change but again stresses increasing differentiation, both of labour and of institutional structures as an equilibrating response to strain caused by such factors as inequalities and conflicting values. Exogenous influences such as environmental challenges and international affairs may also promote such change.

Changes emanating from forces exogenous to a society have been particularly taken into account by theorists of Third World development. Such writers usually espouse an evolutionary view, seeing poor countries as 'modernising' or 'traditional' with technological innovation stimulating change and traditional values hindering it. This perspective has generally been adopted by forecasters, although dissent has been expressed by both development experts and, more recently, by some futures researchers (e.g. Dator, 1974). Sociological research into change has largely stressed internal causes of change, leaving exogenous factors to the historian and political scientist.

Social change theories have also been categorised into 'conflict' and 'equilibrium' approaches. Conflict theories include those in the Marxist tradition, among which are such revisions of Marx's ideas as that of Dahrendorf (1959), who rejects the notion of social evolution towards communism. Social change is viewed as resulting from conflicts generated by the structure of society, its allocation of resources to particular interests and the distribution of power incorporated in it. Conflict approaches, whether seeing social change as evolutionary or not, tend to locate the source of change within a society. Equilibrium notions, on the other hand, like those of Parsons and Ogburn (who sees institutions as moving towards equilibrium with technologies) are applicable to both

69

endogenous and exogenous change. Technological change is frequently the leading factor in descriptions of social change derived from this perspective, just as in most social forecasting. It is of interest, then, that Daniel Bell, a sociologist noted for his interest in futures studies, has attempted to distinguish a radically different basis for social change. Bell describes three types of model of social change important for forecasting (Bell, 1967, pp.975–6; contrast pp.642–4). Essentially, he appears to be distinguishing between planned social change and changes that are 'crescive' (long term technological or demographic changes and their effects), or the result of social demands (i.e. group conflicts). The emergence of national and local planning and forecasting activities, and the greater role of state authorities in many institutional areas, have led several social theorists to focus on social change contingent upon planning (e.g. Etzioni, 1968). This viewpoint accords with many forecasters' interests, both legitimising their activity and potentially bringing them closer to the decision making process. Planned change is viewed as somehow distinctively different from other forms produced by conflict or equilibration. The need for improved social information in an active, planning society has influenced the growth of the social indicators movement (and of technology assessment).

Futurologists largely employ evolutionary, or a mixture of evolutionary and planning, ideas. Conflict is rarely featured explicitly, although sometimes forecasting is clearly an attempt to anticipate criticism of an innovation. Before turning to developments concerning social indicators as aids to monitoring and forecasting change, however, we shall briefly consider what lessons may be drawn from the work of William F. Ogburn, an early advocate and practitioner of social accounting and forecasting who also saw these as necessary inputs to a planning process.

William F. Ogburn: social statistics and prediction

Ogburn's pioneering work in the development and compilation of social statistics has been referred to in chapter 2. His contribution to current futures studies extends beyond his early attempts at social accounting; he also proposed a theory of social change, and both practised systematic social forecasting in a way that was most original for a social scientist (while being quite familar, in a less systematic manner, to science fiction writers such as H.G. Wells), and theorised about the requirements of such forecasts.

Future-oriented perspectives are apparent in much of Ogburn's work,

70

although a shift in emphasis is detectable in his major works from theorising about social change *(Social Change,* 1922), to monitoring social trends (the series on social changes, 1929–1935, 1942, and the 1933 report of the President's Research Committee on Social Trends, *Recent Social Trends*), to forecasting the social impact of new technologies (the Report of the Sub-Committee on Technology to the National Resources Committee, *Technological Trends and National Policy* 1937; *The Social Effects of Aviation,* 1946; *Technology and International Relations,* 1949; *Technology and the Changing Family,* with M.F. Nimkoff, 1955). Duncan (1964) has edited a useful selection of Ogburn's writings which reveals the continuity of theoretical perspectives throughout his work.

Ogburn (1922) viewed man's biological nature as having remained basically unchanged from the time of our ancient ancestors. Social change was to be viewed in terms of the evolution of culture rather than of intellectual capacity. Culture itself evolves through the accumulation of inventions and discoveries, whether technological or social. Individual genius is less significant in the production of inventions than is the cultural base of knowledge on which they are built. As supporting evidence for this assertion, Ogburn points out that significant inventions are rarely made in isolation – an investigation of over a hundred recent inventions revealed each to have been discovered simultaneously, or nearly so, by two or more independent workers. Each invention, furthermore, adds to the cultural base. As the cultural base increases with the accumulation of knowledge, inventions should become more frequent. To support this deduction, Ogburn demonstrated an exponential growth in inventions in various fields. This accelerating trend of discoveries could be accounted for, furthermore, if new inventions were seen as combinations of existing elements in the cultural base. Of course, while exponential growth is made possible as additions to a set of cultural elements multiply the number of such combinations that may be attained, the realities of social demands or other constraints may damp this growth.

As well as accumulation and invention, Ogburn (1922) explained the process of social change with two additional concepts: diffusion and adjustment. Diffusion occurs between cultures that are in contact, where inventions are transmitted across cultural boundaries and brought together to form new cultural bases and speed social evolution. Cultures are organised, however, and need not passively absorb inventions. Inventions may be resisted by vested interests that would lose through change, as well as by habits and conservatism. The organisation of cultures also means that inventions in one part of culture produce pressures for change on closely related cultural areas, and a process of adjustment of parts of

71

society to each other is necessitated. Adjustments may be delayed when different areas change at different speeds; Ogburn introduced the notion of 'cultural lag' to describe temporary maladjustments, which he believed only existed in the short term although they might then prove acute stimulants of change. In a later reference to the early ideas, Ogburn (1957) reiterates his position that contemporary cultural lags are predominantly the product of social organisations trailing behind technological change. He points to such examples as the failure of many Asian populations to adjust birth rates to falling death rates, or urban dwellers to adjust to modern city life, and the lack of civil defence provisions to adjust to the threat of nuclear war. Major upheavals such as the Second World War and the Chinese Revolution, on the other hand, are viewed as often reducing cultural lags and accelerating change. It would be easy for the historian of futures studies, looking back at such work, to read into Ogburn attitudes that better characterise some later forecasters. It would be unwarranted, in fact, to suppose that he was arguing that Asians should adopt Western ways and limit their family sizes without concern for their material circumstances, that the human psyche should be technologically adjusted to cities rather than vice versa, or that we should all be living in fallout shelters. Latter-day technological determinists and technological 'fixers' represent a far less well-informed brand of social commentator than Ogburn, who was himself, foremost, a social scientist.

In the first of his series of reports on social trends, Ogburn (1929) stressed the scale and rapidity of recent social change, and, as he was later to do in the Report of the President's Research Committee on Social Trends (1933), pointed out to social scientists and planners the importance of quantitative research. His theory of social change is one in which continuity is emphasised: new inventions are combinations of existing elements, and qualitative changes are rare. Insofar as prediction of the future, so necessary for active administration, is possible, the best tools available consist of statistical information such as measured trends and time series. His faith in what are now known as social indicators was strong, since he believed that accumulating knowledge of this form would help men understand, anticipate, and eventually try to control, the course of social evolution. Unlike some modern advocates of social accounting, however, he believed that control of social change did not lie in the immediate future. The tasks for now were description, which could be accomplished given sufficient resources, and prediction, for which the development of capabilities and skills should be encouraged.

The volumes of social trend data he edited bear comparison with modern social indicator compilations (see Encel, Marstrand and Page,

72

1975, part 3.5 for illustrations of this), covering such issues as trends in population, production, employment, public health, communications, the family, crime and religion. Even where quantitative data were not to hand (e.g. where religion was considered), Ogburn encouraged his authors to write in terms of trends based upon best available judgements. The view was repeatedly expressed that sharp changes in the direction of social trends are most uncommon events — an argument later used to justify extrapolation as a basic forecasting technique. Statistical measurement was seen as being unbiased: differences of opinion were being ruled out by the collection of reliable data, the conclusions of which were to be unarguable and equally meaningful to those of all political hues (see Ogburn, 1951). The problem of understanding rapid social change was to be handled by dividing society into component parts such as those outlined, measuring the trends visible, and only then interrelating and interpreting findings.

The *Recent Social Trends* report (1933) was financed in the face of the depression, by a government seeking to renew economic growth. As well as the thousands of pages of information in this report and the volumes of special studies connected with it, the authors turn their attention to social forecasting. Ogburn faced the problems here involved more squarely in his later books where he would either study the potential effects of an invention on a wide range of social phenomena (as in *The Social Effects of Aviation,* 1946), or look at the future of one social area in the light of many technological innovations (as in *Technology and International Relations,* 1949). The rationale for his choice of forecasting methods is stated in chapter 3 of the former book.

Two types of forecast (Ogburn refers to 'prediction') can be discriminated; of these, those based on measurement are preferred to those not so based. This corresponds to the distinction drawn in the previous chapter between quantitative, deductive and qualitative judgemental approaches, for his expert judgements were expressed verbally rather than in numerical, form. Where judgement is necessary Ogburn advocates applying modes of thinking drawn from statistical analyses: postulating trends and growth curves, and attempting to validate these against fact or opinions (being wary of conservatism, wishful thinking and bias). Considering forecasts based on measurement, Ogburn concentrates on atheoretical trend extrapolation. He distinguishes between trends and the fluctuation of events around trends: long term trends, rather than recent fluctuations, should be projected; curves showing little fluctuation and slow change in direction are most reliably projected; and short term extrapolations are more reasonable than predictions of the more distant future. He also takes into account the necessity of considering logical limits to trends as well as possible limits stemming from policy decisions, and describes other statistical techniques such as that of forecasting from precursive events.

Ogburn's work, and that of his contemporaries with whom his name is associated, could be assessed by comparing his forecasts in detail against the actual unfolding of events. This would appear to be of interest to those researchers who continue to forecast much in the tradition he set — exploratory forecasters who emphasise the role of technological change. Yet his writing has been largely ignored by those engaged in both futures studies and social indicators research. Even Winthrop (1968) makes no mention of him in reviewing social scientists' contribution to futures studies. The reasons for this are uncertain: partly it may reflect futurologists' reluctance to look to their immediate past, as was described in the previous chapter. The dynamic novelty of forecasting might be diminished if it were admitted that Ogburn was active decades ago, and that techniques have evolved little since. Partly it may reflect the submergence of research on social change in the period during which the structual-functional value-free paradigm ruled sociology, as remarked in chapter 2; besides, Ogburn was more intested in describing actual conditions than in theory building. Partly it may reflect continuing political associations: Ogburn became identified with 'New Deal' planning, and the attempts to tie social research to policy making in the postwar era ran foul of powerful lobbies.

It would be irrelevant to the present discussion to exhaustively tabulate Ogburn's over-optimistic views concerning the helicopter and over-pessimistic views concerning jet aircraft, his accurate anticipation of the use of television and artificial fibres and the development of oral contraceptives, etc. Ogburn himself obviously thought this sort of hindsight review useful — witness the second chapter of the 1937 report he edited *(Technological Trends and National Policy),* in which his collaborator Gilfillian assesses earlier predictions of inventions. Although it may be useful for exploratory forecasters to know what sorts of historical factors produce inaccurate predictions, of more immediate value is an assessment of the overall worth of Ogburn's strategy.

His forecasting work may be divided, as mentioned before, into forecasts of the wide impacts of a specific technology, and those of the likely future of a given area of life in view of predicted technological changes. In the former cases, 'prediction' based on measurement is employed where possible; thus in forecasting the impact of aviation, over fifty variables were tried out for trend analysis and extrapolation. However, he was well aware of the problems of quantifying the effects of future technologies, and argued for the usefulness of drawing up lists of possible effects (such as the 150 effects he listed for the radio), even if these were unmeasured in time or degree. When looking at the future of a social institution such as the family, changes in this institution were taken as 'dependent' variables, with technology as the 'independent' variable producing these changes. (Ogburn, 1955, looked at the effects of a changing standard of living, but this was itself attributed to technological progress.) The strategy followed in these cases was to first locate and describe trends in the past evolution of the institution, to relate these to changes in the 'independent variable', and to use the relationships thus pinpointed to project the likely future course of events given further changes in the 'independent variable'. In Ogburn and Nimkoff (1955) expert judgement is employed to locate significant changes occuring in the American family within the past century. The list of changes thus composed was compressed into eight trends, such as increases in the proportion of working wives, earlier marriages, more emphasis on romantic love and on pressures towards equalising the authority of husband and wife.

The shortcomings of these approaches are several, although they lead to errors of omission more often than those of commission. The modern reader of Ogburn's forecasts will be struck by the accuracy of many of his pronouncements. His work was essentially exploratory forecasting. Discussion of the possibility of social control over technological developments is completely overshadowed by discussions of processes of adaptation to technological futures. (Indeed, normative forecasts are approached most nearly only by the statements he made, in committee reports, advocating the setting up of forecasting journals and institutions.) When he does consider the function of values in producing the future, he regularly ascribes to social institutions the role of producing lags, of resisting inevitable adjustment and change. In line with this are occasional exploratory forecasts of government policy trends, which themselves are seen as responses to changes in the scale of production, and technology. In the main, his social forecasts are much more directed towards changes in culture, lifestyle and behaviour than towards those in social structure, organisation and purpose. While in his theoretical writings Ogburn disavowed the extreme technological determinist position, he clearly asserted that technological change was of greater importance in producing social changes than vice versa, and carried this emphasis into his forecasting.

In forecasting the effects of technological change, then, Ogburn's work differs little from the majority of current technological assessments, and is

75

subject to the criticisms directed against the practice of TA in the previous chapter. Perhaps the modern writers are more concerned with proposing agencies for control of technologies and administrative functions related to innovations, but the focus remains on the consequences of innovation rather than on the directing of innovation towards desired ends. Alternative technologies, such as the conventional aeroplane and the helicopter, are weighed up not in terms of preferable options for policy making, but in terms of likely commercial appeal.

In the extrapolation of trends in such variables as aeroplane usage and productivity, Ogburn's forecasts are easier to compare with actual changes than are his more qualitative predictions. Here the problems of exploratory forecasting discussed in the previous chapter are encountered. While the limits of change imposed by saturation are considered — see Ogburn's debate with Hart in the February 1949 *American Sociological Review* concerning the application of exponential and logistic curves to aeroplane usage data — these projections fail to capture future changes caused by shifting values. The limiting of supersonic travel by environmentalist lobbies, which would presumably be viewed as cultural lag, only highlights the fact that the pressures in commercial airline technological development have recently stemmed from industries in competition for government patronage rather than from an intrinsic momentum in these technologies. The 'energy crisis', which has had repercussions both on transportation and on economic growth, is itself indicative of shifting values in the international system. While it may indeed prove possible to forecast such changes by exploratory means, there is little sign that these particular examples have been taken as serious possibilities by forecasters employed by the national and industrial concerns involved.

In forecasting the future of institutions there is again no attempt to construct desirable futures of directions of change. Even in considering international relations, the goal of peace is treated as a value nations are coming to appreciate more, due to the increasing destructiveness of weapons. The data speak for themselves, about what change has historically been occurring, and what innovations are in the offing. The probable consequences of new technologies are thereby to be balanced against broad historical movements that have themselves, in large part, a technological origin. Pushed to an extreme, futures studies becomes the analysis of the impact of technologies, a kind of super-substitution analysis.

The use of extrapolation of more qualitative trends located by judges has its associated problems. First, there may be a lack of adequacy in the data base as discussed in the previous chapter. In coping with this Ogburn strove to find quantitative evidence or historical research validating the judgements involved, but this was not always available. Quantitative material about technological changes is relatively more accessible than that about social conflict or value changes, and this results in an emphasis on the former – which may be less troublesome than explaining the course of history in terms of numerous cultural forces. Second, there may be failure to spot accelerating trends that are as yet of minor significance. One possible example of this comes in *Technology and the Changing Family* (1955) where increasing use of 'mobile' homes is predicted, but they are expected to serve as accommodation for emergencies or special types of family (such as the childless and the very mobile), and their prominence in recent years is quite unforeseen. Finally, as with other trend extrapolations, allowance has to be made for countertrends or for the waning of forces producing trends – the size of national governing units has not continued to increase since Ogburn's day, despite the continuing development of communications media which should act to erode the 'cultural lags' manifested in political boundaries.

What implications for the present practice of futures studies does Ogburn's research have? For one thing, there is the evidence that a whole body of research and theory can be practically submerged in a change of political and intellectual climate, leaving later workers essentially to build from fundamentals and repeat the mistakes of the past. While technological forecasting flourished, social forecasting had to be laboriously re-established in its shadow. It is, however, unlikely that the current interest in futures studies could fade away without leaving a much more prominent historical record than the work of Ogburn and his collaborators. Research activities are much more widespread and diversified (although it is conceivable that 'futurology' could be so discredited in public and academic opinion as to make speculative studies of the future and macroforecasts, whatever their origin, suspect and judged unworthy of critical attention and serious funding). Furthermore, the growth of state planning has necessitated the development and institutionalisation of forecasting capabilities directed towards social parameters, and this may not be easily reversible. However, the social parameters considered in government institutions are typically very restricted – demographic, manpower, educational, criminological and medical aspects of the future may be considered, but their integration is incomplete, and cultural, aesthetic, psychological and lifestyle considerations are omitted.

The social indicators movement represents an attempt to redress the balance of official interests towards these latter concerns. As such, it is opposed by some commentators who fear the entrance of bureaucratic scrutiny and regulation into these 'residual' areas of life where, it is felt, individual freedom remains largely unchecked. In contrast it may be argued that freedom and diversity in all manner of social choices have been and are being restricted by past decisions (or *laissez-faire* policies) concerning technological and social change. It is not inconceivable that policies could be designed, not to determine the direction of evolution of, for example, culture, families and lifestyle, but to increase the possibility of choice for individuals; to control innovations on this basis rather than allow control to be operated by vested interests for commercial or other purposes.

For such a strategy, social forecasting would need to be sufficiently well developed for citizens to be able to anticipate a wide range of consequence of social changes, and to devise possible changes to achieve desired consequences. This points to a second implication of Ogburn's research: its history suggests that, unless the social components of forecasting are accepted as legitimately inseparable from other factors in the selection of a starting-point from which to forecast, then these social components may be treated as residuals, solely as outputs of technological or other changes. This will mean that the 'independent' variables will be falsely treated as truly independent; that technologies, for example, will not be seen as evolving under the pressure of social choices (albeit choices in which the large majority of the population has no informed participation). In a placid political climate, at least domestically, fore-casters in the West have been prepared to shear off even the analysis of social impacts. This remains a potentiality so long as futures studies are concerned with society only as a dependent variable, as well as limiting the range of social components considered to those that are more gross, highly aggregated, or material. Ogburn shows that it is indeed possible to forecast technology's social impacts in such terms, but fails to reveal whether this is compatible with a more penetrating investigation of social choices.

Ogburn's legacy – the social indicators movement

Ogburn's work on social change was not completely occluded in the 1950s and 1960s. For one thing, he and a small group of sociologists with shared interests continued to publish (e.g. Allen et al., 1957). Some aspects of his theory and methods have been applied by researchers dealing with the diffusion of innovations (see, for example, Rogers, 1971, for a review of the literature) and with the growth of scientific knowledge (such as the work of Price, 1961 on the accumulation of knowledge, and Merton, 1957 on the phenomenon of multiple invention). There was, however, little interest on the part of social scientists in taking a broader look at the future until the mid-1960s.

Concern in the 1960s with the possible consequences of automation on American employment led to the setting up of the National Commission on Technology, Automation and Economic Progress (whose report was published in 1966). This followed the research precedent set by Ogburn's reports in some respects, chief among which was a tendency not to question the inevitability of technological change, although its pace was less taken for granted. Rather than being composed entirely of social scientists, this Commission also contained representatives of business, labour and civil rights; Daniel Bell was a representative of academia. Unlike Ogburn's reports, the Commission set out to examine a normative goal — the maintenance of full employment — and to propose palliative programmes for coping with automation. Like Ogburn's studies, the Commission report advocated the creation of social indicator systems and forecasting capabilities (although these were related to cost-benefit analysis) for planning and monitoring social change.

Arguably, Ogburn's influence is felt, if not acknowledged, by the greater part of mainstream futures research. After all, his work was of major importance in making unfashionable the notion that history is made by unpredictable great men, rather than social forces. Likewise, he played a large part in repudiating the idea that scientific and technological advance is totally serendipitous and unforeseeable, and in laying a framework for studying the cultural impact of technological change in isolation from the wider social system. His insistence on the stability of trends, however, surely contributed to the historicist perspective of many later researchers.

These influences of a fairly diffuse nature reflect Ogburn's impact on the intellectual climate, rather than an absorption of the corpus of his work and a critical assessment of its strengths and weaknesses. It should also be noted that many scholars, especially the more historically inclined, would agree with Nisbet (1968) who argues that any social changes worth looking at will remain unpredictable, being the consequences of 'the Random Event, the Genius, the Maniac and the Prophet' (see also Nisbet, 1969, 1971). It is only recently, with the appearance of such research as that of Hamblin et al. (1973), that effort has resumed on developing a theory of social change along the lines stated by Ogburn.

The Hamblin volume represents a considerable extension of Ogburn's

79

analyses, reconciling them with principles of behavioural psychology and its sociological derivatives. As a first step towards mathematical modelling of certain phases of the social change process, much of this volume is stimulating. Once more the question of social choice is unexplored, although there are some interesting examples of techniques for evaluating the impacts of policy decisions. Furthermore, the notion of 'reinforcement' adopted from behavioural psychology is not related to the societal context within which stimuli are defined. So far, the potential of such approaches to social change has remained largely unexplored by forecasters.

The development of social indicators (SI) research is another matter. I have elsewhere reviewed this field (Encel, Marstrand and Page, 1975, part 3.5) in some detail. The rapid growth of the field is attested by the recent publication of a related journal *(Social Indicators Research)* and newsletter (prepared by the USA SSRC). Among useful sources of material and documentation of SI research may be cited the early statement of Bauer (1966), the collections edited by Gross (1969) and Sheldon and Moore (1968), and the bibliography of research prepared by Wilcox et al. (1972).

SI research, like futures research, has largely been dominated by American initiatives, although the USA in fact lagged behind other countries (the UK, France and Germany) in publishing an official annual compilation of SI material. Some interest was apparent in the USA long before the SI 'movement' took off towards the end of the 1960s. For example, in 1960 *Goals for Americans,* the Report of the President's Commission on National Goals, was published. Unlike Ogburn's *Recent Social Trends* this study set out to describe progress towards n national goals (82 goals were formulated by a small appointed group) rather than to strive to depict trends neutrally. It also made somewhat less use of quantitative material than the earlier report. In subsequent discussions of SIs, a minor controversy has revolved around whether any statistic about society can be labelled as SI, or whether, to warrant the term, a statistic must refer to a dimension of social change concerning which normative judgements are available — such as levels of health, employment and schooling in a society. In the review mentioned above, on which the following discussion builds, it was concluded that this debate is of little significance, given that social phenomena are related causally and changes that are not themselves valued intrinsically may yet be valued as means for promoting other changes.

Some notion of the breadth of concerns with which SI research purports to deal, and for the study of which they have been advocated, may be grasped by looking at what factors were involved in the sudden rise of the SI movement from relative obscurity to a major social research field. The movement represents a convergence of many interests, mostly brought together by the turmoil of America in the mid-1960s. This turmoil had several relevant intellectual consequences. Economic growth could no longer be viewed as a panacea for social problems such as poverty and racism; economic planning criteria became suspect on grounds of omitting social and environmental goods; and economic indices such as GNP were increasingly attacked as insufficient for monitoring national progress. Problems of social change and stress confronted social scientists whose eyes had been fixed on structural-functionalist equilibria, and their value-free stance was challenged by a wave of criticism of academic orthodoxies. A growing school of policy-oriented social scientists were advocating the introduction of 'rational' planning methods into government, both as a logical concomitant of increasing public expenditure on social affairs and as an embodiment of the 'end of ideology' ideal of advanced society (see Waxman, 1968, for perspectives on the 'end of ideology' debate). The sudden resurgence of the suppressed grievances of minorities and environmentalists added more grist to their mills by highlighting the inadequacy of previous social planning. Fore-casters, planners and systems engineers employed in defence and aerospace work saw the likelihood of national interest switching from high technology (at least as applied to such goals as the space programme) to the problems of the ghettoes, of minorities, of public services and of pollution; some may also have viewed domestic insurgency as a growing threat to security.

The development of SI research offered much to these interests. The possibility of augmenting economic measures with social accounting seemed to many to offer a means of solution to the problems associated with (or unalleviated by) growth; one major concern of SI researchers has accordingly been to develop measures of social 'outputs' (e.g. aspects of welfare like health levels) to apply in addition to measures of economic or manpower 'inputs' (e.g. aspects of services like the provision of hospital beds). Social statistics would tell the public and policy makers where social priorities lay, and thus elevate decision making from purely economic considerations or from sheer ignorance. For sociologists and political scientists, SIs promised a wide-ranging data base on which to build theories of social change without abandoning empiricism or the newly found tools of computer data banks, data analysis and simulation; for some, developing or applying SIs would make their work 'relevant', which was what their critics urged. Policy analysts and consultants saw SIs as providing the solid basis for the quantitative comparison of the effectiveness of different programmes and for predicting social progress in terms other than those of 'ideological' theory. The final group mentioned, forecasters, planners and system engineers, saw SIs as integral parts of their systems designs, which typically featured information banks monitoring the up-to-date state of affairs and informing policy makers where action was necessary to forestall unpleasantness.

This is not to say that the SI movement was initiated only by apologists for the existing social order and its social sciences. Administrators are not all more concerned with keeping the system functioning smoothly than with tackling social problems. The concept of SIs has been espoused by severe critics of these institutions as well as by those seeking and anticipating gradual reforms, or hoping merely to improve system management. By revealing areas of stress and harship SIs could expose the real interests maintaining the existing order, and provide material whereby diverse minority interests might by united. Other workers have viewed SIs as the logical next step in the development of their social science specialities, having concluded that only by mammoth and detailed joint efforts of data collection could progress be made in the development of middle range social theories. Many observers welcome the publication of SIs if only as a way to find out what social changes are happening — witness the newspaper interest in and usage of British SI reports. In particular, information about what social changes are occurring in terms of individual wellbeing, as opposed to the more publicised changes in policies and expenditure, is of interest.

As with futures studies, the SI movement represents many diverse interests so that an overall assessment of its significance is difficult. SIs are not neutral; they may be, and are, devised for the administration, legitimation or criticism of a social system, and they may also be employed for ends other than those for which they were devised (e.g. Triesman, 1974, has described *The Radical Use of Official Data,* and much scholarly research uses statistics developed for administrative purposes, e.g. Hindess, 1973). Nevertheless, it is again possible to point to broad emphases within SI research which have a bearing on its potential role in social forecasting studies.

Social indicators for forecasting

The SI movement offers the sustained development of improved and more comprehensive social statistics. As such, it is clearly in line with the requirements of deductive and quantitative forecasting techniques, allowing measurements to supersede judgements and precise expressions to replace broad impressions of social change. In that SI research often focuses on social 'outputs' of welfare rather than on institutional 'inputs' of services, it also offers the possibility of yielding operational measures of social goals such as those considered in much normative forecasting.

To consider some general contributions SI research may make to social forecasting, let us consider the dimensions of forecasting technique described in chapter 3. While some SI material deals with 'categorical' variables for which no clear scales exist, it is fair to say that it is to quantitative approaches in forecasting that SI research offers most, with its emphasis on developing numerical measures of social phenomena which may be used in the comparison of different times and places. As such, SIs share the advantages and disadvantages of operational measures in general (see chapter 2).

Certainly by far the greater portion of SI research has involved deductive measurement and thus offers material for use in deductive forecasting. In some areas of research, such as cross-national studies of political systems or international affairs, indicators are quite often derived from expert judgement as may be noted in such compilations of data as that of Banks and Textor (1962). Even in such areas, as will be seen in a later chapter, the tendency has been towards systematising and coding judgements and developing measures of system structure and behaviour that involve less interpretation than heretofore. The extent of this movement can be seen by comparing the volume just cited with its more recent counterpart, Banks (1971).

A very different type of 'judgemental' SI may be distinguished and is generally referred to as a 'subjective' SI. Such a measure does not attempt to assess expert opinion about a phenomenon, but instead draws on the experience of the individuals concerned, usually through the medium of a questionnaire or interview. Thus there might be expert judgemental SIs (e.g. a health officer's estimate of the level of disease in a community), objective SIs (e.g. data on hospital admissions, morbidity, doctors' records) and subjective SIs (e.g. survey data on people's self-reported health) of the same area of concern. The label 'subjective' is most usually restricted to those indicators, derived from survey research or related techniques, of psychological variables such as opinions, feelings and moods; for example, how satisfied people are with their health, or with local health services. Such SIs are quantified in that their data are usually presented in terms of proportions of people holding a given opinion, or average levels of a given mood in different social settings.

Since they are based on verbal reports of experience, subjective SIs are only to be viewed as judgemental if they are being employed as surrogates for actual measures of the experiences concerned. If they are accepted as indices of verbal behaviour or of subjective experience, which are legitimate concerns of SI researchers, then they are not judgemental – at least, not in the same way as an observer's estimate of what the people surveyed would think and feel. Some recent research has been directed towards relating 'subjective' and 'objective' SIs in communities, for example the studies of Hall and Ring (1974), Hulin (1969) and Reynolds et al. (1974) which relate environmental variables to feelings of satisfaction with the environment gathered in sample surveys.

Turning to other techniques of forecasting, SIs offer much to exploratory futures studies, whether these be empiricist or theoretically oriented. Exploratory forecasting often begins with an inspection of trends, and given more comprehensive and accessible social statistics, trends may be detected and analysed that would otherwise be difficult to ascertain. For example, the 1974 British *Social Trends* (Nissel, 1974) brings together information on trends in variables as diverse as children's reading comprehension, crimes and sentences, housing density and television viewing. The international comparison such volumes make available also lends itself to the sort of forecast that involves predicting one country's future by looking at another country's present.

An interesting example of exploratory forecasting using SI material is provided by Coates (1972), who is concerned with future changes in US crime. Noting an upward trend in officially reported serious crimes, he attempts to identify factors linked to this (such as increasing prosperity, shifting age composition of society, better reporting, and spreading middle-class values) and thus to make policy-relevant statements about future crime rates. It is possible to cite a host of other exploratory studies employing SI data – some idea of the range covered by such studies may be gained by citing the study of Stefflre (1974), who applies trend extrapolation to the forecasting of war casualties, studies reviewed by Wilson (1971) and Brewer (1973) involving urban and regional models (often computer simulations) as forecasting and planning tools for those concerned with housing, transport and other community services, and Inglehart's (1971) work on likely value changes based on European survey data.

Some writers have pointed to roles SI material may play in normative forecasting. SIs may be used as measures of progress towards such normative goals as full employment and adequate health for all the population; they may reveal the state of development of those means that may be used to reach these goals with such measures as levels of occupational demand and the rate of development of health services; and they may clarify debates about what goals are being adopted and what effects particular programmes are intended to have. In this vein, Cetron (1972) is among advocates of the integration of SIs into the assessment of technology, and has described a possible normative TA system. Proponents of broad range social models, to be described shortly, generally envisage SIs playing a normative forecasting role.

Both exploratory and normative forecasting might benefit from one unemphasised effect that sound SI data may have (and indeed already appear to be having). This is to draw attention to some social needs or deprivations that have previously escaped general notice. Examples include the problems of people suffering a handicap or disadvantage who are either not aware of the numbers of other sufferers or who are spatially concentrated but effectively segregated from the rest of society; the relative deprivation of social or regional groups lacking communication channels, pressure groups or acceptable spokesmen; and 'private' problems or grievances. SI material revealing the extent of such needs or deprivations may have exploratory forecasting application (suggesting future areas of social conflict or policy) and normative ones (helping to specify optimal futures and to direct policies according to needs). Recent British census information has been of service to Scottish interests, who have used it to show the unpublicised but severe disparity in living standards between Scotland and England, and the scale of problems faced by Scottish cities, largely ignored by media quick to pontificate on London's problems. SI data may, then, increase problem visibility, and serve as material to be used in advocacy.

SI research has been used in both empiricist and theoretical forecasting techniques. Apart from their applicability in extrapolation, reliable data about social phenomena may be employed in a variety of ways that make minimal theoretical demands. For example, Rummel (1969) has advocated the application of factor analytic methods to cross-national SIs as a means of forecasting nations' future performance. (Factor analysis is a method of summarising information concerning a large number of related variables in terms of a smaller number of dimensions. While it makes certain assumptions about the statistical nature of one's indices and their interrelationships, it has proved acceptable to researchers from many theoretical backgrounds, both as a tool for data reduction and as yielding insight into patterns underlying a mass of data.)

A normative forecaster might employ SIs in comparative analysis in a relatively atheoretical fashion. For example, the existing range of conditions across different countries under which a given level of performance or 'output' obtains might be investigated as a way of looking at alternative routes to a performance goal. Much policy-relevant research, including the literature on programme evaluation (e.g. Rossi and Williams, 1972) employs SIs in a relatively empiricist fashion to assess the social effects of policies or institutional structures without necessarily seeking to understand the dynamics underlying such effects. As argued in chapters 2 and 3, such 'empiricist' approaches necessarily rely on some theory, albeit informal or rudimentary, in guiding the selection of SIs and relationships investigated. When the researcher uses existing measures in an atheoretical manner, as in Rummel's cross-national studies in which practically every available SI was used, this selection is merely guided by what previous researchers or administrators have found relevant. It should also be noted that the ever increasing body of computerised data analytic methods available to social scientists is itself not free of significant assumptions — among the most common of which is that there is no reciprocal causation between variables, a situation that manifestly does not exist in many real-life situations. Progress has been made towards reducing the number of assumptions involved in such methods (and in this respect smallest-space analysis is a real step beyond factor analysis, for example), but so far the assumptions that have been obviated are chiefly those to do with the scaling properties of variables or the nature of the coefficients relating them in a data matrix.

Theoretical forecasting techniques have been the focus of much enthusiam concerning SIs. SI research has been heralded as ushering in a new era of maturity in the 'softer' social sciences, in which economics may be emulated and surpassed in the development and validation of policy-relevant models of society. At first it might seem that the time for Ogburn's caution has passed, and the social scientist may move on from description and prediction to control, using computer simulations and data banks to plot the future course of society given alternative policy choices. Since some confusion is apparent in respect of this issue, it will be necessary to distinguish between restricted range and broad range social models, and consider their separate implications for forecasting.

Restricted range models correspond to small scale econometric models: they refer to discrete sectors of a society rather than its totality. Such a model might relate welfare outputs to service inputs in a logical way, taking account of intervening variables, exogenous trends, etc. Thus Anderson (1973) describes a fairly simple model which might be used by policy makers. He seeks to establish the effects, in a small set of regions with different demographic characteristics, that alternative strategies of provision of medical facilities would have on levels of infant mortality and other health indices. The model is derived from the cross-sectional comparison of these different regions at one point in time in terms of indicators of health, service provisions, and 'background' characteristics. As such, and in common with most restricted range models, it is incapable of answering questions about the effects of a major restructuring of welfare services, since the data base only refers to variation in levels of inputs and outputs within a given structure. The statistical method used to develop the model is causal path analysis, which, based on regression analysis, involves assuming both a particular order of relationships and particular types of relationship (in this case linear) between variables (see Forbes and Tufte, 1968, for cautionary remarks concerning this much used method). In common with other cross-sectional, correlational analyses, a definitive account of causal relationships cannot be obtained since there is no adequate control over the 'manipulation' of variables or the sequence of events, and Anderson's model is in this sense premature. For example, his empirical correlations between health services and health levels may have been due to causality in either or both directions, or to the influence of unmeasured variables causally related to both.

Perhaps most research on restricted range models for forecasting has been in the new speciality of urban simulation, in which local census data are the relevant SI input, and attention has often focused on particular issues like transportation, housing and health. Such work has benefited from the availability of economic and geographical theory and research which relates to the urban situation (and its market structure). Such information is rarely available in other areas for which restricted range models are advocated. Even in the case of urban models Brewer (1973) and others have commented on the inadequacy of existing data, which are often at too high a level of aggregation and too low a level of accuracy. Simulation studies are often very highly demanding of data.

Restricted range models are often developed with forecasting and planning in mind. They may be employed in exploratory modes to indicate the levels of welfare (e.g. adequate housing provisions) or of other important variables that would be attained if particular trends in policies are followed or if policies do not change. For normative forecasting some idea of the relative capability of policies to achieve particular goals may be gained, but the range of social choices revealed by such models is limited by the selection of variables and the degree to which societal interdependencies are elaborated in them. Such models may effectively contain forecasts and constrain policy options within a particular institutional structure which is itself unanalysed. Brewer (1973) remarks that using cross-sectional data in lieu of time series may misdirect attention or import conservative biases. Changes in institutional structures might drastically affect the form of the model itself both in terms of relationships and variables. A parallel in economic theory may be the challenge socialist systems have posed to models developed under capitalist circumstances to account for change.

Many writers have espoused the idea of SI-based broad range social models for forecasting and planning uses, although few have taken a hard look at what might be involved here. Among those who have attempted to map out how construction of such models might proceed, two schools of thought are apparent. On the one hand are scholars who believe that SIs may be employed to validate and calibrate models of existing social structures whether on a grand scale referring to a global view of a nation (e.g. Williams, 1968), or on a more modest scale concerned with specific institutional areas (e.g. Land, 1970, 1971). On the other hand are those who are involved in a more normative enterprise — the design of models of policy making systems to cope with the present mismatch between needs, policies and policy outcomes (e.g. Gross, 1966; Etzioni, 1968). Such writers are more concerned with describing improved social organisation than with simulating or describing existing structures; this may partly be seen as a response to the problem of the 'visibility' of social needs produced by SIs that was mentioned earlier. Such writings belong in the 'post-industrial' school of futures studies, to be discussed in a later chapter, insofar as these models are taken to represent likely futures. Their authors seek to improve the use of SIs in actively forecasting and creating the future, rather than in merely predicting it. While the social information systems they envisaged would be highly involved with forecasting, these authors have not often been temporally specific about such systems: when and how they might emerge is unclear. While Gross and Etzioni appear to envisage their designs as possible within the medium range future, their fruition is seen to be determined by a wide range of factors including continuing economic growth and the development of appropriate values on the part of technical decision makers (e.g. Gross, 1972). There is some irony in this — social information systems are being created, but their operation as tools of democracy waits upon changing social values. The social technologies themselves require social engineering to come into fruition.

Some of the ways in which different authors have seen SIs as contributing to social forecasting have been outlined above, and, despite some reservations about extreme claims, it appears that futures studies could be enriched by the SI movement. However, it is also necessary to look at the criticisms that have been levelled against SI research in order to see what shortcomings and biases might be involved in this interpenetration of research. Previous chapters have looked at broad emphases in the futures literature that determine the sorts of forecast made; the next chapter considers equally significant emphases in SI research.

5 Indicators of the Future?

The social indicators movement and the growth of futures research may both be seen as responses to a need for greater clarity about where our society is and where it could be going. As pressures for planned change and investments in social policy grow, accounts of the current and likely 'return' on policies are sought, and the two streams of research converge at more points.

This chapter reviews a number of criticisms that have been directed at the quality and philosophy of social indicators research, and assesses the extent to which the problems associated with such research may limit future studies. Particular areas where more attention is required are described, and the chapter concludes with a discussion of the potential uses of survey and content analytic techniques as means to understand changing values and culture.

Social indicators in forecasting: criticisms and appraisal

From the concluding section of the preceding chapter it would seem that forecasting has much to gain from the continuing development of SIs. The compilation of SI material should enable forecasters to achieve the criteria of external consistency, adequacy and representativeness more readily. To those who may wonder how forecasting was possible before the SI movement emerged, it must be admitted that social statistics, of course, are no novelty; what has changed is the amount of attention paid to developing systems and compilations of such data by researchers regardless of their immediate theoretical concerns. Such systems are directed towards administrative needs and the research community, and have been described by more than one observer as 'big science' manifesting itself in social research.

Three main lines of criticism relevant to forecasting have been directed at the SI field or at certain trends within it. (Other important issues — such as possible infringements of privacy — will not be discussed here.) These criticisms refer to overstatements of the contribution of SI data to providing the answers to pressing questions, whether theoretical or political; to the uneven pattern of emphasis on different types of social indicator in the research literature; and to an underlying philosophy often attributed to the SI movement, which is seen variously as philistine, incrementalist, scientistic or technocratic.

Sheldon and Freeman (1970) have spoken out with particular cogency against the overstatement characterising much of the SI literature. They identify three areas in which SI research is seen as having great potential: descriptive reporting, social change analysis and social forecasting. For these uses existing data are in general weak, and serious efforts at developing improved measures are needed; they should be the goal of the SI movement. Three main types of overstatement are also identified: that SIs can be used to set policy goals and priorities; that they will enable policies and programmes to be rapidly evaluated; and that they will yield a societal 'balance sheet'. The development of SIs, Sheldon and Freeman argue, reflects pre-existent goals and does not create new goals or values (see Biderman, 1966, for evidence that there has been a 'cultural lag' of SIs behind established social goals). SI data are a tool for policy making and lobbying, and are quite likely to be employed to lend legitimacy to policies already decided on (see also Horowitz, 1970, for studies of the use of social research to justify political decisions). Nor can the collection of SI data answer questions about the impact of social programmes by itself; programme evaluation demands controlled analysis and careful research designs, rather than a simple monitoring of the performance and 'outputs' of society over a period of time when multiple changes are inevitably occurring (see Rossi and Williams, 1972, for discussions of these points). While indicators of those social variables that policy is seeking to influence are needed, and SI research has relevant contributions to make here, evaluating the effects of policy is a methodologically demanding challenge, whose requirements of rigour have not in general been met by the 'policy-relevant' restricted range SI modellers described above. Finally, the development of a 'balance sheet' is seen as being based on a false analogy with economic analysis, where balancing can be accomplished by the use of a single metric (money) and specific models are available to describe linkages betwen factors. This last point will be taken up again in a later discussion of SI 'scientism'.

Other authors (e.g. Shonfield, 1972) have pointed to the crucial difference between social and economic indicators when their applications to decision making are considered — only the latter are embedded in a comprehensive theoretical system. It has been argued in consequence that a comprehensively and programmatically useful SI system can only be set up on the basis of a similarly formal social theory in which, in principle, the relationships between all variables included are represented.

How far may SI research contribute to the development of such theory? It has been argued that if SIs are generated and applied to describe clearly important societal dimensions from present value standpoints, then they will directly bear on those variables central to the explanation of social change – such as human satisfactions, aspirations and welfare. However, this argument equates normative centrality with theoretical significance, and the existence of 'low-visibility' social needs (mentioned in the previous chapter) renders this equation suspect. In the next section the criticism will be reviewed that SI research has tended indeed to overlook whole areas of normative concern, such as family life, values and 'culture'. Again, theoretical perspectives which admit a structuring of wants and demands by social institutions and postulate some kind of 'false consciousness' would suggest that conscious concerns are not of primary significance in producing social stability and change.

As argued in chapter 2, this empiricism cannot generate theories; the information yielded by SIs may nevertheless make possible the refinement and criticism of existing formal and informal views of society. As Biderman (1966) has pointed out, conflicts in social interpretation may often be examined by comparing different indices purporting to bear on the same phenomenon and studying the divergent results they yield. (It is noteworthy that, while economic indicators have played a role in the development of detailed ecnomic theory, economic accounting systems are themselves not theoretically neutral. Thus Western accounting systems are largely based on the data requirements of policy derived from Keynesian theory while Eastern European countries employ quite different frameworks for national economic accounts.) SI research will almost certainly aid in the development of increasing numbers of relatively atheoretical restricted range models of social process, although when and whether these encourage synthesis, or lead to an ossification or fragmentation of perspectives, is uncertain.

SI material has indeed been used increasingly in the testing and development of social models that, while not being necessarily of broad range, are in a sense 'whole system'. The SI movement has coincided with and reinforced a resurgence of sociological and political science interest in the comparative study of national (as well as regional and community) behaviour and evolution, as witnessed by such collections and compendia as Banks (1972), Cnudde and Neubauer (1969), Eisenstadt and Rokkan (1973), Gillespie and Nesvold (1970), and Taylor and Hudson (1972), which focus on the quantitative study of national societies, and volumes focusing on cities and small communities such as Berry (1972) and Clark (1968), and the handbook edited by Narrol and Cohen (1973) dealing with anthropological cross-cultural material. In addition, Garfin (1971) has prepared an annotated bibliography of sociologically oriented comparative studies.

Such research has often centred round a few themes, such as the question of whether social changes reveal an evolutionary sequence, the conditions associated with such different forms of aggregate political behaviour as voting turnouts and civil unrest, the contexts in which particular political structures and policies arise and are supported, and the degree of order apparent in international relationships. The demands of such studies have led to activity in constructing time series of SIs whose historical sweep in some cases rivals that of Sorokin, Kroeber and Quincy Wright, and which certainly involves more detailed operationalisation and accordingly gives less of a role to individual judgement. While relatively few areas of society and culture are the subject of intensive analysis, many scholars are now involved in the study of nation states, and comparative social science and cliometrics are making increasing contact both in terms of interest in SIs and in terms of using formal models to guide research.

While these efforts are both refreshing and commendable, the reviews of research into social development in later chapters leads to the conclusion that such activities have often been impaired by theoretical and empirical poverty. The mutual enrichment of analysis and SIs has been hindered by inadequate methodology and unquestioned theoretical preconceptions, both of which have led researchers to exclude whole classes of variables and relationship from study. While there are signs of distinct progress in this field of research, it is clearly not the case that SIs have led in an automatic way to theoretical enrichment − the main effect seems to have been in the reverse direction.

To claim that SIs will rapidly solve our problems in understanding society, and enable the development of models of social change rich in both theory and data, is an overstatement. Indeed, the social order is so complex that it is exceedingly difficult to test adequately any 'grand theory' of change such as might inform social forecasting. Failure to confirm theoretical predictions is often, and not altogether unreasonably, met by a new elaboration of the theory to take further societal variables into account, rather than discarding a whole set of propositions that seem to have some worth. (In this vein Kuhn, 1962 provides an account of scientific activity that seems more credible than Popper's description of falsification.) It must be conceded, then; that it is unrealistic to expect the growth of SI systems to meet forecasters' needs for a firm theoretical perspective, although SI material may be of use in refuting particular ideas about the direction of social change and the factors involved in social change (e.g. Miles, 1975, criticises the notion of 'future shock', and Chadwick, 1972, questions the assumptions prevalent in futurology about the effects of 'crowding') as well as in providing a data base for forecasting.

The 'comprehensiveness' critique

The second general criticism directed at SIs has been touched on in the preceding discussion: contrary to assertions of comprehensiveness, SI research has been decidedly uneven in the attention paid to different types of phenomena. These criticisms are summarised in the following paragraphs in three groups; for a very different approach to the assessment of SI systems see Klages's (1973) review of the Sheldon and Moore (1968) volume.

SI research emphasises 'hard' data and neglects 'soft' data; research is preponderantly concentrated on 'objective' measures and variables reflecting economic or physical planning concerns while 'subjective' SIs and measures of aesthetic, community life, and related issues are the interest of a small minority of researchers. Thus Abrams (1973), Firestone (1972) and Gerbner (1970, 1973a) are among several commentators who have pointed out that SI research has been focused on material and social conditions (such as trends in family size, housing quality, and leisure time) and only been concerned in a piecemeal and sporadic fashion with psychological states (e.g. feelings of satisfaction or frustration, stress, aspiration levels, values) and associated behaviour (e.g. interpersonal interactions, participation in various aspects of community life, striving to achieve goals) or with cultural products and affairs (e.g. the content of media, the production of art forms and the exercise of crafts). This criticism has much force; the meta-advocacy involved in this lopsided development of SIs implies the perspective that psychological and cultural impacts of social events are of at most secondary importance (see chapter 2; and Shapiro and Neubauer, 1973). Likewise, the hopes of SI researchers that their data can help to develop comprehensive models of social process appear to be tenable only if it is assumed that psychological and cultural variables do not play a significant role in social change and stability.

I have elsewhere (Encel, Marstrand and Page, 1975, part 3.5) reviewed SI research purporting to deal with the 'quality of life'. This notion became elevated to a major theme of political platforms towards the end of the 1960s — perhaps because it is possible to appeal to a wider constituency by promising to improve the quality of, for example, urban life, than it would be to analyse specific problems and injustices. As pundits proclaimed that quality of life was the issue for the future, rather than economic growth or mere materialism, a scholarly literature was rapidly spawned. Volumes have appeared with titles involving the quality of life of the aged, in the cities, at work, etc. and much of this literature stems from the SI movement (e.g. Environmental Protection Agency, 1973), and quality of life and SIs are linked to TA in some volumes (e.g. Stober and Schumacher, 1973). Even with a focus on quality of life which seemingly calls for decisive investment of study in the relatively neglected areas of values, lifestyle and culture, the SI movement has revealed tendencies towards employing 'hard' and 'objective' indices. Most of the discussion focused in terms of quality of life has involved the same indices of economic and material welfare with which SI research has been saturated. However, it is in this field, perhaps, that the most concerted efforts towards developing 'subjective' SIs have appeared (although contenders might be the study of political attitudes and orientations and associated concerns for one's country or community, e.g. Knutson, 1973; Robinson and Shaver, 1969a; and the research into the budgeting of time reported by Szalai, 1972).

The volume edited by Campbell and Converse (1972) for the Russell Sage Foundation was intended to be a review of the potential and state of the art in subjective SIs similar to that provided by Sheldon and Moore (1968) for the foundation on objective SIs. While particular chapters covered the survey investigation of such matters as the use of time, family and kinship, and political attitudes, the volume was rounded off by a discussion about the measurement of subjective aspects of quality of life. Campbell and his co-workers have since gone on to carry out a number of studies in this field, and workers in other countries have taken up research promising to yield cross-national, longitudinal, and disaggregated data on related subjective SIs. Among such studies may be cited the British work reported by Abrams (1973) and Hall (1973), Allardt's (1973) work in four Scandinavian countries, and work in the USA reported by Andrews and Withey (1974). The Gallup organisation has been commissioned to carry out various international studies of feelings of satisfaction and optimism, some of which are extending the pioneering studies of Cantril (1965), and the EEC is concerned with monitoring feelings of satisfaction and changing concerns in the different countries of the community (the survey involved is called the Euro-Barometer!). There is even a simulation model (of Oregon State) which includes quality of life variables monitored in regular surveys (reported in Institute for Social Research, 1974).

This area aside, there has been little systematic research into developing subjective SIs with a view to monitoring social change. The other areas mentioned — the study of political values and the research into time budgeting — remain largely unrelated to the SI movement, as do the efforts of polling organisations to keep abreast of social events.

The study of changing values and attitudes through SI material of various kinds, though overshadowed by other concerns of the SI movement, is of importance to forecasting — where, for example, exploratory forecasts based on assumptions of cultural stability may be upset by shifts in values and beliefs. Accordingly the concluding section of this chapter is devoted to a lengthier analysis of the state of the art of two main research approaches to developing indicators of such variables: content analysis and survey research. It seems fair to conclude that at present the SI movement is impoverished in its relative neglect of such variables, and that this will restrict its usefulness as an aid to forecasting and informed discussion and, following the arguments in chapter 2, possibly distort both the sorts of models of society developed and the prescriptions for change that are proposed. This might mesh, for example, with a Skinnerian vision of society in which considerations of internal psychological states are inadmissible aspects of the future.

A second line of criticism is that much SI research, while addressed to matters of social goals and needs, is tangential to the three values of equality, justice and freedom (Encel, Marstrand and Page, 1975, part 3.5). Presenting SI data in highly aggregated forms — such as measures of per capita GNP, numbers of physicians per thousand population or the total housing stock of a community — overlooks the distribution of values within a society. Following Allardt's (1973) argument, equality and justice may be related to this distribution of values, and the co-variation of values with each other and with other characteristics (e.g. are the most wealthy people also those with the most satisfying jobs? Are these variables related to race?). It would be valuable, then, for SI data to be reported as a matter of course in aggregated, distributional and co-variational modes. (I am not suggesting that the problems of defining justice are resolved by this procedure, since questions of compensatory or punitive co-variation remain to be answered; however, without such disaggregation of SIs, they are simply ignored away.)

This is not to say that issues of equality and justice are foreign to the SI movement; on the contrary, one claim of its proponents is that, by providing adequately disaggregated social information, such issues are brought to the fore. Thus Coleman (1969) sees SIs as giving policy makers essential data on the occurrence of social needs in particular groups. This should help prevent past 'mistakes' — he cites the case of unsuccessful programmes against unemployment that had failed to take into account the racially structured nature of unemployment in the USA. However, the disaggregated data collected in official censuses tend to deal with a very limited set of variables, and more widely ranging statistical compilations have predominantly focused on highly aggregated information. This reflects, no doubt, the problems involved in managing large quantities of data and the expenses involved in surveying populations. In recent SI publications there seem to be trends towards devoting more space to analysis of the status of groups such as women and the aged.

In the main body of SI research, issues of distribution are either restricted to questions such as educational opportunity and equality of income, or else segregated off as a special class of SI. So, for example, J.O. Wilson (1973) in comparing 'quality of life' characteristics of American states, develops seven indicators based on aggregate data concerning issues like health, economic growth and education, but treats racial equality in a separate indicator rather than as a component of each other issue.

Freedom is a value area almost completely ignored in the SI literature, presumably because of the thorny ideological and metaphysical issues involved. Some cross-national political science research has involved developing measures of press freedom, freedom of political opposition and related matters, of which many, but not all, are judgemental. There is also a body of research in which nations are compared in terms of occupational stratification (e.g. Fox and Miller, 1966). These have only limited relevance to the possibility of indexing changes in people's freedom in respect of such matters as education, mobility or community organisation, a possibility discussed at more length in Encel, Marstrand and Page (1975, part 3.5). Perhaps the nearest approach to this question is that taken by some SI-inclined geographers and urban researchers, who have investigated the development of indicators of accessibility of various services. Thus Wachs and Kumagai (1973) pointed out that measuring the amount of existing travel in particular social groups may lead planners to overlook the presence of by no means inevitable constraints on the mobility of different groups in making 'demand' projections; they consequently proposed and tested out some measures of accessibility. Such directions for research are promising, but fairly unexplored at present.

A final criticism that may be levelled against the comprehensiveness of the SI movement is the lack of integration, in the great majority of SI studies, or measures of system 'outputs' and related indicators, with considerations and indices of social contexts, of organisational, institutional, and collective variables.

The development of SIs relating to social units has been guided to a large extent by particular research interests and existing sources of data rather than by motives of comprehensive social accounting. While social commentators are quick to grasp and ponder the significance of developments in organisations ranging from the contemporary commune to the multinational corporation (e.g. Coleman, 1970, and Conger, 1973, both writing of 'social inventions'), such changes might not exist as far as the SI movement is concerned. The focus of much SI research on comparing individual outcomes is a welcome addition to, on the one hand, macrosociology with its abstract societal systems, and on the other, immensely detailed studies of very localised situations and interactions. However, it would seem that the SI movement is hoping to engage in social accounting and even modelling without taking into account the fact that people are not isolated atoms, computer terminals or laboratory rats. Social phenomena occur in a web of social relationships, and these are structured and manifest in social organisation. Thus the significance of an 'output' depends on the setting in which the person receiving it is located. A satisfactory wage for a worker who lives in one town may be nothing like that for a worker on the same job in a different town; or for a worker with a large family (statistical poverty definitions have not always taken family size into account as well as income!). Whether education is time-serving, schooling or something else will depend on the structure of the school or college, about which graduation certificates are inarticulate.

At this point it is important to note a distinction between two types of SIs that may be applied to collectivities which is made by Etzioni and Lehman (1969) and Lazarsfeld, Pasanella and Rosenberg (1972, section III). This is the distinction between aggregated and global measures. The former are based on an aggregation of the characteristics of the individuals making up the collectivity, such as describing national wealth in terms of per capita GNP; global measures are not produced out of individual characteristics, but instead refer to properties of the entire collectivity such as its formal organisational structure and decision making procedures, its physical capital, etc., and, as Etzioni and Lehman remark, are quite often based on judgemental indices.

One broad area where development of both sorts of organisational indicators has taken place, as remarked earlier in this chapter, is in studies of nation states, their legislatures, regions, cities and local government areas as well as of 'anthropological' cultures, and such studies have tended to grow alongside and be assimilated by the SI movement. This assimilation has approached integration most closely in research concerned with relating policy decisions to global or aggregate characteristics of the organisation. 'System outputs', usually conceived of in SI writings as the concrete outcomes of these policies for people, have only rarely been considered. This research has often been explicitly informed by a 'political systems' perspective either derived from or resembling Easton's (1965) analysis. The growth of literature in this field seems not to have caught the attention of futures researchers to any extent, despite its potential attraction as a source of hypotheses about future policy changes in exploratory forecasting. Clark (1968, chapter 22) has reviewed various research programmes concerned with community decision making. His own recent work (Clark, 1970, 1973) involves developing typologies of urban communities based on both aggregate and global SIs (e.g. population size, economic characteristics), relating these to factors like the centralisation of decision making and the sorts of actors most influential in this respect (as assessed by surveys of élites), and relating the preceding variables to the pattern of expenditures on various urban functions (such as urban renewal, police and fire services).

Few other studies have been able to look simultaneously at collective characteristics, decision making and policy outputs. Among local and regional studies relating socio-economic variables to policies, of particular interest is the work of Davies (1968) in which the question of measuring justice in policy allocation is taken up using aggregate SI data, and the review by Hofferbert (1972) in which policy outputs and social and environmental impacts or outcomes of policies are distinguished, and which suggests that, within the contemporary US urban and regional systems, socio-economic variables are more closely related to policy differences than are political variations. Forecasters bemused by the complexity of political change might take this as a cue to predict future policies from economic growth alone, but they would be well advised not to do so! (For cross-national and longitudinal extensions of such research see Hayes, 1972, and Hogan, 1972). Among studies of nations, the work of Cutright (1965, 1967) is well known. He relates development of and expenditures on social security programmes to measures of political structure and national economic development. In a study of Canada from 1867–1968, Kornberg, Falcone and Mishler (1973) related socio-economic variables, measures of the composition of the legislature and of political changes, and policy decisions and expenditures, tentatively concluding that the process of socio-economic development was closely tied to passing of legislation and expenditure on various programmes. None of these studies really begins to look at the effects of policy variables on other types of SI, unfortunately.

A second group of studies bearing on organisational indicators is less closely linked to the SI movement. This group consists of studies of groups of various sorts and of voluntary and business organisations. The literature on these topics is diverse: studies may focus on the structure of a group or organisation, on the performance of its functions, or on the interactions between its members. The aim of research may be to develop a taxonomy in which different kinds of groups may be classified, or to probe in detail one particular variable; and the concepts and measures employed may stem from various psychological and sociological traditions. Bereiter (1966) reviews some psychologically based studies of group characteristics using factor analytic approaches, and the volume edited by Graham and Roberts (1972) brings together perspectives from several other streams of thought. Price (1972) has also prepared a handbook of measures of organisational characteristics. Rather than attempt to summarise this literature here, a few studies will be cited to illustrate the sorts of considerations and analyses that may be involved.

With respect to voluntary associations, the work of Harp and Gagan (1971) is of some interest: they apply scalogram analysis to a set of indices reflecting different types of association. Scalogram analysis may be briefly described as a method of ordering a set of variables, each measured in a number of instances, so as to reveal whether any sequence apparently underlies their co-occurence. Their data, based on studies in over 400 New York communities, suggest that such associations may be reliably coded into a number of categories that form a scale running from 'expressive' to 'instrumental' organisations. The former apparently emerge first, for communities were very unlikely to possess instrumental associations without possessing ones of intermediate status, and were unlikely to possess these without having expressive associations, while the reverse was not true: expressive associations could exist on their own. It would be of interest to see this work linked to survey studies of association membership (e.g. Hyman and Wright, 1972), especially since the development of such associations is assigned an important role in some theories of social change. The growth of social movements is a related area with much bearing on the study of the future; the work of Kanter (1972, 1973) on past and present communes is notable for combining theoretical and empirical analysis, although her work could not really be regarded as SI research in more than a marginal way until attempts are made to systematically monitor developments in numbers, forms and fates of communes.

Studies of business and administrative organisations are fairly numerous, often focusing on variables like bureaucratisation. Two will be mentioned here: Herriot and Hodgkins (1973) studied a large number of educational systems at different levels of analysis (from national through regional, state and district to the level of actual schools) relating the socio-economic development of the system's environment to the system's inputs (e.g. expenditure per pupil, qualifications of teachers), throughputs (e.g. pupils' performances) and outputs (e.g. level of graduation of pupils). Their conclusions were that, at all levels of analysis, the 'modernity' of a system is correlated with the 'modernity' of its environment, which could suggest a predictable path of development for educational systems. Of relevance to the question of technological determinism is the careful study of Hickson, Pugh and Pheysey (1969), who studied fifty-two organisations in Birmingham, England. These authors related operations technology (involving measures of automation and types of workflow sequence) to measures of organisational structure (such as concentration of authority and the standardisation and specialisation of functions). There was little suggestion of a strong technological influence on organisation in these businesses. What effects did seem to exist were mainly confined to smaller firms whose organisation was centred around the work flow of production and distribution.

It is likely that studies such as this will be eventually integrated into the SI literature, possibly through the investigation of the quality of working life. Several large studies have been carried out relating working conditions to subjective SIs such as job satisfaction and alienation (e.g. Mueller, 1967; Tudor, 1972). What is perhaps the most elaborate large scale survey of this sort has been replicated and thus provides a source of trend data (see Quinn, Mangione and Manokovich, 1973). The study of occupations may also provide concepts whereby SI research dealing with individuals can escape its single-frame orientation towards present status: research into occupational mobility may enrich our understanding of people's evaluations of their circumstances and consequences of policies. For example, it has been reported that one British programme designed to help working class children attain higher educational standards was mainly influential on children of the 'lapsed middle classes'; and inter-generational occupational mobility has been found to be related to work satisfaction (e.g. Laslett, 1971).

As for SIs dealing with the relationship between nations, reference will be made in chapter 7 to 'international indicators'. There has been little quantitative study of the system of international organisations: an exception here is Skjelsbaek (1970).

Three broad criticisms of the emphases of SI research have been put forward. Each carries much weight, although the problems posed do not seem to be insuperable, since it has been possible to cite examples of research in neglected areas. These emphases limit the potential contribution that the SI movement can make to futures studies, since SI data are practically non-existent on several key questions. While the above argument does not mean that the efforts put into SI research are wasted — on the contrary, the field contains much valuable theory, experience, and data — it suggest that the social forecaster or planner who intends to employ such material should be well aware of the possible distortions these emphases might produce in futures studies designed with other emphases in mind. When SI research is commissioned as part of a forecasting or planning project, the past emphases of the movement should not be allowed to determine automatically the types of data collected.

Social indicators as ideology

Three related ideological underpinnings of the SI movement have been the target of criticism: what are seen to be its incrementalist, scientistic and technocratic orientations. The first two charges certainly apply to some proponents of SI research and some conclusions derived from it, but it is questionable whether these two orientations are truly characteristic of the field. Technocracy is a harder charge to rebut. A more pervasive claim against SI should be mentioned at this point; it is that SIs are essentially a philistine attempt by scientists and technicians to reduce the quality of life to mere numbers. This is partly associated with the charge of scientism, the attempt to reduce value issues to matters of logic and mathematics, which will be considered later. In part it reflects the suspicion that social scientists have frequently minimised men and women in their theories, treating people as mere materialists, naked apes or roles, and that social statisticians are unlikely to be any more responsive to the aesthetic, altruistic, playful and spiritual sides of human nature. Indeed the SI movement has shown little interest in what humanistic psychology calls 'growth needs' (as opposed to 'deficiency needs'), as described earlier in this chapter. The possible result of this, a subordination of such concerns in debate and decision making to hard 'unarguable' statistics, must be recognised.

As for incrementalism and the charge that SI research is tied to strategies of piecemeal social reform, at least one leading SI researcher has described the position of a cerebral, analytic new politics, which holds that the development of social intelligence will remove any necessity for radical restructuring of society to redress injustices - Bertram Gross (1969 preface). This view actually seems to follow from his earlier (1966) echoing of Ogburn's appraisal that the tasks for SIs at present are to aid description and prediction, that control will not be feasible until we have valid understanding of the effects of choice. Harrington (1968a, p.47) talks of the political climate with which the establishment of the SI movement was associated as one in which important people were advocating 'a social revolution but without the inconvenience of changing any basic institutions'. To the 'end of ideology' social scientists and planners, who viewed social problems as technical matters which could be solved if only sufficient data and expertise were available, rather than as products of deeply rooted aspects of a given social order, SIs were such essential sources of information for 'fine tuning' of society. Would the statistics generated for these aims necessarily satisfy only conservation needs? Harrington himself sees SI research as potentially threatening to established interests and the *status quo,* although this would require more explicit documentation of responsibility for social ills than the SI movement has yet provided. For example, rather than merely documenting the extent and growth of urban malaise, social statistics should involve measures of the ways in which government subsidises this malaise (e.g. by its treatment of the automobile, 'invisible' benefits for privileged groups, etc.). He warns that, just as a reactionary interpretation of Keynesian doctrine was employed against the poor, so may SI research be used to support, obscure or rationalise injustice. Elsewhere (Harrington, 1968b, p.4, *passim*) he has remarked that the injustices of US society have been extensively documented by government reports for a long time, yet they remain unresolved. Harrington is by no means alone among commentators welcoming SI material and employing it to make his points. Such commentators encompass a wide range of political persuasions, which in itself suggests that SI research is not inevitably or even preponderantly associated with incrementalism. It can, however, be framed in terms which anticipate incrementalist conclusions, for example, by being constrained to the analysis of incremental changes only.

Scientism is manifested in many ways throughout applied social science, and appears in SI research in various forms. For example, I have described three approaches researchers have adopted in attempting to develop unitary measures of the 'quality of life' from SI data (Encel, Marstrand and Page, 1975, part 3.5). Researchers have attempted to build an index by weighting SI scores by idiosyncratic assumptions (these may be based on personal preference, half-baked social theory, or simply avoiding the issue by assigning equal weights to each measure), statistical techniques (including factor analysis), or opinion polling (to establish the average public rank ordering of concerns). In each case a value judgement about the aggregation of concerns is disguised as a scientifically neutral approach.

Development of such composite 'welfare' indices is something of a fringe activity in SI research. The proliferation of factor analytic 'investigations' directed towards various entities and theoretical constructs has been directed as much by the hope that sophisticated computer-based manipulations can extract order from chaos as by any desire for policy relevance or value-free summarising of social conditions. Many of these outpourings are of more significance as academic games yielding rapid publication for the mere stake of a research assistant's day spent at the computer, than as attempts to gain practical or theoretical insights. These games' players make use of SI data others have collected to get themselves into the SI movement amid a welter of methodological jargon. While a great outpouring of trivial exercises in high analysis has taken place, it cannot be presumed representative of the SI literature. In fact, one of the more prominent assertions made by SI workers is that the development of better social statistics will provide an alternative to the purely economic definition of social concerns prevalent in the past. Again it is necessary to express reservations. SI data are often employed in cost-benefit analysis, in which social changes are scientistically translated into monetary values. SI researchers, while hoping to reduce reliance on an economic (or other arbitrary) metric, have failed to outline methods other than these economic or statistical reductions of data for aiding decision makers and the public to cope with a mass of detailed and subtle social statistics.

The question of technocratic underpinnings is related to the above. In our society, the definition of theoretical constructs, the development of SIs and the processing of associated data are usually seen as requiring technical skills that are restricted to professional élites. This assumption is dubious, although certainly such skills are formally exercised in the main by such élites. Attacking this state of affairs, Maruyama (1973, 1974) has stressed the value of 'endogenous' research, by which he means social research carried out by members of the communities involved rather than by outside experts. He also advocates the development and evaluation of SIs within communities by the people to whom they relate. (See also Cortazzi and Baquer, 1972, for a report of 'action learning' research, based on the premise that members of an institution are best equipped to study it.) These points are well taken but there are problems associated: What constitutes a 'community'? Under what conditions are community members prepared to make efforts to prepare SI data for the use of what kinds of policy making process?

The existence of expertise in itself need not make SI research technocratic. Technocracy is involved when the decision process is mystified in the name of 'rationality, and made invulnerable to criticism; when judgements made on the basis of covert assumptions about the importance of issues and the modes of analysis appropriate; when policy decisions are regarded as too complicated for lay participation or where exercises in participation are arbitrary from the citizen's viewpoint in terms of timing, choice of alternatives, etc. Elsner's (1967) history of the Depression era technocracy movement reveals that its founders and spokesmen advocated the development of improved social statistics (for example, date on consumer choices), and anticipated some aspects of contemporary, programme evaluation notions in their proposals for social planning.

SIs are hardly a matter of public debate, and even when Mondale's Social Accounting Bill has been discussed in the USA, interest appears to have been limited. In the absence of popular pressures, it is not surprising that SI research is left to the experts. A partial exception, which suggests alternative routes for SI studies, is the report by Koelle (1974), describing how a citizen sample (albeit small and unrepresentative) determined a set of SIs to encompass the notion of quality of life. Some one hundred aspects of this notion were discriminated and operationalised by these respondents in successive Delphi-like 'rounds' of consultation. While this research makes it abundantly clear that ordinary people can be involved in the design and selection of SIs it is apparent that researchers in general are not enthusiastic about such an approach. Among factors that may play a role are the undeniable time and money costs of survey-type consultation (which suggests that surveys are not the most appropriate tool for this purpose), the stresses of public exposure, unwillingness to risk favoured theoretical constructs being dubbed 'irrelevant', or even being discarded and élitist.

The SI movement is partly nurtured by the desire to translate essentially political decision making into scientific terms. While it is impossible to reduce value issues to considerations of technique or logic alone (values and purposes inform our premises, while formal logic enables the development of conclusions consistent with them), some authors have pointed to a threat in technocratic ideology. It is possible that the vocabulary of social and political discourse could be restricted by technocratic SI (and futures) work. This point is argued forcefully by Wynne (1975) in his critique of TA and associated methodologies, including SI research. He points out that they may obscure important aspects of decisions, and cites as an example the current formulation of the problems of nuclear power as one of safety, ignoring the social implications involved in the associated intensification of organisation for security, for example. The formulation of problems is itself a political process, and leaving it to 'experts' — even if set up in adversary groups — is no insurance against conceptual and linguistic poverty.

Marcuse (1964) anticipated the problems of SI research with his warnings against 'one-dimensional' thinking. In his depiction of one-dimensional society, critical analysis can hardly be brought to bear on major social choices due to a subordination of problem definition to social control disguised as technical rationality. In the case of SI research this can lead to a definition of problems in terms of selected indices developed by experts who are increasingly isolated from reality (see Lasch, 1970, chapter 3). This does not necessarily imply thoroughly pessimistic scenarios of extremely totalitarian or conspiratorial social control; but it is necessary to be aware that social choices may become framed in terms of a restricted and restrictive set of SIs (rather as a few economic statistics constituted a vocabulary for public economic debate in the recent past). Emergent issues might lack statistical representation and response from data-based decision instruments — an example might be the 'cultural lag' of American housing statisticans who failed to take the growing use of mobile homes into account in compiling their reports. Furthermore, established interests might remain openly unchallenged and criticism rendered unintelligible and 'irrational' to the majority of those aware of it; and our visions of alternative futures may be constrained rather than enriched by the prospects of increased comparability of here and there, then and now, which the SI movement offers, if this comparability is itself confined.

It is possible that SI research might, even under its current constitution, paradoxically play a role in averting such a 'technicist' future? Outside the mainstream of the SI movement, Harrington (1968a) has already been mentioned as a commentator who, while aware of the dangers of one-sided social information and the ability of systems to ignore data selectively, sees some grounds for optimism. Likewise Horowitz (1968, chapter 22) considers publicly available SI data as likely to be employed as a means of pressure on legislators to justify their decisions, and Ferkiss (1969, chapter 7) has even proposed that a rediscovery of politics could be produced by the requirements of modern planning techniques for precision in the statement and choice of priorities.

One factor crucial to the tenability of this view is the degree to which SI information is readily available to publics aware of its significance and willing to challenge imbalances. At present there seems to be, along with the oft-remarked disillusion with technology, a distrust of techniques such as are embodied in statistics. (For example, refusals to respond in surveys and censuses are believed to be increasing). Yet the available official and non-official statistics give much material for public concern and for egalitarian interests. To some extent national governments seem to employ SI material as a means to prod local authorities into redressing imbalances — for example, while it may be founded on dubious assumptions about the genesis of and solutions to urban deprivation, Britain's Department of the Environment has made efforts to provide cities with data, derived from census reports, about the extent and concentration of particular forms of urban stress. While SIs may not be accounting for responsibility in Harrington's sense, they may play a role in enchancing public awareness of social needs, and hardly amount to a 'whitewashing' exercise.

Some efforts are visible in Western societies to develop social data representative of a wider range of interests than are captured in mainstream SI work. Apart from academic researchers motivated by political and/or scientific desires for knowledge, pressure groups of various kinds are active. Thus in Britain the journal *Social Audit* monitors the social and environmental performance of British industries, and *Poverty* publishes the results of the Child Poverty Action Group's quantitative investigations into such matters as the expenditures of low-income families and the functioning of welfare benefit tribunals. Consumer groups, environmentalist groups and particular communities have developed social statistics to fight their cases, and there are signs of trade union interest in such research. As yet, however, the notion of SI 'advocacy' groups is practically science fiction, although the recent formation of a Radical Statistics Group may be a precursor of such developments.

One reason for this is the attraction of existing SI material itself for broad interest groups. Official statistics — except those employed in public speeches — show little sign of censorship in the sense of deliberate exclusion of material reflecting poor performance. What omissions there are in the SI literature, as documented earlier, seem to follow from a narrow definition of the movement's scope (and the scope of political action) rather than from recognised political interests. SIs themselves, though produced 'technocratically', are not unilaterally used for the technical legitimation of political values; and while they may be employed in technocratic decision making, they also provide a basis for informed criticism of policies. However, critics such as Wynne and Marcuse are arguing less about a stifling of debate as about a repressive tolerance which is able to contain intense debate within strict limits. Increased pressure to develop SIs appropriate to the study of neglected areas of social choice would be some safeguard against the restriction of debate by statistics; the development of real public participation in choosing SIs is the only real answer to the claims of expertise. Only then can SIs widen debate, and only then will people grasp the nature of SIs as parts of a system rather than as intrinsically isolated, if relevant, statistical 'facts'.

Indicators of psychological states: survey research and content analysis

It will be worthwhile to devote some space to two approaches to developing indices of psychological states and attributes since so many of the preceding comments have focused on the patterns of emphasis in SI research. In concluding this chapter, the role that such approaches might play in changing these patterns of emphasis will be considered with reference to forecasting.

Among psychological states are such constructs as feelings of relative deprivation, satisfaction or anomie, while psychological attributes may include values, perceptual habits and personality characteristics. Such variables are most generally assessed in psychological research by the study of the behaviour of those people concerning whom the assessment is to be made. Thus there are pencil and paper measures, measures of behaviour in more realistic situations, and physiological indices of 'internal' states. It is also possible to use such variables as hypothetical intervening constructs, which are not themselves measured (see chapter 2). On the basis of a theoretical specification of the measurable factors involved in influencing a variable, its level or rate of change is inferred. For example, Gurr (1968) has proposed a theory of political violence in which relative deprivation plays a role. In the absence of sufficient 'direct' evidence of the strength of such feelings in a population (elsewhere he cites survey data as appropriate, e.g. Gurr, 1970a), he developed a measure based on a large number of factors believed to contribute to a state of relative deprivation (such as lack of educational opportunity, low economic growth, high inflation and political restrictions).

While such attempts at operationalisation as Gurr's are of continuing value, the inferential gulf between measures of precursive conditions and the salient theoretical constructs remains a wide one, spanned only by the assumptions of an elaborate theory. Fewer researchers are likely to accept such a theory than are prepared to go along with the assumptions of more direct operationalisation. As an early step in empirical analysis such surrogate measures are useful in testing the broader implications of a theory, but a task for later analysis is that of validating the steps, intervening between operational measures. In the case of Gurr's theory, for example, survey studies such as those of Grofman and Muller (1973), while admittedly confined to narrower geographical and behavioural aspects of political strife, suggest that the relationship between felt deprivation and unorthodox political action is very different from the linear form suggested by Gurr. Gurr himself (Gurr and Duvall, 1973) has rejected his earlier model of civil strife, partly because of the inferential gulf between social conditions and relative deprivation. His more recent model de-emphasises the role of psychological variables.

The two more 'direct' approaches to psychological variables that have received most attention from social scientists and SI writers are first, the methods of survey research, and second, the content analysis of documents and other cultural artifacts. While not necessarily so con- strained, these approaches are generally restricted to the analysis of verbal behaviour, perhaps because of the peculiar face validity of such behaviour in respect of psychological constructs. In comparing and contrasting these two approaches I here draw on my previous discussions of survey research as a tool of social forecasting (Encel, Marstrand and Page, 1975, part 3.4; Miles, 1974). These papers should be consulted for reviews of forecasting applications of survey research: the present discussion will contain relatively more examples of the somewhat neglected approach of content analysis.

There are a number of methodological and substantive issues involved in the application of SI material developed by these approaches to problems in forecasting. The first issue involves research reactivity. Survey research generally involves collection and analysis of individuals' responses to interview questions (even if these questions be open-ended), whereas content analysis of cultural products involves applying a coding scheme of some form to existing material originally prepared for purposes other than research. Thus, as generally performed, survey research runs a clear risk of being reactive; that is, the process of data collection, being readily apparent to the people who are the source of the data, may lead to a distortion of some kind. Respondents may attempt to create a good impression, to hasten the interview, to please the inverviewer, or to build up a particular public case. Content analysis is much less reactive, partly because it is less frequently employed and publicised, and, more importantly, because it is generally applied to materials that were created for wide consumption in any case (such as newspaper articles, novels and

110

speeches). It only involves an unpredictable sample of the total body of material produced, and is often applied long after their production.

Survey research need not be constrained to interviews, verbal behaviour or artificial settings, but the vast majority of studies conform to these limitations. Other types of survey research could provide useful material for behavioural SIs. For example, in measuring racism researchers have looked at the propensity of employers to offer jobs to similarly qualified applicants of different races. As an index of trust levels in different communities researchers have investigated whether car doors were left unlocked, and, of course, the methods of participation observation developed by sociologists might be employed in a systematic fashion. The 'Mass Observation' project carried out in Britain in the 1930s and 1940s, in which a large number of volunteers recorded the events and conversations they experienced on a particular day, remains perhaps the most extensive work of this kind, although its usefulness as a source of SIs would be impaired due to the lack of theoretical constructs guiding observations. There has been very little discussion about developing behavioural indicators in the SI literature, although the related question of developing an ecological perspective has been repeatedly raised in recent years in the literature of quantitative social research (e.g. Willems, 1973). What is at issue here is whether ecological SIs might be recorded on a continuing basis. Survey researchers would then be involved in sampling contexts or situations as well as people in static frames. Content analysis may be applied to material developed deliberately for the purposes of such analysis — essays written by schoolchildren, or people's life histories as told in interviews, for example — but the present discussion will refer mainly to the analysis of existing cultural products. For discussions of research using unobtrusive measurement, the review prepared by Webb et al. (1966) is recommended. Reviews of research using naturalistic research methods — that is, studies carried out in natural settings rather than in the artificial contexts of interviews or laboratories — include Brandt (1972) and Willems and Rausch (1969). The extent to which the validity of SIs drawn from these two approaches is reduced by reactivity would seem to be greatest for survey data. In other words, such data may lack internal validity, and convergent validation of conclusions based on respondents' verbal reports is desirable.

A second issue relates to the sampling procedures to be employed to obtain SIs by these methods. It is possible to dispense with sampling and attempt to assess the whole population — as in censuses or studies of a country's entire television output, for example — but the expenses involved are generally prohibitive and will not be justified if an appropriate sample can be constructed. Sampling, of course, first requires a definition of the population with which research is concerned. In survey research a detailed literature on sampling techniques has developed and the requirements for a valid sample are fairly well understood and often met in practice (see, e.g. Moser and Kalton, 1971). Problems of self-selection may yet occur, especially when investigation is concerned with the attributes of a small group within the population (e.g. élites studied in research into bureaucracies, administrations and business and community decision making). It should be borne in mind that many studies purporting to reveal trends in attitudes or behaviour have been based on samples of uncertain significance (particularly classes of students from particular colleges). Earlier survey studies are less likely to have used current criteria for establishing a sample, which may reduce comparability.

Content analysis faces sampling problems of a magnitude similar to that involved in survey research, but, since content analysis has proved a far less popular research approach, its sampling problems have received much less attention. Delimiting a human population need not, however, be any more straightforward than doing so for a population of documents or records. In survey research one's sample can be set up to reflect accurately the proportions of groups within the actual population, even if the relative size of different groups is not mirrored in social action (e.g. legislation does not necessarily follow from changes in public opinion). However, cultural products have already been subject to a form of sampling, in that the generation of such products is by no means uniform across a human population, and there is often a further selectivity in which products survive. It would be simplistic to expect the distribution of surviving products to mirror the distribution of influence on social action, if such a thing were unitary in any case (e.g. the influence of newspaper editors on reporting and comment does not necessarily mean that they have equivalent influence on policy making). Sorokin's macrohistorical studies, referred to in the preceding chapter, illustrate this problem. His measures of cultural values, if they have any validity, largely correspond to the values of upper classes, and the processes involving other segments of society are thereby underplayed.

Once a population has been defined, the procedure of sampling can be fairly automatically based on random selections from this population, possibly modified to make most practicable use of its existing structural properties. Survey studies are usually focused on some population defined by criteria extrinsic to the research issue, such as national boundaries, although even in this case there are questions to be answered about the treatment of non-resident nationals and resident foreign citizens, etc. Content analyses more often use pragmatic or explicitly theoretical grounds for defining a population. For both research approaches, the selection of population and sample will determine the generalisability of any results and the comparability of different studies. That most survey research, for example, has been carried out in contemporary Western countries, may be good grounds for caution in projecting relationships here established into future societies.

An issue closely related to that of sampling, and throwing some light on it, is the aggregation question (see chapter 2). In survey research attempts are frequently made to present data in a disaggregated fashion – by, for example, providing age, sex, racial, class and regional breakdowns of results. The very characteristics that prove useful for disaggregation are also of use in sampling. The representativeness of a sample may be checked by comparing the proportions of different groups captured in the sample to the proportions known from other sources to exist in the population at large. Surveys may be deliberately performed in such a way as to capture specific proportions of different social groups, and their results weighted to reflect the actual proportions where disproportionate sampling is practically or statistically unavoidable (e.g. due to the need to sample a substantial number of even a very small minority group in order to reliably assess the characteristics of its members). If the population concerned is changing in terms of such groups, such weighting is sometimes employed as an extrapolative forecasting device. Thus if the proportion of older people is predicted to increase in some societies, then attitudes and opinions that current data indicate are characteristic of the elderly might be forecast to become more prevalent. Again it must be admitted that much of the survey material regularly reported is not presented in disaggregated form. Thus public opinion is often represented as a crude percentage of the whole population rather than in terms of specific groups. Increasingly, academic and scholarly research is prepared so that disaggregation in terms of standardised categories is possible, and with the advent of computerised data banks this trend seems likely to continue.

The question of disaggregating SIs based on cultural products has received less attention. Yet disaggregation is a valuable tool of social analysis – for example, as a means of assessing system equivalence (see chapter 2). With disaggregated data it is possible to search for consistencies in the relationship between common categories and a variable whose validity in indexing a construct is at stake. Content analytic studies have, in general, merely defined some particular population of cultural product — for example, TV dramas, editorials of daily newspapers, government policy statements, with specific historical and geographical limits — and analysed some sample of this either as a whole or broken down into 'natural' categories such as different TV channels, newspapers, or political parties. Other disaggregations might be suggested with uses in particular analyses: by audience size, characteristics, and attentiveness, by manifest functions (e.g. advertising a specific product, entertainment, education), by nature of media flow and gatekeeping. As Firestone (1972) argues, a theoretical basis for sampling is necessary, and the same may be said for disaggregation and aggregation of SI material. Gerbner (1973a) has suggested a foundation for content analytic studies that involves linking these analyses of message systems with studies of institutional processes involved in mass communications and the images of society cultivated by public messages. He admits that such linked analyses are incomplete and rare indeed — the focus of communications research has been on its 'effects' defined in such limited ways as attitude change and persuasion (see, e.g., the readings selected by Schramm and Roberts, 1971). His own work (Gerbner, 1970, 1973b) is much more concerned with the 'hidden curriculum' of transmitted symbols than with the analysis of particular messages of direct persuasion. Thus, rather than study what overt persuasive messages or information campaigns are presented, he has looked at such factors as the characteristics regularly attributed to different types of people (e.g. teachers, blacks) and the contexts in which particular acts occur (e.g. Where is violence portrayed? How intense is it? Who is affected?) over large samples of films, TV plays, etc.

A fourth issue, related to both sampling and aggregation, is the time-boundedness of research. One of the virtues of the SI movement is in the attempt made by researchers to collect time series data, which are important to forecasters both for revealing trends and for providing data appropriate for testing theories of social process. Both research approaches face problems with establishing time series — surveys because it is not possible to give interviews retrospectively, as it were, and content analyses because of the selective survival of cultural products.

The problem of building longitudinal data concerning changing values and attitudes has engaged several SI workers. Duncan (1969) put forward the case for investing in trend studies in which earlier research projects of good quality serve as base data for replications. Hyman (1972) has described the methodology of survey replications, and Smith (1974) has prepared an annotated bibliography of selected American studies employing replications of survey material. Recently researchers interested in subjective SIs have begun to collect information at regular intervals concerning feelings of happiness, satisfactions and frustrations, worries about various aspects of life, etc. Reference to such projects has been made earlier in this chapter, and I have reviewed some studies of life satisfaction, including some longitudinal data, in Encel, Marstrand and Page (1975, part 3.4).

In that review I also described a tactic that has sometimes been used by researchers in the absence of true time series data. Where the psychological attributes under investigation are believed to be stable, the attempt may be made to infer longitudinal trends from the location of cross-sectional differences between age groups. Although fairly widely employed as an extrapolative forecasting technique, especially in journalistic analyses of changing social values, such a tactic needs careful justification; otherwise the validity of any inferences of generational change is weakened by the unassessed possibility of maturational changes producing differences between older and younger respondents. The opposite criticism may be levelled against studies using such variables as educational level to discriminate between groups at one time in a correlational fashion, and projecting differences thus located to forecast the population attributes in a future where everyone is highly educated. In this latter case, the actual causal role played by education *per se* is assumed important but not validly assessed, whereas in the former case the role of age was assumed to be negligible. In the absence of longitudinal (and where possible, experimental or quasi-experimental) data, multivariate analysis offers a means of, if not validating inferred relationships of this sort, at least invalidating some contending possibilities. In multivariate analyses statistical controls are employed in an attempt to sort out the distinct relationships between many variables, as well as any interaction effects that may be present. Such analyses are becoming more available with the growth of computing facilities, and may be expected to help clarify the significance of ambiguous research findings.

Survey researchers are often at a loss for time series data. The history of survey research itself is short, the development of adequate techniques of sampling and attempts to reduce response biases in interviews are recent, and from the perspective of the SI movement many of the questions asked and most of the data collected in the past are trivial and of transitory significance. On the other hand, content analysis may be applied to any suitable surviving cultural product, and has thus frequently been used to study social changes. Unfortunately few of the studies available could really be considered as yielding more than an inkling of what SI series might be valuable. Often a study is restricted to describing, for example, changes in the presentation of one institution or type of character in one format (such as short stories) in one magazine for one time period. Such studies are usually descriptive.

Some content analytic studies have had a deeper theoretical basis than the expectation that particular trends might be found, but they are in general so isolated that no firm conclusions can be drawn as to their external validity. Given the relative underdevelopment of content analytic methods and the limited number of studies that have been performed, it is hardly surprising that researchers should feel cautious about accepting statements about either specific societal trends or about 'universal' relationships and social laws, when these are based on analysis of a small sample of one particular class of cultural products by fairly novel techniques. It may be useful here to examine a few of the applications of content analysis to the study of social change which do have a theoretical rationale, in order to see how conclusive and suggestive their results are, and how these might relate to forecasting.

Sales (1972) presents an ingenious study based on the notion that authoritarian psychological attributes increase in times of economic threat. Comparing the years preceding the Depression to years during it, he finds statistically significant changes in many surprising measures — including the toughness of comic strip heroes, the cynicism expressed in magazine articles, and the featuring of astrology in magazines. He concludes that a hypothesis of increasing authoritarianism in this era is supported. Though suggestive, and clearly of interest to forecasters who are concerned with the possibility of future massive economic threats, this study is by no means conclusive. One of the main problems is the lack of control over other possible influences on the measures cited (see Campbell and Stanley, 1966). Sales's indices might, for example, be continuously responding to one of Sorokin's long run trends rather than displaying any specific effect of the Depression. Studies involving other cultures and times would be useful tests of this thesis. Sales's rationale for predicting the effect of threat on authoritarianism was based on existing psychological theory and thus his findings have some support beyond the narrow limits of his comparative technique. Furthermore, he does use some controls for his measures (e.g. changes in astrology articles are compared to changes in astronomy articles).

In discussions of the utility of content analysis the work of McClelland (1961) and related researchers (e.g. de Charms and Moeller, 1962) is almost invariably cited as making a considerable contribution to our understanding of the processes of cultural change and the sorts of values that are required for national economic development. (For attempts to apply the ensuing value prescriptions see McClelland and Winter, 1969.) The content analytic aspects of this work have largely been concerned with the coding of school texts for motivational emphases, particularly the stressing of achievement motivation. (Not only school readers have been analysed; folk ballads, popular plays and other verbal material has been studied, and attempts have even been made to analyse the characteristics of non-figurative art in achievement motivation terms.) These workers have reported cross-national differences and longitudinal variations within nations, and have related these to, among other variables, subsequent rates of economic growth, extending Weber's notion of the 'Protestant ethic'. The studies produced by achievement motivation researchers have revealed impressive correlations between motive levels in cultural products and subsequent changes in political and economic activity, some of which are summarised by Firestone (1972). Such relationships may be used in forecasting in an exploratory manner, to predict future national changes from current motive levels, or even to forecast on the basis of extrapolated trends in motive levels. There are also normative applications. The McClelland and Winter (1969) attempts to instil achievement values in a sample of businessmen in order to create economic change present a microcosm of social engineering which could be extended in various ways.

Rather than ponder the implications of this approach to cultural change, it is necessary to point out here that while some important relationships are being assessed, their nature is in doubt — for reasons beyond Inkeles's (1971) query about what highly achievement motivated adults are doing writing children's readers rather than becoming business tycoons. Essentially, the stories analysed in these studies do not reflect the motives of the children whose later activity causes social change. Instead, just as Gurr's social conditions are expected to cause relative deprivation, these stories are believed to instil achievement motivation in their young readers. In principle it should be possible to investigate the actual motives expressed by citizen samples in cross-national and longitudinal comparisons. In a very different content analytic study, Greenstein (1964) analysed children's essays, written over a period of half a century in American schools, concerning whom they would most like to resemble. He concluded that there was no decline of children's expressed achievement values corresponding to that located in their textbooks, although other trends were apparent (notably increased preference for popular over serious entertainers). This would suggest that the values expressed in these books and subsequent social changes are both products of a common cause rather than being directly linked through the readers

E

117

of these books, although the matter is by no means closed since there may be doubt about the validity of Greenstein's coding as a true index of achievement values. Cross-national motivation studies using content analysis have also generated some controversy. (For example, see Barret and Franke, 1970, for a refutation of one of the studies cited by Firestone, in which attempts were made to link national motive levels to 'psychogenic' deaths.)

A recent study represents an attempt to apply the sorts of techniques developed by McClelland to futurological ends. Fowles (1975) analysed by content advertisements in *Life* for the years 1950, 1960 and 1970. The degree of expression of eighteen motives was coded and changes over these periods computed. Diferences between the motivational profile of the advertisements in 1950 and 1960 were related to social changes occurring between 1960 and 1970. The degree of fit obtained was sufficient to give Fowles confidence to forecast the social environment of 1980 from 1960–1970 advertisement changes. His forecast is that 1980 America will be relatively anomic, privatised, more concerned with scientific than with social progress, neither resistant to nor supportive of minority demands, and so on.

Certainly this is an adventurous study, but methodological problems alone would make his forecast suspect. For example, the readership of *Life* is hardly a representative or a static sample of the American population – perhaps TV would be a better medium in these terms. Fowles furthermore fails to provide a convincing rationale for his selection of social indicators to support his contentions about social change. Extension of this study to a wider historical or cultural sample would necessitate a confrontation of these methodological issues, and might open up some interesting perspectives on social dynamics. However, the assumptions of such a study should not be allowed to foreclose either the possibility of potentially malleable variables mediating (or indeed, producing) any relationships that were established, or the possibility of using other media and institutions to transmit values.

A fourth crucial issue in survey research and content analysis as SIs and forecasting tools relates to problems in the specification and operational-isation of theoretically significant constructs, and variables significant to long term forecasts rather than immediate practicalities. As already mentioned, many surveys are concerned with trivia or transitory issues, while few have been directed at psychological constructs of any depth – thus opinions are sounded more than values. Values may be conceptual-ised as central goals towards which people strive, which are manifested in attitudes towards objects and actions only with the mediation of beliefs about the relationships of these objects and actions to these goals (Rokeach, 1973). The methods employed in psychological and anthropological research are generally cumbersome, and while new methods are being employed in the studies of Rokeach and Parker (1970) and the life satisfaction literature, their validity is uncertain. Values are not necessarily readily verbalised by those holding them, and their assessment in interviews by relatively direct approaches, such as asking respondents how important they feel particular goals to be, is potentially reactive. Survey studies of attitudes and beliefs are far more common, and are of course valuable as SI sources in their own right. It may be that an understanding of the dynamics of value change would be necessary to forecast attitude change in more than a superficial way, but SIs of personal values remain in their infancy.

Commentators often infer values on the basis of what they see as meaningful combinations of attitudes and beliefs. Duncan, Schuman and Duncan (1973) demonstrate the difficulty of inferring changing social values from changes in discrete attitudes in their analysis of American survey data collected over eighteen years. Thus two items are cited in terms of which greater 'liberalism' becomes apparent between 1956 and 1971; belief in non-intervention in South American affairs and willingness to let one's child bring home a black playmate. The authors question an interpretation of these shifts as signifying a deeper trend towards more liberal values, showing that in neither year were the two measures significantly correlated; nor was a simple account of the changes compatible with a presumed underlying connection between the attitudes (such as their differentially reflecting the same value). Duncan, Schuman and Duncan thus rightly caution against the premature inference of underlying connections between variables, when pairs of variables follow similar trends in aggregate summaries of data. Explanations of social and political evolution in terms of value change in mass publics must be treated with caution, especially when underlying values are not directly assessed or the assumptions relating them to operationalisations are not spelled out in a testable way. (Of relevance here is the critique and empirical analysis made by Mann, 1970, of the 'value consensus' approach in political theorising about democracies.)

Among content analytic approaches to value change, the work of Namenwirth (1973) is of particular interest. Explicitly focusing on public expressions of élite values, rather than trying to summarise the mood of a total society, he has analysed over a century's American political party platforms, using a computerised system to count the frequency of mention of particular concerns. Clear trends were established in the expression of values in these documents, with both long and short term cycles apparent. Namenwirth attempts to explain these changes in terms of Parsonian theory in which the expression of values is seen as a functional social response to phased problems confronting the society. The temptation to extrapolate from these trends is great, and Namenwirth himself sees particular values as reaching peak expression only in the forthcoming decades. Laird (1973) has in fact developed a simple computer simulation model of value change based on this work with which he forecasts, for example, increasing emphasis on long range goals and moral issues over the coming decades, and a possible American economic decline in the late 1970s or early 1980s, followed by an upsurge in instrumental values, caused by overemphasising non-economic goals!

Returning to the broad issues of operationalisation and specification in researching psychological variables, survey research presents the observer with a familiar set of measures. Although a great deal of effort is wasted and opportunity for replication lost by workers laboriously constructing (and often only minimally validating) new measures of familiar constructs, there have been considerable efforts to disseminate standard indices with evidence of their reliability and interrelationships (e.g. Robinson and Shaver, 1969a, b). Content analytic techniques are largely experimental, and the foci of different measures range from the messages in single sentences and paragraphs, through theoretic analyses as involved in the McClelland work and symbolic analyses à la Gerbner, to studies of the structure of literary genres. One step forward, the development of computerised techniques for analysis of verbal documents (Stone et al., 1966), not only reduces problems of inter-observer coding reliability but also makes possible rapid reliability and validity testing of alternative coding systems and levels of indicator aggregation. However, such methods are currently best suited to relatively simple analyses of the frequency of particular concepts or statements and the ways in which ideas are paired and concepts evaluated than they are to studying broader aspects of styles or plots. The volume edited by Gerbner et al. (1969) provides some indication of progress in such respects, but suggests that content analysis has much ground to catch up before its battery of measures can rival that of survey research. Thus it is difficult to present a review of the relevance of existing content analytic research to futures studies that might parallel my relatively optimistic treatment of survey research (Encel, Marstrand, and Page, 1975, part 3.4).

It would be possible to discuss a number of further issues relating to both these approaches, such as the role of multivariate analysis and the possibilities of comparative research. However, it is already possible to

120

reach some conclusions about research into the psychological aspects of social change.

Earlier in this chapter it was remarked that the SI movement has largely neglected the enterprise of measuring such aspects, and that this was likely to hinder the development of models of social change appropriate to human forecasting and to involve threats to the comprehensiveness of forecasts and the debate surrounding them. In this section it has been apparent that, despite the creation of many useful survey instruments and the wide implications of many of the studies reviewed, social research has been fairly limited in scope. The difficulties involved in studying for example, large numbers of interactions in everyday settings, large samples of cultural products and the deep structure of individual values, are enormous. These difficulties may be more of a barrier to further expansion of SI research than disciplinary or ideological biases − although it must still be admitted that, with the exception of the few works in the Campbell and Converse (1972) tradition, even those limited subjective SIs in existence are rarely taken into account in the SI literature.

Two tasks lie ahead of SI research in respect of the issues raised in this section: improving existing techniques for studying psychological variables; and acknowledging those insights that have been gained to date. Futures researchers may indeed benefit from the contributions of quantitative social research, and should certainly use such material wherever possible to appraise their concepts and assumptions. Basing forecasts on the inevitably tentative conclusions of social scientists requires much caution, and every effort should be taken to assess this indeterminacy, and to acknowledge the wide realm of variables that are not touched on in a futures study, though they will undoubtedly be impinged on by and impinge on the future itself.

6   Post-Industrial Futures

In this and the following chapter attention is directed towards some area of social forecasting prominent in social science. In such forecasting we might expect to see the interdependence and influence of societal variables on each other used as a major basis of analysis. Simplistic technological determinism would seem unlikely, even if technological change is seen as an ongoing source of stimulation for social change.

One of the most widely diffused notions employed by social scientists looking at the future of Western societies is the concept of 'post-industrial society'. This chapter begins with an overview of the main attributes claimed for this slippery concept, which has been subject to numerous interpretations. Subsequently essential issues of the social structure and sociopsychological features of post-industrial society are explored at more length. The conclusions stemming from these reviews suggest that the terms in which the future of industrial society are framed by at least one group of influential writers are inadequate; this inadequacy leads to only partial descriptions of the future they anticipate, and obscures the possibility of constructing alternative futures.

Concepts of post-industrial development

The notion of 'post-industrial society' (PIS) has appeared in many futurological and social scientific writings, as Daniel Bell, with whom the term is perhaps most closely associated, points out in the introduction and first chapter of his *The Coming of Post-Industrial Society* (a synthesis of essays written in the decade before its publication in 1974). Marien (1973) also details a range of uses of the term and related notions. Different perspectives have been brought to bear on the current changes experienced by Western industrial societies, just as earlier social theorists grappled with the spread of industrialisation and the growth of modern bureaucracies, and PIS has proved sufficiently compelling to feature in some very divergent analyses. Writers are frequently vague about which factors are causes and which effects in their descriptions of the trends characterising PIS, and also disagree about the validity of particular assertions about present or emerging aspects of such a society. Whether or not PIS is already in existence is a matter of some contention, depending on the precise definition adopted. American society is often described as having largely completed the transition to a PIS, based on the decreasing proportion of the population employed in industry. (Most observers describe PIS as being a service-based society. The following review is not, in the main, concerned with those forecasters of scarcity, alternative technology, or an ecological revolution, who have used the term 'post-industrial' to refer to a society of, for example, self-sufficient personal subsistence in rural communes.)

A broad listing of these factors (compare Trist, 1972) must start with the shifts in the labour force from production of goods to production of services common to advanced industrial societies – which alone is seen to justify the label PIS – and the increases in numbers of technical, managerial and professional workers. These shifts are generally related to continuing economic growth, and are often viewed as being linked to increasing social equality, which may be viewed as either a side-effect of industrialisation's impact on the occupational structure or as a consequence of changing political values. Bell and other commentators of an 'end of ideology' disposition see the growing scientific and technical knowledge élites as comprising a new class which will displace the established sources of power as PIS blossoms into a social order based on rational, technical decision making. Technology assessment, forecasting models and systems analysis will replace *ad hoc* adaptiveness and experimentation as political approaches to social change. In Bell's terminology the 'axial principle' of PIS will be the centrality of theoretical knowledge as the source of innovation and of policy formulation. A dominant role will be played by professional and technical people, armed with a new 'intellectual technology'. Education in the new skills involved here is the route to power; society will be managed by those who understand how to manipulate masses of SIs into policy directives by using computers and high-powered analytic techniques. Other commentators, however, do not view the coming PIS as post-ideological, and have viewed the new white-collar workers as a new working class aligned against the capitalist system or as a co-opted technostructure subordinate to an executive élite.

Along with the growth of knowledge élites comes the extension of state planning activities as a component of PIS. The increasing propensity of liberal democratic governments to assume responsibility for directing economic and social change is taken as an inevitable response to the increasing complexity and interrelatedness of advanced industrial society. The accompanying centralisation of decision making in mixed economies is a concomitant process which (to the post-ideology school) actually protects pluralism by reducing the power of business groupings as central government takes up the causes of the less influential and articulate, which it has been able to diagnose with SIs and community councils. The growth of long term planning in large and/or affluent corporations equally is seen as having irrevocably changed the shape of the economy, and the interests of such corporations are seen as being increasingly coincident with, and informed by, government aims to maintain economic growth and stability. However, there is a stream of criticism directed towards multinationals, which are free to play a different game (mostly by commentators from outside the PIS stream of forecasting, e.g. Bannock, 1971; Tugendhat, 1971; Turner, 1974). Private corporations will remain of importance to the economic structure for a long time, but the 'managerial revolution' has already largely come about. The decoupling of ownership and authority in modern businesses is transforming the values in terms of which companies operate away from mere profit maximisation to social concern and the exercise of social responsibility. Related to this is an increasing involvement of private corporations with public services which Harrington (1968b) wryly describes as the 'social—industrial complex'.

Value change in the PIS is not restricted to managers and politicians (who have adopted long term time horizons). Affluence, security and leisure are seen as producing various psychological consequences in the PIS population. While high and rising material aspirations will be the norm, ideological conflict will decline and consensus on broad objectives mark political life. Humanistic values will prevail over questions of economic status, according to one set of writers; others disagree and foresee a culturally impoverished one-dimensional society.

In the foregoing account, conflicts and differences of emphasis and evaluation have been passed over hastily to give a crude picture of the issues frequently encountered in the social scientific literature on PIS. Divergent interpretations and forecasts are very apparent in these writings, especially with respect to counterpressures and the extent of class and value conflicts within PIS. For example, commentators disagree on the possibility of a new white-collar class displacing established élites without a struggle, and of humanistic values being compatible with a highly bureaucratic and centralised society. Where authors agree on a phenomenon − for example the decline of overt political conflict − their evaluations of it may range between extremes of optimism and pessimism. Contrast, for example, the attitudes of Marcuse (1964) and Lipset (1963) to the 'end of ideology' in contemporary PIS. Specific disagreements are also evident — for example, whether PIS is to be a monolithic 'mass society' or a mosaic of diverse sub-cultures, whether minority demands will be repressed or acceded to. Rather than outline each of the large number of perspectives on PIS, I shall illustrate the problems involved in assessing the quality of social forecasts first by reviewing those ideas on the structure of PIS represented in the work of Bell and the associated writers currently dominating the futures field, and, second, by studying the contributions of social science to forecasts of the values of PIS based on contemporary value changes.

Before we turn to such specifics, some points made by Kumar (1972) are worth noting. He relates the study of PIS to the social conflicts of the 1960s, which shook establishment sociology's conviction that Western capitalist societies represented a mature and (structurally) fairly static cumulation of economic development processes. The 'post-ideology' analysts of social process had adopted a diluted Marxian view of the historical development of society in which the eventual revolution of the proletariat was rendered unnecessary by reductions in inequality. With the thesis of PIS a new stage was appended to this sequence of societal developments, and a model of the future conceived to accord with present trends. Kumar finds much to fault in the adoption of this viewpoint in futures studies. He protests against the technological determinism, evolutionary analysis and passive acceptance of technocracy inherent in much of this work. Fundamentally PIS is an exploratory forecast based on extending certain past trends into the future, and Kumar challenges futures researchers to think of discontinuous futures and to attempt normative forecasting. The comments of Goldthorpe (1970) described in chapter 1 are here echoed. Both writers warn against the limitation of images of the future that are threatened by the ready acceptance of historicist views of PIS.

Trends and countertrends in post-industrial society

This section focuses on the particular stream of research into PIS exemplified by the work of Daniel Bell and his associates — a group consisting mainly of American writers, many associated with the journal *The Public Interest* and, earlier, with the notion of the 'end of ideology' (see Bell, 1960; Waxman, 1968). References to Daniel Bell in this section relate to his 1974 PIS volume. If this PIS literature is based on exploratory extrapolation of present trends (although in reading Bell it is difficult to separate description of the forces bringing PIS into being from prescriptions for a more comfortable infancy), then it is important that its data inputs be examined. In particular, which of the host of trends displayed by Western societies are chosen for extrapolation?

In a paper entitled 'The Historian's Role in Futures Research' Waskow (1968) argued that the study of alternative futures migh valuably proceed from the study of competing major trends, and his work may prove a useful guideline here. In his discussion he points to three major directions of development in the USA and other advanced industrial societies, which throw some light on the issues of PIS. They are the hypertrophy of war and the associated growth of powerful élites based on military organisations; the increasing numbers in the 'new class' of the highly educated; and the emergence of underclasses cut off from the mainstream of affluent society and social mobility. For each of these directions there are countertrends that may negate their development. Studying projections and possible negations of major trends is seen by Waskow as a useful approach to the task of extracting the most salient aspects of alternative futures from the vast number of possible forecasts that might be made. A focus on 'trends' notwithstanding, Waskow's search for conditions which might negate their future development shows his analysis to be more than historicism.

Bell's analysis mainly elaborates the second of these trends. This emphasis is justified by asserting that the idea of PIS is really being employed as an ideal type, an 'ordering device' to make actual social change more intelligible. However, his book is subtitled 'a venture in social forecasting' and his analysis of current affairs is repeatedly in terms of post-industrial tendencies in current society rather than of the gap between present reality and the PIS ideal, even if the many tables and trend lines reprinted in his volume rarely include long term projections.

In respect of the first of Waskow's trends — the concentration of power (especially in matters of foreign policy and expenditure on high technology) in what C. Wright Mills (1956) called 'the power élite', also known as the military—industrial complex — Bell is almost silent. To quote Lasch (1973, p. 63), 'Bell argues at one point, following the lead of that deep thinker Herman Kahn, that "military technology has supplanted the 'mode of production', in Marx's use of the term, as a major determinant of social structure" (p. 356). This formulation begs the question of whether military technology is not itself determined, or at least heavily influenced, by the 'mode of production' — in which case we do not need an 'updated' Marxism to understand the role of military technology in the capitalist economy'. In fact Bell's analysis cited by Lasch merely points to the underwriting by the State of private R & D on military matters and to the introduction of systematic policy analysis (PPBS) into government for defence decision making (the letters PPBS stand for planning programming budgeting system — a way of systemising policy making by comparative estimation of costs and benefits of alternative policies). A high national priority on the need for security is seen as leading to investment of economic and technical resources in defence and to the growing demand for scientists and technicians capable of planning. In his coda Bell discusses the interaction of scientists and society in the development of nuclear weapons and in the Oppenheimer affair. These discussions demonstrate that, while scientists initiated discussions about technology and strategy, decision making power was firmly in the hands of military and political leaders; the American military is also acknowledge to have achieved a unique freedom from reliance on outside science. These considerations play no role in the body of the forecasting exercise, however.

As for Waskow's third trend — the emergence of an 'underclass' in Myrdal's (1963) term — again the reader must turn to Bell's coda for anything more substantial than hopes that SI data will document the plight of the underprivileged, thus helping PIS choose appropriate social goals by focusing attention on areas of need, and that the pluralist basis of decision making will ensure that minorities are taken into account. Here he takes up his assertion that PIS will (or should) assume a meritocratic form in which academic credentials are the basis of advancement, but obscures questions of the institutionalisation of racism and poverty by attacking 'populism' by the method of *reductio ad absurdum* which somehow again becomes an argument for increasing meritocracy.

The most thorough critique of this orthodox perspective on PIS is presented by Kleinberg (1973), writing before the concatenation and publication of Bell's essays as a single volume. Kleinberg looks at the work of a number of PIS writers and not only directs attention to the two trends neglected in their forecasts, but also criticises as invalid their interpretations of SIs concerning the growing 'knowledge élite'. He concludes that this theory of PIS (which he sees as a revision of the theory of the end of ideology, itself a revision of earlier liberal—pluralist analyses) is seriously flawed. Its main value is to foster awareness of the intertwining of government, industry, commerce, science and education in progressive co-ordination and planning for modern societies whose overt class conflict has been reduced and welfare state paraphernalia have been institutionalised. As such it points to important social changes, but this can be a far cry from giving an accurate forecast. Kleinburg's book represents a critical alternative venture into social forecasting based on this awareness without recourse to ideal types. Indeed, the 'ideal type' of PIS is here seen as serving an ideological function of rationalising the existing decision making system and its values by forecasting a utopia of sorts which will come into being 'crescively' without needing revolution or radical action.

Kleinberg's approach illustrates the value of bringing a critical social scientific analysis to bear on questions of the future, as well as specifically revealing the flaws in received notions of PIS. This summary must be very sketchy, since his book is itself extremely rich in case studies, statistics and illustrative analyses. It is important to note that rather than provide a geographically unspecific portait of PIS, suggestive of tendencies in all industrial societies which will lead them to structural convergence, Kleinberg explicitly deals with futures of the USA only. In fact, French and British economic planning are taken as comparative models pointing to alternative directions in which American decision making might evolve (Kleinberg, 1973, chapter 8).

The central issue in his analysis is the nature of the role that may actually be played by technical decision making and a knowledge class in a future society in which the extremes of power élite and underclass coexist. In the conventional PIS view, continuing growth is seen as providing opportunities for redistributing wealth and improving the quality of life while maintaining social consensus. Far from being a broker between powerful interests, an increasingly centralised state will play an active role in planning and in ensuring the representation of plural interests. With increasing societal feedback from SIs, and the application of forecasting and planning techniques developed in military contexts, social goals will be attained; education and the service sector continue to expand as public programmes employ workers freed from industry by a gradual spread of automation.

Kleinberg questions the existence of a 'knowledge class', given that there is little evidence for shared interests in upper white-collar groups. Not only could members of the National Commission on Technology, Automation and American Progress (1966) not reach consensus on a key issue of PIS — the cushioning of structural unemployment due to technology by relief, as opposed to increasing public employment, divided business from labour and civil rights representatives (themselves hardly radical) — but the parts of the report that were agreed upon were too controversial for executive response. To assume that technical decision making in PIS would faithfully reflect the needs of a plural society, achieve political consensus or even prove instrumentally effective are all articles of faith against which Kleinberg marshals much evidence.

Rather than view the institutions proposed for PIS as signifying an 'active state', responsive to a broad range of social groups, Kleinberg sees the operation of commission (such as the Technology Commission and France's commissiones de modernization), of executive–administrative government, and of all levels of the 'Great Society' package, as representing a special kind of 'élite pluralism': While conflicts of interest can and do occur in the élite pluralist forum, the range of alternative decisions that are up for consideration are strictly limited by the shared interests of these élites. The conflicts that occur are seen as often reflecting competition for government largesse and preference rather than different senses of social priorities. (These interests may be shared, on occasion, by the co-opted 'representatives' of minorities. In respect of the co-optation of minority representaitves see Bensman and Vidich, 1971, chapter 12; and Lasch, 1970, chapter 1, who also illustrate (especially in Lasch's chapter 3) the co-optation of intellectual élites in the service of power.) The political feasibility of technical decisions is questioned; American legislatures are capable of blocking executive actions, and have historically been resistant to social programmes (whose costs are minimal compared to defence expenditures). Their effectiveness must also be in doubt. For one thing the terms of reference and problem definition in systems analysis is not itself the product of technical choice; this is evidenced by the military perspective which was consistently and practically automatically brought to bear on matters of overseas development by the 'Great Society'. The fact that the Technology Commission could not follow the logic of PIS to recommend a programme of expansion of public service employment similarly bodes ill for technical decision making as a means of escaping the narrow constraints imposed on policy options by established interests. Furthermore, government agencies and large contractors have shown great flair for setting obstacles in the way of implementing distateful decisions reached by such analysis. Reforms of military planning, in the McNamara era, cited by PIS writers as examples of the coming style of policy making, failed at the level of politics, generating collusive counterstrategies from the military–industrial complex. The knowledge 'class' is hardly represented in these practical processes of making and implementing decisions. The 'knowledge explosion' (which Kleinberg shows to have been remarkably directional in terms of defence and aerospace requirements in any case), produced technicians subservient to existing interest groups rather than a new class.

Lasch (1973, p.64), argues that the 'academic boom of the Fifties and Sixties reflected short-term political decisions, not underlying sociological tendencies'. For comparative data on public expenditures on research, see Freeman et al. (1971); several points are worth making from these sorts of data. Different countries are displaying markedly different 'knowledge explosions' in terms of manpower and expenditure indicators, so the notion of a unitary form for PIS seems untenable – instead local trends are of considerable importance. Furthermore, the USA and UK have both shown declining government support of industrial R & D in recent years, and likewise military, aerospace and nuclear expenditures have declined in relative terms as percentages of public expenditures. Lasch's point seems apt: the support of research has less to do with 'the centrality of theoretical knowledge' than the Cold War, the space race and, in Europe, the 'technology gap'. Whether all members of the 'knowledge élite' are totally subservient to political masters is of course another matter. Both government-funded academics and community workers have a good deal of discretion as to their activities, and both groups have been often portrayed as harbouring many opponents of the establishment.

Kleinberg's own forecast takes into account alternative possible paths of PIS development, with the drift being towards a 'technocratic corporatism'. (For a forecast of the British economic future which also foresees corporatism as a likely outcome of present trends, see Pahl and Winkler, 1974). Present-day America has not realised the pessimistic forecasts of the 1950s and become a 'garrison state'. Kleinberg views it rather, as a 'contract state' in which the economy is dominated by a small number of large corporations and strategic élites, who contend for government support (e.g. underwriting of research costs, training of manpower, awarding large contrasts) within a framework of shared interests.

The supposed growth of interest in social welfare on the part of private and non-profit organisations is hardly a welcome development in view of the model established for programmes of national security. The consequences of contracting out of public programmes would include reduced accountability, and business's profit orientation would be manifested in glossy high-technology projects unrelated to social needs (again, see Harrington, 1968b, on the 'social–industrial complex'). The evolution of economic planning is more likely to follow paths of collusive co-ordination for the benefit of particular private interests, of piecemeal attempts at central policy making whose value and effectiveness would be curtailed by a fragmented administration, or of some mixture of the two, than the rational centralisation of the orthodox PIS literature. The conventional forecasts involve élites willingly conceding much of their power to the underprivileged, and even a formulation like that of Etzioni

(1968), in which massive mobilisation of 'active citizens' and minorities is envisaged, seems to sidestep the conflict inherent in such futures, whether it be minorities or their technocratic champions that confront established interests.

The future of the 'underclass' is a matter about which Kleinberg is equally pessimistic. He sees the relatively abortive careers of the radical right and black nationalist oppositions in the past decade as manifestations of status politics, certainly not displaying the features of a common class consciousness. These movements, and that of the relatively privileged student left, have failed to find much common ground, are internally fragmented, and lack any effective theory. Ironically, social theorists, in forecasting the reform of social structure by the PIS technocracy and in restricting themselves to prediction and description rather than the posing of alternative futures, avoid questioning the functions served by the established distributions of power. PIS theorists are prone to denounce opponents of the trends of centralisation and bureaucratisation as nihilists and romantics, to foresee conflict between a rational social structure and a hedonistic culture – this hardly aids the appraisal of futures based on alternative power structures.

Kleinberg's own projection for the underclass is vague, partly because he concentrates on an issue usually dismissed by PIS writers: possible massive increases in structural unemployment caused by automation and cybernation. This might be averted by the possible generation or coincidental occurrence of new military crises, or by increasing public service employment. If the option chosen, or drifted into, relies to any large extent on merely cushioning unemployment with relief or income maintenance programmes, then sharp class differences would appear in PIS, reversing the trend towards such differences being obscured by overlapping multiple strata. Even in the absence of such a thorough-going transformation of the occupational structure, the masses excluded from meaningful participation in a technocratic society may show 'restiveness'. This would involve at least the granting of token reforms, and, more likely, increasing cultural repression and state surveillance of the individual.

Kleinberg's book can be taken as a further stage in a continuing debate about the transformations of advanced industrial societies. The end of ideology viewpoint is described by Kleinberg as an answer to C. Wright Mills's critique of pluralist theories of modern society. The PIS approach emerges from this viewpoint as economic growth and political centralisation proceed against a context of sporadic political turmoil, the Vietnam war with its policy making and political consequences, and a

132

growing concern with 'quality of life'. While Kleinberg's arguments and data are often convincing, this debate between optimistic and pessimistic forecasters of PIS social structure is conducted on increasingly sophisticated ground. (So, for example, earlier questions of the convergence of industrial societies are relegated to footnotes.) The perspectives that must be chosen between or reconciled involve, for example, Bell's view of PIS as displaying an increasing disjunction between culture and society (which enables him to argue away particular social trends, especially those of opposition to technocracy), as against the interpretation of contemporary cultural fragmentation as directly bound up with the values of mass consumption and military security that support élitist decision making in the recent evolution of PIS, which is made by Harrington and Kleinberg.

Again, to what extent are 'technical' considerations predominant in setting the agenda of decision making, and to what extent are the decisions reached constrained by technical perspectives? How far and when is the use of expertise mere legitimation as opposed to a central element in the direction of resources? A resolution of these alternative perspectives is hardly likely to be settled by available SI data!

As seen above, Kleinberg questions the significance of the occupational shifts that have been interpreted as intrinsic aspects of the coming PIS. Other trends in modern society that are often projected into PIS are also suspect. For example, Goldthorpe (1967) has argued against three supposed features of advanced industrialism: that the stratification system becomes decreasingly differentiated with income redistribution and growth in higher level occupations; that there is increasing meritocratic consistency between occupational level, educational attainment and prestige; and that rates of social mobility become high as PIS is approached. His critique is particularly directed against those 'convergence' theorists who reasoned that an underlying logic of social development will produce similar stratification systems in all industrial societies. It is also relevant to the more recent formulations of PIS theory.

In respect of the supposed trends towards equality in PIS, Goldthorpe reviews several studies suggesting that in recent decades, at least, there has been little evidence for an overall trend towards greater income equality; both egalitarian and inegalitarian tendencies seem to operate at different points in the stratification system. His own studies (see Goldthorpe et al., 1969) suggest that stratification systems are not becoming more integrated; the affluent British working class has not adopted traditionally middle class lifestyles. (The work of Jencks, 1972, among other studies, suggests that the meritocratic ideal is far removed from reality in any case; educational credentials only account for a small proportion of the differences in wealth and power between people.) Social mobility, furthermore, seems to depend significantly on factors other than the industrial system, since mobility indicators paint very different pictures for different countries.

'Convergence' theories are not always restricted to predicting that similar stratification systems will characterise different advanced industrial nations. The forecast has also been made that the political systems of countries will converge as their economic growth continues — a perspective with which issue is taken in the following chapter. When applied to PIS, this perspective has been used to suggest that the USSR will come to develop a political structure similar to that of the USA — a suggestion of which Russian scholars and politicians themselves strenuously attack (see the collection edited by Gouré et al., 1973).

If, as Goldthorpe argues, the 'effects' of advancing industrialism are mediated to a crucial extent by cultural values and political factors, then it appears pointless to talk about PIS in general. Forecasts of the future of industrial societies need to take into account a wide range of causal variables rather than succumb to a simple 'industrialisation' model. This is really just technological determinism serving to mask cultural diversity, and simultaneously obscure the differing presents of different modern nations, and the alternative futures open to them in PIS.

Values and post-industrial man

The post-ideological school of forecasters has not, in its recent work, been particularly specific about cultural and psychological aspects of PIS, preferring to concentrate attention on a single axis of social change. Perhaps this reflects bewilderment at the ingratitude of their students (who will form the new class) and the underpriviledged (to whom justice will be provided in the post-industrial future), who not only reasserted ideology, disrupted the supposed tranquillity of the cities and campuses, and invalidated forecasts based upon the notion that 'the fundamental political problems of the industrial revolution have been solved' (Lipset, 1963, pp.442–3), but who also attack many of the basic tendencies of PIS: its centralised decision making, its mystifying techniques of allocation, its powerful executive. For Bell (1974) and Trist (1972) there is a cultural lag between PIS social structure and culture, including values. Trist belongs to a school of theorists prepared openly to prescribe the values needed for man to coexist with PIS rather than to focus on trends and conflicts in a detached way.

Bell (1975) has recently expounded further views on PIS values, in which he reasons that the new social reality will crucially influence human consciousness. Work having become service work, involving the encounter of people rather than games against nature (for the pre-industrial person) or against technics (for industrial people), old constraints of season and scheduling will be replaced by new ones involving group integration. In an effort to ascribe meaning and purpose to life, Bell believes, a revival of religion may arise — one which may actually resolve the conflicts of affluence, community and open political decision making. This hope that religion may solve the problems of apparent discrepancies between public values and the societal (or ecological) predicament is one often voiced at present (e.g. Cook, 1974, and other contributors to the same conference). Sometimes this appears as mere lubrication for technocracy. Perhaps the best exposition of the view is in a science fiction novel entitled *The Electric Crocodile* (Compton, 1970) in which a secret TA unit, wielding immense power over the direction taken by scientific research, embarks on a forecasting project aimed at locating the optimal religion for resolving PIS conflicts.

Several types of literature about PIS values may be discriminated. Firstly there are (or were) post-ideological writers, who foresee a society of little conflict in which the basic structure of values in the population has undergone little change and people are increasingly satisfied with their material standards of living. A second group of theorists, often supported by survey or impressionistic evidence, has suggested that at a psychological level people are becoming increasingly less rigidly concerned with issues of material wealth and status, and more aware of spiritual and community needs. A third set of writers has engaged in analyses of what sorts of values would be supportive of PIS, and write as if such changes are practically inevitable. In contrast are theorists who doubt that people are really capable of coping with the degree of social change involved in present-day life and PIS; the complexity and speed of advanced society is seen to conflict with deeply-rooted human needs and thus to produce adaptive (or maladaptive) responses of various kinds. This is the thesis of 'future shock'. Finally there is the controversy over the possible change in values shown by the leaders of modern corporations, the thesis that the managerial revolution means that PIS will essentially be a post-capitalist society, and the notion of a 'new working class'.

Since the theory of PIS emerged out of the end of ideology school, it is not suprising that, at least until the mid-1960s, advanced industrial

135

societies were generally anticipated to be fairly tranquil. In the words of Harrington (1965, pp.104–5), 'the end-of-ideology is a shorthand way of saying the end of socialism, at least as that idea was conceived of by the nineteenth century party of the poor'. There are strong echoes of Ogburn's prediction (1955) that rising standards of living would mean a decline of socialism, at least in its radical forms. One of the most concise statements of the thesis of tranquillity was made by Lane (1965) who asserted that in an age of affluence (characterised by such features as economic growth, relative equality, welfare state practices and a managed economy) various political attitudes and values would emerge, and who attempted to test this assertion against trend data from US survey research from the 1940s to the 1960s. He reported data supportive of predictions of increasing trust in other people, increasing sense of personal control of one's fate, increasing optimism about the future; decreasing political partisanship (so fewer people believed that it would make any difference who won the national elections, evaluations of incumbent presidents are less tied to party preferences, etc.); a decline of religious hostility in politics; and changes in class awareness so that, for example, fewer people thought their taxes excessive in later surveys. He failed to find support for his notion of declining political alienation, which had in fact risen by the mid-1960s. More recent reports render his other findings suspect as indicative of growing feelings of trust and efficiency in political matters, or of a growing sense of optimism – for trend studies showing the opposite to have been true in the USA (even, apparently, before the economic troubles of the early 1970s). Such studies are those of Duncan, Schuman and Duncan (1973), Harris (1973) and also Rotter's report, (1971) which, while based on student samples does employ a measure of fatalism/personal control which has received extensive validation and has been related to various forms of behaviour. Surveys of happiness and life satisfaction conducted in the USA over several decades also suggest a fluctuating rather than continually increasing sense of well-being (see Miles, 1974, p.248).

Lane's forecast that increasing affluence would lead to a PIS founded on consensual values clearly failed to anticipate some very important factors. Among these were the counterculture, Vietnam, the revolution of rising frustrations in the ghettoes (partly fuelled by repeated promises that equality was just around the corner) and openly corrupt politics. Might his forecast prove valid in other circumstances? The German time series attitudinal data reported by Conradt (1974) point to trends over the past two decades towards increasing popular support for the existence of competing political parties and belief in the freedom of political expression. Consensus on 'the rules of the game' of politics is interpreted by Conradt as indicating support for the performance of the incumbents of political office and their policies. Research on consensual political values and attitudes has often stemmed from a theoretical perspective stressing the role such psychological variables play in maintaining the political system. However Mann (1970) has pointed out that consensus is certainly not the rule for values related to liberal democracies, and cannot be the key support of institutions. Finding that working class survey respondents frequently supported 'deviant' values and beliefs concerning political action, the legitimacy of the class structure, the trustworthiness of others, and personal political efficiency, he proposed that 'false consciousness' may play an important role in maintaining existing political institutions.

In a series of studies, Norval Glenn (e.g. 1967, 1974) has reported data questioning another aspect of the consensus image of PIS values — the notion that mobility, education and the mass media will produce a society in which differences in values and attitudes between different social groups decline. From a number of American surveys he finds that while some survey responses appear to show declining differences between such groups as the old and the young, men and women, rural and urban dwellers, and occupational, racial and regional groups, other survey responses show increasing differences. Nor does the work of Alford (1963) on social factors related to party preference in Australia, Canada, the UK and the USA suggest that there is any consistent decline in class-based voting choices in these countries over time. The 'massification' view of PIS is not supported; whatever pressures might be acting to homogenise values in society, counterpressures clearly exist.

Associated with the end of ideology school is a further image of PIS value change — the notion of working class embourgeoisement. According to this hypothesis, increasing affluence should lead workers not only to share the consensus on political activities and institutions, but also to increasingly adopt values and life styles that have previously been identified with the middle classes. As mentioned earlier, Goldthorpe et al. (1969), having investigated affluent British workers in survey studies, concluded that predictions of embourgeoisement were ill-founded. The workers they studied, for example, retained an instrumental attitude to their work rather than perceiving it as being of intrinsic value, did not adopt middle class life styles, and continued to support left-wing parties. Whether or not embourgeoisement has actually taken place — a question whose answer will depend upon the sorts of data one chooses to cite as relevant — the hypothesis is itself flawed as a tool for understanding PIS (on this point see the reviews by Jelin, 1974, and Mann, 1973). This is because it abstracts changes in values from their historical context and fails to analyse the relations and conflicts existing between social classes at the particular time when they are said to be converging. It falls into the historicist error of seeing the 'ideal type' of PIS as some kind of historical inevitability, whose form will not be effected by cultural or political variations.

The second viewpoint concerning PIS values is often encountered in reference to 'youth culture'. The development of youth movements (e.g. hippies, the counterculture) and the interest of large numbers of young people in the environmentalist, women's, and personal growth movements, have been among the factors leading serval observers to diagnose a radical shift in values across the present generations and to forecast a future dominance of 'Consciousness III' (Reich, 1970), the values of a post-industrial (Keniston, 1968) or post-transition (Kelly, 1972) society.

Of particular interest in the present context is the work of Inglehart (1971), since it not only shares many of the assumptions of these analysts but also attempts to test them out and engage in extrapolation forecasting on the basis of survey data. His theoretical analysis is similar to that of many commentators, favourable and unfavourable, on youth culture – a developmental psychological explanation is called into play. However, his young people are not, for once, assumed to be rebelling against over-liberal parents.

Young people today are raised in conditions of affluence and security unknown to their parents, according to Inglehart. As predicted by the theories of the humanistic psychologist Maslow (1954) among others, when basic physical and safety motives are abundantly satisfied other motives emerge. Critics of youth culture view these as unrepressed destructive, envious or romantic motives. Inglehart (1971, pp.991–2) looks at the growth of '"post-bourgeois" values, relating to the need for belonging and to aesthetic and intellectual needs'.

Inglehart reports on surveys carried out in six European countries, in each of which younger people tended to choose 'post-bourgeois' values more frequently than older people, with the differences being particularly striking in those countries whose economic growth had been most rapid (Italy and West Germany). Treating these cross-sectional data as reflecting real trends over time rather than the product of short term fashions in expressive style or of some maturational process – he cites national differences and some German time series survey data to support this – Inglehart forecasts that the values currently characterising youth will be shared by majorities of these European populations within a few decades.

Reservations have elsewhere been expressed about Inglehart's approach (Encel, Marstrand and Page, 1975, part 3.4; Miles, 1974). Briefly summarised, these involve doubts about the depth of the values indexed by his measure (respondents were asked to select two out of four alternative national priorities, relating to combating inflation, maintaining order, increasing participation in political decisions and protecting freedom of speech); doubts about the stability of these values (the time series data, while showing a trend towards 'post-bourgeois' choices, also reveal that adults do shift their positions); doubts about whether there is absolute decline in acquisitive, materialistic values in 'post-bourgeois' man (other survey data indicate that the younger 'post-bourgeois' respondents hardly feel saturated with money and possessions, and, on the contrary want relatively more improvement in their status than others); and consequently, doubts about the permanance of a shift towards post-industrial values, particularly if economic growth were interrupted, an option that may be chosen by, or forced upon, Western Europe.

The most intriguing question raised by Inglehart's work is the nature of the judgement his survey instrument assessed. Various studies indicate that young people, and the 'post-bourgeois', tend to have more unsatisfied material wishes than other respondents. Apart from studies reviewed in the above, the work of Katona, Strumpel and Zahn (1971) may be mentioned. Studies carried out in four countries revealed that younger respondents tended to express more unsatisfied purchasing wishes, and that age differences were most acute in the USA (which is generally supposed to have made most progress toward PIS).

Surveys provide little evidence for significant declines in consumer desires on the part of the young, despite the undoubted increase in the formation and membership of various 'drop-out' and alternative social groups and lifestyles — although these have often been viewed as opening up new markets for a hip capitalism, since the fringes of such sub-cultures often greatly outnumber the core. The notion of human needs rather mechanistically arising as prior needs are successively satisfied in any case ascribes universality and biological necessity to a Western consumer ethic that may alternatively be viewed as the product of a particular social system with powerful instruments for marketing and merchandising lifestyles and values, if not always particular products. Rather than support this notion, Inglehart's work points to an absolute increase in expressed desires for political liberty and participation that suggests that some autonomous process is implicated in these value changes. This process might relate to such features of PIS as the growth in numbers engaged in higher education, the development of electronic mass communications, and the changing style of technocratic decision making, as much as to affluence *per se*. But at least of equal explanatory significance to such trends must be the world political context: a history of world wars, cold war, imperialist wars, depression, recession, liberation and repression.

The recent beginnings of regular replications of surveys may soon throw light on whether the apparent increasing concern with participation and free speech is part of a deep-rooted trend or whether it is susceptible to short-run economic or cultural fluctuations. Inglehart's questions have been employed in British quality of life surveys, where it may be possible to gain a surer sense of their significance — which of several constructs they might tap — by studying their relationships with other measures. For the present it is extremely difficult to assess whether such forecasts as Inglehart makes concerning future political party affiliations are likely to be realised, even if economic growth were to continue with little setback — let alone if a transition to post-affluence, such as Gappert (1974) talks of, is realised.

Gappert's work belongs to the third class of studies of PIS values, those concerned with describing the sorts of values and institutions that would be associated with societal stability in PIS, although it is exceptional in that he predicts it as undergoing declining affluence. For example, since there will be insufficient capital to build enough conventional suburban housing for the increasing number of families, multi-family buildings will become more common; consumer values will be replaced by needs for intimacy and an ethic of leisure. Sharpening class conflict might be resolved by welfare reform, age conflict by intra-family transfers of wealth and antibureaucratic tendencies by social accounting, TA and participatory community planning. This social tinkering will be rounded off with self-change by psychotherapy and meditation to help citizens adjust to scarcity. Whether these prescriptions would satisfy the young, both with their material and post-bourgeois needs, the poor who might object to learning to live 'poor with style', and the more established interests, remains to be seen, and Gappert himself sees the transition to PIS as 'turbulent'.

In common with other appraisals of PIS value changes that stem from analyses of the adaptations needed to cope with changing social conditions, Gappert presents a strange mixture of the exploratory and the normative in his work. Rather than attempting to evolve alternative futures which might be attained within the constraints he anticipates for PIS, he is projecting a future based on a mixture of desires for as much social stability as possible given external pressures, hopes that this stability

140

would be maintained by a series of piecemeal anticipatory strategies, beliefs in the improbability of military or repressive responses either internal or international, and alertness to 'novel' lifestyles.

In contrast with Gappert's paper, Rainwater (1972), in an issue of *Society* devoted to emerging American lifestyles, presents an exploratory forecast of life in affluent PIS which entails little turbulence (except that involving the still-deprived black underclass). One aspect of his forecast is the assumption that increasing economic security will encourage people to experiment with different lifestyles before committing themselves to a particular mode of living, and one result of this might be increased tolerance of diversity (and incidental absorption of feminist and counter-culture values).

Emery (1974) is among several prominent 'systems' researchers who have produced futuristic analyses of needed PIS value change. Others include Ackoff (1974), Beer (1975), and Trist (1972). (For a viewpoint that, while not framed in 'systems' language, follows the same pattern of approach to conclude that counterculture values will predominate in the future, see Simon, 1974. Interestingly, his post-industrial man shares, in common with several other species, a present-focused time orientation that meshes strangely with the future orientation of administration as described by Bell and others, even if it reflects the 'here and now' themes in the counterculture.) Unlike Gappert, Emery considers alternative macrosocial responses to PIS, which he characterises as 'adaptive' or 'maladaptive'. However he argues that adaptive responses are likely to predominate in Western societies (although the USSR, for example, is likely to adopt a 'maladaptive' response), and correspondingly devotes more analysis to the forms that adaptation should take. In what seems to have become the established tradition of systems theory, these alternative responses are based on conclusions drawn from the study of personality rather than from political analysis. While of much intrinsic interest, these forecasts again intermingle prescription and anticipation, and the implications for normative policy of the adaptive scenario (questions of what in chapter 3 were termed the criteria of clarity and closure) are ill defined.

The 'systems' writers generally take an optimistic view of PIS, and consequently see the human values and the institutions of such a system as in harmony. Jobs will be flexible, work democratic and life-enhancing, education continued throughout the lifespan and carried out in groups, family patterns will be more open and less isolated. The values fulfilled through such institutions will include Trists's self-actualisation, self-expression, interdependence and capacity for joy, Emery's humanity, homonomy and beauty. The approach of these forecasters, then, is to identify qualitative social changes that could be needed if an adaptive PIS were to be developed according to such values; there is little consideration of how these changes might be brought about.

The thesis of 'future shock' as a psychological result of the complex and ever changing PIS is dismissed by Emery (1974, p.30– who does not believe 'that individuals or organisations are "future shocked" into inadaptibility by decreases or increases in their range of choice (i.e. hardship, success or good luck). It is our contention that change only begins to have this effect when it increases the degree of "relevant uncertainty" – unsureness and consequently anxiety about what can be expected in areas that really matter to the person or organisation'. The best-known exponent of the thesis is Toffler (1970), who talks of super-industrial society, although Klapp (1969) gives in many ways a more coherent, 'grounded' and readable approach. In a similar vein, Popper (1957) attributed historicism itself to the stresses of a changing, open, society.

According to future shockers, uncomfortable uncertainty is generated by rapid rates of social change such as characterise PIS. This has various bad results, including stress and psychosomatic disease, the proliferation of sub-cultures providing a sense of stability, tradition, meaningfulness or identity, and the growth of economic social movements and violence. Elsewhere (Miles, 1974) I have reviewed studies supporting Emery's contention that massive change in lifeways is not in itself likely to lead to psychological malfunctioning. For example, Inkeles and Smith (1970) found no consistent evidence that migration and modernising experiences, such as contact with factories and media, and urbanisation, had deleterious effects on mental health. The classic study of Goldhammer and Marshall (1953) found no evidence for a long term increase in psychoses over the past century in the USA. It may be speculated that the sorts of change that form the empirical material supplied by Toffler and Klapp, such as it is, seem to be leading to feelings of malaise and need to establish identity through the medium of adopting a new set of group norms, and are in fact not those changes portrayed in optimistic depictions of PIS.

In the conventional portrait of PIS there is affluence, equality and increasing development of social services and welfare provisions, making life better for citizens. The sorts of change leading to psychological malaise would instead seem to be those involving multiple crises of transition (e.g. economic deprivation, sudden separation from family) in the absence of resources (financial or communal) or assistance to cope with disruption (see Fried, 1964). While increasing family instability is often forecast, economic deprivation and the absence of social services are not part of orthodox PIS, although a rapid rate of change is.

142

Leighton (1969) compared samples from Nigerian towns and villages and rural Canada on psychiatric symptomatology measures, finding that the populations showed fairly similar kinds and general proportions of disorder. The environment least conducive to mental health appears to have been that displaying social disintegration rather than social change. Thus in Nigeria disorders were most prevalent in disintegrated traditional communities rather than in new communities. Bronfenbrenner (1974) believes that American society is providing its children with increasingly disorganised and isolated living conditions, and calls for the greater integration of adult and child life (e.g. parent participation in crêches and the involvement of older children in caring for younger children, less segregation of activity areas on age grounds). Some theorists of PIS values (e.g. Kelly, 1972) see the counterculture partly as an attempt to cope with such stresses; such social innovations as encounter groups and the 'personal growth movement' have similarly been related to the limitations of what Bennis and Slater (1968) call 'The Temporary Society'.

Some authors have interpreted current political violence as an anomic response to change. Despite some scholarly versions of this view (e.g. Olson, 1963, writing of 'rapid growth as a destabilizing force' extends this account well beyond the notion of unspecific change itself as a causal factor to take into consideration such features of rapid social change as economic gains and losses, and rising aspirations), empirical data do not support it. A cross-national time series study by Flanigan and Fogelman (1970) involved relating measures of political violence to changes in economic development as indexed by the proportion of the work force engaged in agriculture in sixty-five countries. The conclusion was that more rapid development was likely to be associated with less political violence. Lodhi and Tilly (1973) studied crimes against property and persons, and collective violence, in relation to urbanisation in French departments over a lengthy period. Collective violence was found not to be related to urbanisation, but to power struggles at the national level, and to fluctuate widely through the period. Tilly (1969a) reports that collective violence was lower in France during years of rapid urban growth, and that riot participants were integrated workers whose upward mobility was restricted, rather than members of underclass – their actions were rational politics rather than anomic outlash under stress. (See Levy, 1969, for evidence on American trends in political violence.) This evidence suggests that change which opens up opportunities and increases the range of meaningful choice is anything but stressful.

The final set of perspectives in PIS values are more restricted to a particular social group than the analyses reviewed above. One general theme of PIS theory is the argument that in advanced capitalist countries there has been increasing separation of ownership and control of large corporations. (In fact this assumption is open to question, as has been shown again recently by Zeitlin, 1974, who makes a case for the continuing existence of a capitalist class with much power over corporate affairs). Owners delegate power to corporation managers and the values guiding their organisations increasingly give less emphasis to mere profit making and capital accumulation. PIS theorists thus update the idea of a managerial revolution as propounded by Burnham (1940). A related trend is often depicted: the managers of organisations are seen to be becoming more concerned for their employees, and more environmentally and socially conscious.

Blackburn (1972b) has strongly criticised these post-capitalist interpretations of PIS. Whatever the truth about the separation of ownership and control, he is able to produce evidence that company directors on average have considerable financial interests in their companies' affairs, that the imperatives of owner-managed and professionally managed companies both share and focus on growth as well as profit making and capital accumulation, and that in practice there is little difference between these two types of company. The account by Harrington (1968b) of what 'social involvement of business' actually looks like in practice strongly suggests that the idea of managerial attitudes and values changing in general on any large scale is merely a legitimation of profit making through tailoring business to the apparent needs of welfare agencies.

Another social group which is sometimes taken as a signficant focus of PIS value change is that consisting of technically and scientifically skilled workers in the more automated and advanced sections of industry. This 'new working class' has been at the centre of some European analyses of PIS (e.g. Touraine, 1971), in which its involvement in knowledge- and science-based production is seen to make its members particularly salient in PIS class conflict. Their alienation and involvement in issues of control, coupled with their financial security, may be seen as facilitating the growth of class consciousness and militancy in PIS. Mann (1973) has criticised these theories on both empirical and theoretical grounds in his review of studies of the contemporary Western working class, finding that their apparent applicability to recent events in France may be interpreted in terms of local factors which have reinforced demands for control on the part of such workers. In other Western countries the 'new working class' has shown more signs of increasing participation in existing structures rather than in opposing them, and even in France a sense of class identity is lacking. These questions are by no means closed, however, and deserve

144

closer inspection than I have been able to afford them here, as well as requiring further and more detailed research.

This chapter has reviewed a number of prominent perspectives on the post-industrial future in the light of existing criticism and empirical evidence. This existing evidence rarely allows any of the crucial issues to be finally settled, but it has served an important function. It has demonstrated that frequently the portrait painted of PIS is a caricature, consisting of certain features magnified out of all proportion and consequently minimising other initial features. The literature of the social sciences may not be sufficiently rich to lend extensive forecasting much validity, but it can help the forecaster dispose of simplistic ideas and consider ranges of alternatives. A dialogue between forecasting and the social sciences has only recently been resumed. To be constructive it must not be restricted to a single theme, nor to topics that do nothing to disturb existing prejudices about the future.

7 Political Research and Images of the Future

Contemporary political science has been strongly influenced by operationalism and the social indicators movement. Some political researchers have seen this as ushering in a new era of comparative political analysis in which laws of social evolution might be established, with consequent revolutionary effects on political prediction and planning. Considering the range of topics dealt with by political analysts, this is no insignificant claim.

This chapter begins with a brief account of research into extremes of this range: individual political participation and international relationships. The body of the chapter contains a more detailed analysis of the merits of the claim of a new era in two particular areas where much cross-national political research has been directed: the development of political institutions and the origins of domestic political conflict. The controversial nature of research in these areas suggests that, if political forecasting is feasible, it must be explicitly concerned with politics. Forecasters should beware of uncritically taking over conservative or simplistic evolutionary models in which political choices are treated as mere outputs of economic change.

Politics and prediction

Contemporary empirical political research spans a wide range of topics, ranging from studies of individual decision makers and of the interactions within political organisations facing particular environmental challenges, through research on the political activity of mass publics and on the characteristics of national political systems, to analysis of the whole world system of nations. This chapter is to be largely concerned with two areas of research employing what Narrol (1972; Sigelman and Narrol, 1974, in bibliographies of such studies) terms holonational analysis — that is research in which nation states have been the unit of analysis. These two areas of research involve first, the processes of development and change in political structures, and second, the genesis of political violence and civil strife; these are both areas in which SIs of a global nature, as described in chapter 5, have been established to describe national characteristics.

Before reviewing this research, two other fields of study are worth investigating in terms of their implications for futures studies. One is the study by techniques of survey research of the political behaviour of ordinary citizens – the matter of political participation rather than of partisanship will here be taken up. The second field is the study of relations between nations and of the changing pattern of such relations over time, which is of course relevant to the forecasting of international conflict and the prospects for regional integration.

The question of political participation is of some interest to futures researchers. The findings of several studies would seem to indicate positive relationships between the standing of individuals on socio-economic variables such as membership of voluntary associations, social class characteristics, and educational attainment, and their levels of political participation. Following from these cross-sectional findings, projections of increasing levels of affluence and schooling have often been linked to forecasts of future increases in political awareness, interest and participation. Such forecasts are of doubtful value until the possibility of other factors (such as age which is associated with educational level) playing a significant role is assessed, and cross sectional data are supplemented by longitudinal information.

The survey conducted by Almond and Verba (1963) in five countries – Germany, Italy, Mexico, the UK, the USA – had a substantial influence on later treatments of participation. In this study social status was found to be positively correlated with psychological states such as feelings of personal competence in political affairs, as well as with actual political participation, and the five nations were compared in terms of a notion of development of political culture. Later researchers have employed their cross-sectional data to build more precise statistical models of individual political involvement, based on causal path analysis. Different aspects of the respondents' social and economic background are here analysed together in a controlled way so that the distinct relationships of each to attitudinal variables and participation could be assessed (Nie, Powell and Prewitt, 1969). These data were also used by Muller (1970) in an analysis of feelings of political competence. He found that factor analysis of a set of attitude questions employed by Almond and Verba revealed a similar structure of three factors in each of the five countries. One set of questions relating to levels of political involvement and attentiveness were found to group together; other groups included questions reflecting the belief that one could influence government, and questions concerning perceptions of the impact of people in general on government. Such studies suggest fairly stable constellations of political attitudes and relationships of such attitudes to social background and to political participation and point to likely effects of national and regional contexts, at least for parliamentary democracies. The socio-economic mobilisation model implied here — where socio-economic status influences psychological states, which in turn produce predispositions to voting — might be employed in forecasting participation (if not partisanship). Indeed, Lerner (1958) has made use of similar hypotheses in writing about the likely effects of socio-economic 'modernisation' on political development in the Middle Eastern countries.

The survey work of Verba, Nie and Kim (1971) in five countries — Austria, India, Japan, Nigeria and the USA and later extended to include the Netherlands and Yugoslavia (Verba et al., 1973) — represents something of a break with this body of research. These authors found that a number of distinct forms of political participation could be distinguished (by factor analysis). While particular modes might not be present in a national setting which offered no real opportunity for its expression, there was much similarity in the forms of participation distinguished in the different countries. In particular a factor comprising different forms of voting, which are typically aggregated together with other forms of political participation, was found to be distinct from factors involving such acts as campaign activity, contacting of officials on a personal basis and engagement in community affairs. The socio-economic mobilisation model of political participation was not found to apply equally to all modes of participation; in general it seemed to have most applicability to campaign and community activities. These studies, with their findings of a good deal of similarity in the contexts of action in widely different nations, suggest that some forecasting of levels of different forms of participation may eventually be practicable. To satisfy the criteria of an adequate forecast, such work would have to be based on longitudinal extensions of the work reviewed above which would look at the effects of (planned or unplanned) contextual change, and will have to take into account aspects of political structure, partisan involvement and the politicisation of 'personal' needs, rather than relying on a simple economic/educational determinism.

Two further points should be made about such studies. First, they have so far been focused on 'orthodox political behaviour'. Those few survey researchers who have investigated participation in other modes of political activity — such as demonstrations and riots — have found that such behaviour is not mere anomic aggression engaged in by maladjusted or unintegrated 'outsiders', but is itself comprehensibly linked to attitudes and values in much the same way as 'orthodox' participation (e.g. Caplan and Paige, 1968; Muller, 1972). Forecasting involving merely conventional political participation should be recognised as engaging in a particular form of meta-advocacy (see chapter 2).

Second, if the hope is to be able eventually to forecast changes in institutions and policy on the basis of this research, it will be necessary for much more detailed comparative examination of the linkages between public participation and élite decision making than this field has yet received. Clearly it is wrong to assume that different modes of participation exert the same influence on policy makers, or that all participants have equal influence.

To turn to studies of the international system, various planners and scholars have been involved in forecasting potential conflicts in terms derived from the social sciences for many years, and were among the first beneficiaries of the resurgence of empirical political analysis. In volumes such as that entitled by Hekhuis, McClintock and Burns (1964) are found papers like Pye's 'The Underdeveloped Areas as a Source of International Tension Through 1975', in which questions of underdevelopment and international integration mingle strangely with considerations of strategy and deterrence. Futures researchers have often been involved in studies of international relations and conflict, as was pointed out in chapter 3. This work proceeds with many techniques and degrees of refinement (see, for example, the review of simulations by Guetzkow, 1969); the SI movement may be expected to make an impact on such studies, whether they are conducted as theoretical exercises or tools for policy making. Research in this field often adheres to partisan viewpoints. Thus the definition of international stability is frequently oriented towards the interests of a particular nation. With SI research, a somewhat less narrow range of issues may be explored. Nevertheless the interpretations offered in current research often fall into the old patterns. Thus Park (1973) reports a study of interactions between Asian countries based on indicators of such behaviours as military coups, trading, and diplomatic interchanges. Over time the clustering of countries was found to have changed – Park proceeds to interpret this as reflecting an abatement of 'identity crises' (turning Asian countries to China), which were replaced by pragmatic 'political realism' (alignment with the USA).

Recently political scientists have been involved in developing such 'international indicators' reflecting the behaviour of nations towards each other, and attempting to build theories of the foreign policy behaviour of nations from such data (e.g. Kegley, 1973; McClelland and Winter, 1969;

150

Rummel, 1972). These writers have attempted to discern patterns in foreign policy behaviour, and to account for the relations of particular pairs and groups of countries in terms of indices of national attributes. Such work has already been employed for forecasting international affairs in order to 'enable governments, industry and private groups to prepare for expected changes and, in some cases, modify undesired trends in the global system' (Wynn, Rubin and Franco, 1973, p.244). This quotation comes from an account in *The Futurist* of a private research firm's ventures into quantitative forecasting of conflict based on McClelland's data. While vague about what particular assumptions and techniques they employ, other than that regression analyses formed an analytic base in terms of which such variables as differences in power, defence expenditure, geographic contiguity and history of conflict were related to international behaviour, these authors do offer some titbits from their results. For example, they conclude that India seems likely to be at war with Pakistan and/or China, and Ethiopia with Somalia and/or the Sudan in the 1982–1991 period. As well as conflict, other characteristics forecast included likely alignments with the USA or USSR, and economic growth.

It is not possible to evaluate these forecasts in any detail on the basis of this report, but there are obvious reasons for caution in accepting their conclusions. It seems unlikely, for one thing, that adequate forecasts could be made in the absence of a satisfactory theory of international relations. One may also ponder the potential effects that knowledge of such forecasts might have on the parties involved. International conflict, with its heavy risks meaning that frequent conscious attention is paid to it by policy makers, is one field in which Popper's notion of an 'oedipus effect' is likely to be particularly cogent.

One of the few futures studies to focus on the international system in a holistic way was presented to a futures research conference by Johan Galtung (1969). Although his work in this case is based only minimally on quantitative data, Galtung does raise interrelated questions concerning the international impact of PIS (thus complementing the concerns of the previous chapter) and concerning the future relationships of the developed with the developing nations (a topic relevant to the rest of the present chapter). Along with the usual features of PIS, Galtung describes fundamental erosion of loyalty to the nation state, at least among the 'most advanced' population sectors of 'neo-modern' countries. Among other consequences this should lead to an interpenetration of neo-modern nations with increasing organisational links (multinational companies, unions, pressure groups, etc.) and co-ordinated policies on such issues as

151

arms control. The Third World is expected to undergo economic development, and the populations of its nations to increase in national loyalty, although ethnic conflicts within and between these countries should continue. Galtung then proceeds to delineate alternative futures for relationships between these two groups of nations. For example, poorer nations may conduct their dealings with richer nations individually, or they may organise into 'trade unions' to set prices for their goods. Galtung reasons that the latter kind of scenario was most likely, with the possibility of international wars or 'preventive military operations'.

Galtung's forecast is not alone in projecting alternative futures for the international system. Other futurological works which make use of this focus and take some account of structural features of PIS include Emery (1974) and Kahn and Wiener (1967). However, Galtung's work is particularly explicit in its assumptions, and does appear to have received some validation in the light of the actions taken by Third World petroleum exporters and the attempts of other nations to cartelise their natural resource and agricultural productions. Rather than exhaustively survey Galtung's forecast, which includes some telling and some less substantial analyses, I would like to refer to the work of Harrington (1968b, chapters 7—9) which has a bearing on Galtung's 'most likely future'. On the basis of data provided by Shonfield (1969) and others, Harrington pointed out that the developed nations were increasingly trading among themselves and, with the crucial exception of oil, the produce of the Third World is becoming less relevant to PIS. (Other commentators have reached or implied similar conclusions from perspectives markedly different from Harrington's — for example, Rostow's, 1971, extension of his 'stages of growth' model of national development suggests that PIS is motivated by a search for quality rather than for increasingly high mass-consumption, and would presumably have little interest in the Third World were it not necessary to keep in check the expansionist urges he attributes to industrialising countries!) The parallel between the rich and poor world and the capitalist and working classes may be invalid in this case. PIS and even advanced industrial societies may be sufficiently independent of the rest of the world to simply ignore 'trade union' activities, in which case Galtung's speculation about nuclear terrorism as a possible consequence of continued world inequality may prove relevant. Still, it is worth noting that forecasting teams have been employed by developed states to investigate the possible extent and impact of future cartelisation — one aspect of Galtung's work that is perhaps too sketchy.

Futures research could provide imagination and wider horizons to research on international development, and political economy could give futures studies a firm analytic basis. So far the dialogue between these fields has been limited, and, as the following sections will describe, uncritical, at least in the case of futurologists' assimilation of ideas from political science. If the consequences of present trends and countertrends are to be grasped, and if alternative futures are to be seriously investigated, such a dialogue is essential.

Indicators of political structure

It is fortunately possible to sort many of the numerous recent quantitative studies of political institutions into a small number of groups. One set of studies involves attempts at compiling political data in a catholic manner (rather than to specify *a priori* theoretically significant variables or to fashion indicators to constructs), and subsequently applying to these data 'theoretically neutral' techniques of statistical analysis. Other studies focus more specifically on particular theoretical constructs — for example, there are many studies involving measures of party cohesion and party competition in parliamentary systems. Some of the theoretical constructs proposed here have been linked to notions of political development and thus are clearly connected to the forecasting of political change. Among the most relevant of these are literatures relating to constructs of polyarchy and parliamentary democracy, and to the institutionalisation of political systems.

The 'take-off' of empirical comparative politics may be placed around the time of publication of compilations of SI material for nation states by two groups of political scientists (Banks and Textor, 1962; Russett, 1964). The later products of these groups (Banks, 1971; Taylor and Hudson, 1972) reflect two of the directions followed by research in the subsequent decade. These later volumes place less emphasis on judgemental indicators, and strive to present time-series rather than cross-sectional data alone. The Taylor and Hudson volume disavows, furthermore, the cross-sectional correlational and factor-analytic methodology featured in Russett's first edition of the *World Handbook of Political and Social Indicators*.

'Atheoretical' attempts to locate significant regularities in the widely varying, complex political structures of nations received much of their impetus from the first editions of these volumes. The work based on the Banks and Textor book is of most relevance here. Studies employing Russett's data have tended to mingle indiscriminately political,

153

socio-economic and other indicators, a feature also found in the work of Rummel (1972), itself involving a large data collection enterprise, and some earlier factor analytic studies of national differences, e.g. Cattell (1950).

Gregg and Banks (1965) present a factor analysis based on sixty-eight SIs and a sample of 115 nations. Of seven factors located, three accounted for more than half the total variance in the correlation matrix. These were labelled and interpreted as follows: access (a set of indices discriminating constitutional regimes, neutral military forces and interest group articulation from authoritarian, hierarchical and single-party systems), differentiation (a factor characterising different types of ex-colonies in terms of length of independence, degree of development of post-colonial bureaucracies), and consensus (political system stability and Westernisation versus political violence and military intervention). Banks and Gregg (1965) complemented this analysis by clustering nations into groups exhibiting similar features, again by factor analysis. Five groups accounted for most of the variance: polyarchic, élitist, centrist, personalist and traditional. These labels were derived by inspecting common political features of the nations involved. The first group are almost entirely economically developed and Western, the second group African and the third group Eastern European.

The value of such studies is debatable. It may be argued that throwing together a large number of variables of doubtful theoretical significance is likely to obscure central relationships; certainly not all the variables included in these studies were actually measures of structural forms or institutions, nor were all the relevant variables that might be listed included. However, one finding at least is significant. These studies point to the existence of several dimensions of political variation of present-day nations; it thus seems unlikely that social forecasting could assume a unilinear trend in political development, or a single, all-important construct in terms of which variations could be understood. Indeed, these results suggest that even the assumption of a dominant and reversible path of political evolution is an inappropriate concept for exploratory forecasting; nations may apparently change direction in terms of several quite independent dimensions.

The work of Kumar (1972) will be recalled from the previous chapter. As described there, he reviewed the perspectives of futures research on industrially advanced societies (where he criticised PIS theories). However, he advanced a similar critique of social forecasting as applied to the Third World. Social scientists approaching the question of 'development', whether social, political, economic or all three, have tended in his view to fall back on evolutionary and stage theories similar to those advanced in

154

the nineteenth century. (Rostow, 1960, 1971, is probably the best-known advocate of a stages approach to economic and political development processes.) Third World countries are viewed from this perspective as being propelled by internal dynamics from a traditional or under-developed pole to a modern pole, perhaps with the initial take-off fuelled by inputs of foreign aid and technology. Kumar criticises social scientists for accepting a unilinear model of social change, which makes the task of forecasting merely prediction based on a series of stages or states. The extent to which this charge applies to quantitative comparative research will be assessed below.

In this section several approaches to developing indicators of political structure will be reviewed, and in the next section attention will be focused on the empirical bases of theories and models of development. This distinction is not always easy to maintain, as in the case of studies founded on explicitly evolutionary indices. For example, Snow (1966) employs data from Banks and Textor (1962) in a scalogram analysis of Latin American nations. Since scalogram analysis may be used for the purposes of ordering a set of attributes into a development sequence, and then using a nation's position in this cumulative sequence as a summary SI of development, theory and measurement are here closely bound together.

Snow chose twenty variables representing political characteristics of twenty Latin American nations. This choice of variables from a larger pool was made on grounds that Snow does not make absolutely clear, but which presumably reflect his underlying model of development. It is noteworthy that half these variables display heavy loadings on Gregg and Banks's (1965) factor of 'access'. Only variables that discriminated between these twenty countries were used in the analysis, which may accordingly have little to say about sequences or indicators of political change in other countries. Snow found, in fact, that his set of variables did form a scale. The most 'primitive' features of development were the establishment of freedom of political organisation for autonomous groups and moderate interest articulation by political parties. Nations not possessing such attributes were very unlikely to possess attributes of 'higher' development. The 'highest' aspects of development discriminated here were possession of a modern bureaucracy and of a stable political party system. Nations with such characteristics were very likely to possess all those preceding them on the scale.

Snow's work would appear to support the notion of unilinear evolution, and thus to provide a secure basis for exploratory forecasting. Since, for example, his scale implies that a politically neutral military is the rule for those nations in this sample which have stable party political

155

systems, it might be possible to make such contingent predictions as 'a change in military political orientation will affect prospects for establishment or retention of a stable party system'. This type of exploratory approach may have some value, and scalogram analysis might also be useful in normative forecasting where indicators of normative goals were included in a scale and the forecaster sought a listing of features supportive of attainment of such goals. A number of reservations should be expressed, however, concerning the scalogram method itself (let alone the particular SIs employed).

The scalogram method requires that each component variable be represented in all or nothing terms, each of which receives equal weight in forming a composite score. The numerical values attached to composite 'development' scores are not strictly comparable, then. By restricting the measurement of variables to a binary form much information is lost, and it can only be said that a particular goal is or is not achieved rather than that the level of performance in terms of this goal reaches a specific value. The scale itself dictates no evolutionary imperative. It is not merely quibbling to point out that from cross-sectional data alone an observer could not judge in which direction along the scale nations tended to move. Over time nations have indeed gained and lost some of the attributes from which the scale is formed. (The work of Carneiro (1970) is notable in this context, for he has tested out a scale of cultural evolution based on cross-cultural comparisons against data on the historical changes in Anglo-Saxon England, and actually reports a good deal of correspondence between his cross-cultural and longitudinal scales.) As Kumar (1972) argued more generally, the forecasting assumptions captured in a stages model (and thus in the scalogram technique) fail to reveal and may actively mask the possiblity of alternative developmental paths. Nor can it suggest the direction of evolution once the stages of the scale have been passed through. The scale is bound to existing, binary, attributes and there is a danger of assuming that development culminates at the highest stage and that no change thereafter occurs. Snow's work can be seen to represent a kind of ahistorical historicism. It is historicist in that a scale purportedly reflecting a historical sequence of change forms the basis for more universal statements about change in principle applicable to the future. It is ahistorical, however, in that its cross-sectional data base not only fails to capture actual historical developments, but overlooks the different environments in which nations at a particular scale level exist at different times.

Several other authors have attempted to develop measures of political structure which are related either explicitly or implicitly to the notion of

156

'development', although the confinement of scalogram analysis is rarely endured. (Sigelman, 1971, uses scalogram techniques on a larger sample of nations and a much smaller set of variables, in an attempt to demonstrate the necessity of modern administrative institutions for political development.) The index Cutright (1963) proposed as a measure of political development has attracted much interest. It was originally described as a measure of political complexity, the development of specialised institutions, but Cutright (1965, 1967) more recently called it the 'Political Representativeness Index' and described it as measuring the extent to which a government is likely to be subject to effective pressure and demands from non-élite groups; others have employed it as an operational measure of democracy.

This versatile instrument is based on scores awarded to nations for possessing given parliamentary and executive attributes for each year throughout periods. For parliament, more points were awarded if the major party is not overwhelmingly strong in the lower (or only) house and if seats have been attained by electoral processes; for the executive side of government more points are awarded if selection has been by direct vote in a free election or by a (non-overwhelming) elected party. This measure was modified in various details for particular studies. In Cutright's early study data were based on a twenty-two year period in which national scores could range from 0 to 66. Later studies (e.g. Cutright and Wiley, 1970) develop measures that can be applied to shorter time periods.

Although widely employed and cited, the validity of the Cutright index as a measure of either complexity or even of some restricted notion of democracy is questionable. The existence of a Western-style legislative and executive, as assessed by Cutright's procedure, may conceal pseudo-representation and reinforcement of élite power (the same argument may be directed against some of the variables used in Snow's study). Thus Bill (1971) describes Iran's legislature as actually buttressing the traditional power of the monarch while appearing to satisfy democratic criteria. The possibility of 'system interference' (described in chapter 2) is strong in this case, particularly since the institutions concerned did not evolve spontaneously in many countries but were instead 'transplanted'. A further criticism of such measures is that, as Neubauer (1967) points out, it fails to discriminate between Western democracies that in practice vary widely. Many receive a score of 66 points, although there are significant ways in which these countries differ — for example, party systems reflect class interests in very different ways in different Western countries.

Other problems may be cited which are also relevant to the issue of using this index in forecasting, which is what Cutright (1963) essentially tried to do. For example, the index assesses average or cumulative performance over time and unless a fairly lengthy time period is involved or the forecast is believed to be remarkably accurate, scores attained at a future point will reflect the entire period back to and beyond the present, and the index is slow to respond to even dramatic changes. While Cutright is probably right not to adopt a binary or grossly categorical approach to indexing the construct 'democracy', the problem of aggregation over time and over different phenomena is not given sufficient attention. It might be more worthwhile to articulate several components of the construct and develop indices of these rather than to treat a set of fairly crude observations as simply additive. Measures deriving from research into party fractionalisation might then contribute to the analysis of parliamentary democracy (see Rae and Taylor, 1970. Pride, 1970, brings the two concepts together in an empirical analysis).

Two measures similar to that employed by Cutright have been developed by researchers working with time series data. Flanigan and Fogelman (1967) apply an 'index of democratization' to data for twenty-nine nations for each decade of the period 1800–1960. Its component indices, scored on internal scales, are: democratic succession of executive officeholder, political competition in an elected legislative, the degree of universal suffrage, and freedom of political activity from suppression. Flanigan and Fogelman (1968) later extended analysis to a set of forty-four nations. It is noteworthy that no tendency is apparent for countries to follow a single pattern or trend in these variables of political structure in either the short or long term.

Banks (1972a) constructed an index for an even larger set of countries, covering a similar span of time, using a factor analytic approach. He actually found some empirical cohesion among a set of variables related to the construct of 'democratic performance'. These four variables were measures of electoral selection of executive, effectiveness of legislature, electoral selection of legislature and the frequency of elections for the legislature. Banks summarised the performance of all nations on a single graph. While a general upward trend was apparent for most of the nineteenth century, in this century the average score has displayed peaks and troughs which would hardly encourage trend extrapolation.

Reservations similar to those expressed in relation to the Cutright index clearly apply to the Banks and Flanigan and Fogelman indices. Perhaps what is most important is not that the measures so far developed have several serious flaws, but that the attempt is being made in a concerted fashion to apply quantitative techniques to such material.

A further group of studies has directed attention to Dahl's (1956) construct of polyarchy, attempting thereby to escape the evaluative connotations and divergent implications of the term 'democracy'. Thus Neubauer (1967) has developed an index of polyarchy based on four equally weighted indicators: the degree of adult electoral suffrage, equality of representation (degrees to which seats are allocated in proportion to party votes), electoral competition (taking into account alternation of parties in office and the closeness of the vote) and information equality (taking into account the capital city's population, its number of separately owned newspapers and their average circulation). Neubauer's index is aimed at assessing pluralistic development in Western-style democracies between which the Cutright index fails to discriminate well, and in a set of twenty-three such countries Neubauer found the measures to have a very low correlation.

A different approach to polyarchy is attempted by Jackman (1974), who also employs four equally weighted SIs to develop a composite index: electoral participation, competitiveness of the party voting system, electoral irregularity and Press freedom. Actual turnout in elections as here used may correspond more closely to Dahl's construct, but suffrage seems to be the better measure for studying structures of political institutions and opportunities rather than public behaviour. Neither Jackman nor Neubauer achieve adequate operationalisation of Dahl's stipulation of equal information (the former is judgemental and the latter ignores the class biases of newspaper ownership and relative cost), which points to the fact that 'polyarchy' is an ideal type construct which is difficult to reflect in a package of equally weighted SIs. Again it can be argued that theorists of political change would be better advised to understand the component SIs before aggregating them together into an index of uncertain reliability.

There is some evidence that the set of variables constituting 'polyarchy' is not empirically coherent. A study by Kim (1971) involved the factor analysis of political indicators for forty-six Japanese prefectures. Three factors emerged, grouping separately variables which related to party competition, electoral participation and representation equality. Such variables have been found in contrast to be empirically related in similar studies of US states (e.g. Sharkansky and Hofferbert, 1969). This suggests that any coherence these variables have is a function of characteristics of the wider system rather than reflecting inflexible causal links between them.

The final group of studies of political structure to be reviewed here consists of quantitative analyses of the concept of institutionalisation, in which researchers have drawn liberally from the work of Weber and such

159

later writers as Eisenstadt on bureaucracy and organisations. The work of Polsby (1968), Welfling (1973) and Duvall and Welfling (1973) thus involves developing indices of the boundaries which divide institutions from their environments, the stability and complexity of inter-relationships of sub-systems within organisations, and so on.

Polsby does not attempt to develop a composite index, but instead studies the evolution over time of the US House of Representatives in terms of a fairly large number of indicators dealing with the legislative system. His measures of boundary formation relate to the terms of service, reappointment and career characteristics of legislation; his measures of internal complexity relate to the mode of election and designation of leaders, reliance on the whip system and levels of expenditure; and his measures of universalism (formal criteria in dealing with filling roles and with deviation from rules) include violations of seniority and seat contests in committee appointments. Not surprisingly, the House of Representatives has shown a trend towards greater institutionalisation over time in terms of such measures. Some reversal of these tendencies was found during the civil war which suggests the dependence of such evolution on a supportive environment.

Welfling's work is concerned with thirty-one African legislatures over several decades, and her indicators deal with the institutionalisation of party systems within these parliaments. She also differs from Polsby in providing evidence for the empirical relation of the thirteen indicators employed (ten of them are shown to be closely related in principle components analysis). As a measure of boundary characteristics, the proportion of legislators elected as party representatives is taken; for stable internal interactions, changes within parties such as splits and mergers, and changes in the relative strength of different parties; for institutional adaptability, the reliance on such techniques as postponing elections, arresting opponents, etc; and for scope, electoral participation. (The three SIs poorly correlated with the remainder fall into these last two groups.) While most of the countries studied showed no general trends, Welfling (1973) reported that six revealed declining institutionalisation scores and two increasing scores over time. One construct validation of her index is also reported in this study: the occurrence of military *coups* in these countries was found to be highly related to the level of independence and subsequent trend in institutionalisation.

One aspect of 'institutionalisation' that does frequently reveal an upward trend is reported by Flanigan and Fogelman (1967). They developed an index of government publications for the nations they studied, and census, statistical and trade and commerce information produced in serial publications is found to be increasing with a fair degree of consistency. Over time this measure correlated fairly highly, in the UK and the USA, with data on the proportion of the population employed by the government, which again suggests relationships between different aspects of institutionalisation.

Related to institutionalisation are studies of party systems, especially those going beyond mere classification of nations into partyless, one-party and multiparty types. Some authors have developed measures of party cohesion based on voting that reveals consensus or follows the party line (e.g. Ozbudon, 1970). In an ambitious study paralleling the Flanigan and Fogelman work, Pride (1970) attempts to operationalise notions of party system aggregation and penetration, basing this work on measures of number of parties, fractionalisation, party types, and so on. The evolution of nations in terms of such SIs was found to be closely tied to the specific historical conditions in which the party system was established (e.g. whether this was before or after the onset of urbanisation).

Whereas most of the studies reviewed in this section have rested on frankly developmental indices, it is noteworthy that there has been very little indication of any general evolution of nations towards greater levels of political 'democratisation' or 'institutionalisation'. This fails to accord with the historical experience of Western nations. The contradiction might be resolved by attributing the lack of aggregate trends to the decolonisation of the Third World and subsequent political upheavals. Again, it might be attributed to an ethnocentric transposition of Western views and ideals to inappropriate social contexts. Questions have been raised above as to whether many of these indices tap the same underlying variables in different cultures. A related problem with using such measures is that their inbuilt evolutionary assumptions are liable to be accepted without scrutiny. In fact the measure may have little relevance to a given nation's developmental course — nations retaining the political structures involved may be stagnating or actually undergoing political decay not captured in such measures. These indices themselves are biased in favour of 'liberal democratic' parliamentary institutions rather than alternative political structures in which levels of political participation, involvement and 'access' may be greater in the many social settings. To assume that these institutions are universally related to opportunities and actions in a given way is very dangerous. The following section considers the uses of such indices in models of political evolution, and such models in political forecasting.

Modelling and forecasting political structure

As would be expected, given the confluence of comparative political research and the SI movement, studies of political structure are often relevant to forecasting. Thus Cutright (1963) talks of certain nations being under pressures which would be resolved either by economic growth or declining political development in terms of his index. Thus India and the Philippines are liable to future political 'backsliding'. Similarly, although in a more sophisticated analysis, Hakes (1973) compares the prospects of different African states in terms of future avoidance of military *coups* and maintenance of parliamentary structures. He regards Tanzania and Malawi, respectively, as having the best and worst prospects for stability. Although the indices of political structure that are employed are often implicitly developmental, work reviewed in the previous section demonstrated that forecasting on the basis of extrapolation or assumed evolutionary pressures was neither practicable nor desirable.

Cutright (1963) based his study of democratisation on the work of Lipset (1959), extending it in two main ways. First, his development index is less based on judgement than Lipset's classification, and second, it provides a continuous measure which enables levels of political development to be plotted against other variables. On cross-sectional data for seventy-seven nations (African states and very small countries excluded) Cutright found a close relationship between his index and a measure of national communications development (based on measures of newspaper, telephone and mail usage). He argued that deviations from the linear trend might prove useful guides to forecasting political change and/or desirable communications policies.

It is worth recalling that Neubauer (1967) regarded the Cutright index as only capturing some of the more formal institutional trappings associated with parliamentary democracy, and developed his own measure based on the theory of polyarchy. This index not only bore no significant relationship to Cutright's, but also displayed no meaningful relation to communications development. Neubauer interpreted this latter finding as indicating that differences in polyarchic democratic development in Western countries reflect cultural differences and accidents of leadership or politics.

McCrone and Cnudde (1967), Smith (1969) and Winham (1970) used Cutright's measure in testing a more complex theory of political development based on Lerner's (1958) work. In the context of a study of attitudes and values in modernising people in Middle Eastern countries, Lerner had proposed a theory accounting for the growth of political participation. He argued that urban living both necessitates and allows increases in literacy, which in turn stimulates the development of the mass media. Literacy and exposure to media provide people with cognitive skills and information needed for meaningful political participation and thus facilitate democratic political development.

McCrone and Cnudde (1967) applied causal path analysis to Cutright's data plus indicators of urbanisation and education, as a test of Lerner's formulation on cross-sectional data for seventy-six nations. (With causal path analysis it is in principle possible to sort out direct relationships between a pair of variables, e.g. urbanisation and political structure, from those mediated through a third measured variable, e.g. communications development.) Their conclusions essentially supported Lerner's formulation. The statistical model developed suggests that the intercorrelations between the four SIs can be best accounted for by assuming that urbanisation acts on education levels, these in turn act on communications development, and this on the Cutright index, with only a weak relationship remaining between urbanisation and political development. Before hurrying to build computer simulations based on this model (while this may seem far-fetched, Harbordt, 1971, actually built relationships based upon Lerner's work into simulations for world forecasting), it must be pointed out that Smith's (1969) causal path model, derived from slightly different SIs, takes on a different form — urbanisation strongly influences both political development and communications development, which now itself only acts on the Cutright index through its effects on education. Winham (1970) employed data for the USA from 1790 to 1960 using a version of Cutright's measure which was weighted by voting turnout. His causal path model is even more complex, with reciprocal causal relations and communications development actually appearing to influence urbanisation.

Neither Cutright's regression line nor such models based on Lerner's theory are adequate bases for forecasting political change. The specific criticisms to be advanced against these models in the following paragraphs apply in a more general sense to most attempts to build models of political evolution on cross-sectional data, examples of which abound in political science and sociology journals. Sigelman (1971), who himself conducted a scalogram analysis of political development using such data expressed surprise at the McCrone and Cnudde 'causal' analysis. In their model, communications development (indexed by 1960 data) emerges as a cause of prior political development (indexed by aggregating data for the period 1940–61)! Moul (1974) has been among the strongest critics of cross-sectional analysis as a means to infer longitudinal development. He has pointed out that this involves assuming developmental equivalence, in which spatial and temporal differences are taken to be interchangeable. Differences between nations at any one time on a given variable are viewed as being analogous to differences within a nation over time. Moul, however, demonstrates the faulty logic of using such assumptions in causal analysis with a hypothetical instance in which cross-sectional analyses at two points in time are shown to yield the same correlation between a pair of variables, which is quite the inverse of the actual relationship of these variables over time. (See also Pride, 1971, and Sunshine, 1973, for discussion of causal analysis in cross-sectional and time series political research.)

Indeed, Winham's work indicates that the USA itself does not historically reveal the relationships of McCrone and Cnudde and Smith when time series data are employed. Flora (1973) provides even more reason for caution in his longitudinal study of ninety-five countries. He finds that cross-sectional analyses at different points in time indicate different relationships. (Thus between earlier and later sampling points appears a cross-sectional correlation between urbanisation and literacy.) From analysis of trends he finds that the present most industrialised nations reveal an early long term growth in literacy preceding large scale urbanisation, while the newer nations of the Third World have experienced more rapid urban growth than spreading literacy; again the assumption of developmental equivalence is challenged.

This last study demonstrates the utility of studies based on time series SI data as a means of approaching political change and escaping the limits of cross-sectional analysis, although it also points to possible divergences in the paths followed by nations whose economic development started at different times. Some researchers have employed indices of political structure in longitudinal analyses. For example, Cutright and Wiley (1970) studied all forty nations that remained self-governing through the period 1927–1966 and concluded that political development was fairly predictable from knowledge of socio-economic factors (literacy levels, energy consumption as a measure of economic development, and economic security as indexed by a measure of development of social security programmes). One of their findings was that, over this period, the cross-sectional relationship linking the Cutright index to energy consumption and literacy levels was essentially stable, suggesting that a nation's political development might be forecast on the basis of estimates of its future standing on these two variables — at least if it be one of this set of nations. The question of developmental equivalence is not settled by this analysis, however.

164

Whereas Cutright and Wiley found that political development was related to earlier levels of economic development, and that political change was related to the other contextual variables, other studies suggest that political variables themselves are a determinant, rather than a by-product, of socio-economic development. For example, Banks (1972a) studied the performance of thirty-six nations over the greater part of a century, and found earlier political development to be significantly related to later measures of communications and government revenue and expenditure over this period, and likewise with urbanisation and school enrolment until the early decades of this century. For this set of American, European and Latin American countries, then, political development would seem to be less open to forecasting from other SI material than its socio-economic consequences would be from political indicators. The different measures of political change employed by Cutright and Wiley on the one hand, and Banks on the other, make the contributions of their work to understanding political change hard to compare, on top of the remaining methodological problems these studies pose. The former authors look at change in terms of the Cutright index (finding change most likely to occur in nations previously characterised by low levels of economic security and high levels of literacy), while Banks developed a separate measure of political change based on the incidence of *coups*, major constitutional changes, and changes in the cabinet and executive.

These studies point to the necessity of considering political structure and its socio-economic environment as interactive, rather than the former being the passive output of the latter, as implied by some cross-sectional studies. Flanigan and Fogelman (1967, 1968) found both socio-economic and political factors important to the successful establishment and maintenance of parliamentary democracy in their comparative and longitudinal studies. Economic development was associated with more sustained democratisation, and attempts at democratisation made in the nineteenth century met with immediate success more frequently than those made in the twentieth century. Civil strife under industrial conditions and more rapid socio-economic change were found to be associated with less successful attempts, and experience with participatory institutions for at least two decades before the onset of full democratisation as measured by their index seemed to be a necessary but insufficient condition for sustained democratic rule. With similar data Pride (1970) concluded that nations in which parliamentary democracy had been established prior to the onset of significant population mobilisation (shift to urban living and non-agricultural employment) tended to remain stable democracies, while nations in which this sequence was reversed tended to remain non-democratic. Large numbers of parties, high party fractionalisation, and the existence of mass and devotee parties during early development were all found to be associated with less stability of democratic institutions.

Such findings might suggest the possibility of an exploratory forecasting of national political change (or rather of stability) since nations may be grouped, as Flanigan and Fogelman (1967) have done, into classes such as stable highly democratic, stable non-democratic and two unstable types — although, as was pointed out earlier, the indices involved may not tap many aspects of the construct 'democracy', and thus any forecasts would only relate to a limited set of institutional events. Equally, these studies may be seen to undermine the evolutionary assumptions of much analysis of political change, since the interplay of political and socio-economic factors here evident makes it clear that political development is by no means bound to follow from economic growth alone — particularly since the mobilisation process in the Third World is taking place in ways unprecedented in Western experience. Furthermore, Banks (1972a) points to effects of the international environment as well as merely the internal socio-economic environment of political institutions. Political changes in both the Latin American and Amer-European group of nations showed similar aggregate patterns over time, and decreasing foreign conflict tended to be accompanied by increasing average levels across countries' democratic performance, as did increasing levels of political change (years occurring in either World War were omitted from this analysis).

The 'development' model for the Third World seems to have been generally accepted in the futures research literature. A paper like 'Fascism: the past and the future' by Joes (1974) appears in a political science journal, and its gloomy analysis of trends is even there a rarity. Equally absent from most futures studies are considerations of peasant revolution as forecast by Wertheim (1974). A partial exception to this rule is the work of Emery (1974), who considers possibilities of fascist and Chinese-style regimes developing in different parts of the Third World. It is important to consider the limitations of political development research to evaluate the quality of forecasts relying on such notions.

Moul (1974) has criticised empirical studies of political development for this frequent exclusion of international factors from analysis. Along with cross-sectional sources of data, this leads to a neglect of what anthropologists term 'Galton's problem' — the possibility of attributes of societies displaying spurious empirical relationships which are produced by their similar historical patterns of diffusion rather than through direct causal association. (Several papers on this issue as it can be dealt with in

166

cultural anthropology are reproduced in Narrol and Cohen, 1973, but the solutions applicable in the study of fairly isolated cultures hardly apply to the international community.) In particular, 'Westernised' political structures in the Third World rarely arose spontaneously, but instead reflect their colonial pasts.

Moul goes on to argue that studies of political development must be based on a global perspective. This can be seen to apply to futures studies as much as to the research tradition he is focusing on. Even longitudinal analyses of the political evolution of Western states must be treated cautiously as a basis for inferring the future of the Third World, for in their early stages of economic development these states were, in Moul's terms, not underdeveloped but undeveloped. This accords with comments made above concerning novel patterns of mobilisation in the Third World, and amplifying them by relating them to the question of the structure of the international system. For example, Moul argues that the colonial powers attempted to reproduce their own political institutions in their colonies, but to maintain the economies of the colonies complementary to and servicing their own. Stauffer (1971) extends these arguments to focus on the constraints placed on political development by alliance systems which include developed countries, and which may attempt to limit the types of political movements and policies considered legitimate. Increasingly, conservative élites come to be supported by such alliances in Third World countries in the name of stability — often with severe political repression as a consequence.

Such points are also taken up in Bodenheimer's (1971) extensive analysis of theories of political development. Four themes are identified in the bulk of the literature: a notion of cumulative progress along a continuum of development (often mirrored in quantitative indices like those described above); a concern with stable and orderly change related to the search for universal laws as a basis for prediction and policy guidance; the end of ideology thesis, whereby countries are believed to be evolving towards a pluralistic consensus; and the assumption of diffusion. of cultural forms, technology and values from modern to traditional sectors within countries and from developed to developing countries.

The swingeing attack on each of these themes of development theory which Bodenheimer launched has much import for SI and futures research in this field. The notion of cumulation, for example, is associated with assumptions of unilinear evolution towards 'modernity' based on immanent factors within each country. It bypasses the possibilities of stagnation and decadence, of radical departures and new directions in political and economic development. It is ahistorical in that the changing

167

international context of political evolution is ignored; it takes indices as being of uniform validity in different cultures (this applies not only to 'political' indicators, but to SIs of education and communication, for example where the content and context of these experiences is largely ignored); and it leads to a focus on piecemeal and reformist change. As for the concern with stability, this meta-advocacy downgrades alternative norms such as participation or justice. Instability is often viewed as disrupting development in theoretical analyses. Bodenheimer asks whether stability itself, the paucity of real socio-economic change, may not be the main problem. Current research perspectives such as structural—functionalism, tend to rationalise the *status quo* and lead to views of the future in which its maintenance is taken as a *sine qua non.*

The end of ideology thesis once more makes its appearance, this time in 'the pious hope that development can be achieved without paying the high cost of removing the social and economic obstacles, that the impoverished masses can somehow be upgraded without infringing on the interests of the established élites' (Bodenheimer, 1971, p.20). It is assumed in the orthodox view that the class structure is becoming more flexible, despite evidence of increasing polarisation and inequality. The agents of progressive change are again seen to be established élites and conflict is treated as irrational and pathological (even despite the absence of the societal consensus claimed for the developed nations). As for the assumption of diffusion, Bodenheimer cites evidence revealing the exploitation of the traditional sector by the modern sector in Latin Ameria, and of similar inequities in the international system (see also, for example, Stauffer, 1971). The orthodox vision of archaic feudal areas being modernised by the material benefits and spiritual example of industrial capitalism is thus challenged by a view of the latter having actually blocked the progress of the former by economic exploitation and internal colonialism. The assumption of the diffusion of political institutions leads to a confusion of form with substance which means 'that the only possible example of *substantive* democracy and mass mobilization in Latin America — Cuba — is generally classified as a totalitarian dictatorship' (Bodenheimer, 1971, p.29).

This summary of Bodenheimer's paper omits both the empirical support marshalled for her views and her analysis of comparative political research as reflecting these four themes: the notion of cumulation is mirrored by an emphasis on cumulative amassing of large quantities of data, stability by the concern for universal predictive laws, ideology by value-free science, and diffusion by the transference of a Western conceptual framework to the Third World. The implications of her analysis (and those of similar workers; in addition to those she cites, see e.g. Cockcroft, Frank and Johnson, 1972) are clear enough, however. Unless futures research is to be unwittingly bound to these four themes in studying political evolution, it is necessary to look at the global context of national affairs'— an approach also recommended by Emery (1974) from his systems perspective. Existing conflicts of interest between nations and social groups, rather than assumed evolutionary pressures, may be taken as fundamental factors whose resolution in different ways might be seen as determining options for future development. Futures studies based on analyses that gloss over such conflicts will be foreclosing this range of options. The futurologist Jim Dator (1974) has favourably reported on Bodenheimer's analysis to a major conference of futures researchers, so there are some grounds for expecting the controversy in political science to be reflected in a new critical approach to political forecasting.

The studies by Welfling (1973) and Duvall and Welfling (1973) on the institutionalisation of party systems in black African states referred to in the previous section only partially escape the criticisms reported above. Their institutionalisation construct is clearly directed towards stability and Western notions of multiparty democracy. There is, however, longitudinal consideration of one feature of the international context of political structures by Duvall and Welfling (the impact of the ending of colonial rule is studied by quasi-experimental analysis), and of the effects of other political variables (the relationships over time between institutionalisation and civil strife are analysed), as well as those of the more conventional indices of social mobilisation.

The substantive results of these studies are interesting, suggesting for this set of nations, for example, that patterns of party institutionalisation are predictive of *coups* and that such patterns also determine the effects of civil strife of subsequent trends in institutionalisation. No significant stable relationship between social mobilisation (indexed by communications and educational levels) and institutionalisation was found, in contrast. The use of quasi-experimental analysis (see Campbell and Stanley, 1963, Caparaso and Roos, 1973) is also an advance in comparative political research, opening up possibilities of developing generalisations out of scattered instances of change. (An alternative approach to this possibility is presented by Almond, Flanigan and Mundt, 1973, in a volume of quantitative comparative studies of particular historical examples of political structures undergoing crisis, looking at formation of coalitions and crisis resolution, and the resultant changes in polity and environment.)

Such studies are of significance in further ways. While they may not launch a frontal assault on orthodox notions of political development, works such as Welfling's do face up to the issue of political decay and stagnation. Also of relevance here is the work of Adelman and Morris (1973) that reveals relationships between measures of social equity, political participation and economic growth that diverge from evolutionary assumptions in important respects. For example, they find that political participation in seventy-four underdeveloped countries is more closely related to social factors (e.g. mobility) and political variables (e.g. the strength of the traditional élite) than to economic development.

Of most value is that these studies show that events are very much more complex than earlier research would suggest. This leads to these authors' rejection of simplistic models of political change, but not to the abandonment of quantitative methods. Instead a present generation of researchers seems to be developing research methods that are increasingly capable of coping with fairly large numbers of variables, reciprocal causality, cross-cultural validation of indices and the like. Although such developments are themselves valuable, and may lead to some convergence with futures studies techniques such as computer simulations, they pose a problem for the forecaster. On the one hand it is necessary for futures studies to take into account more complex configurations of variables and reject oversimple images of political change. On the other hand, the welter of indices and relationships that characterise the more advanced forms of empirical political research can easily conceal unwarranted assumptions, unwanted meta-advocacy and error. The forecaster should not be parasitic on primary researchers; dialogue and confrontation between images of the future held by specialists and generalists would be valuable to both parties.

Civil strife: theories and forecasts

Research into what is variously termed 'civil strife', 'domestic conflict', 'political violence', 'instability' and 'collective violence' will here be given a more condensed appraisal than that with which a few aspects of political structure were treated above. Some of the vicissitudes, controversies and advances in these two fields have been so similar that detailed repetition is unnecessary. In particular, the increasing recognition of the shortcomings of cross-sectional analyses and the emergence of longitudinal studies pointing to different theoretical orientations are shared by both fields.

One distinction between the two fields that should be noted at the outset is the fuelling of research interest into civil strife by domestic turmoil in Western nations in the mid-1960s. This gave rise to a large literature on such conflict focused at sub-national levels which complemented the cross-national research. Graham and Gurr (1969) have attempted to make cross-national research relevant to the American experience. Among interesting studies of ghetto riots in American cities are Berk and Aldrich (1972) who look at the types of businesses chosen for vandalisation in disorders, Morgan and Clark (1973) who attempted to account for the severity and frequency of disturbances in different cities using aggregate data of such variables as inequality of housing provisions, and Betz (1974), who rather convincingly linked disorders to subsequent changes in welfare policies by city authorities. Rossi, Berk and Eidson (1974) combine survey data from different social groups (including merchants and various city officials) with a variety of objective SIs in a study of disorders in fifteen cities. Several journals have devoted whole issues to this area.

In the study of civil strife, as in that of political structure, a number of relatively atheoretical factor analytic studies based on cross-sectional data appeared as the quantitative mood spread among political scientists; these studies, however, have had more impact on subsequent research. One reason for this is undoubtedly the degree of consensus that was attained by researchers using different sets of SIs, different selections of nations and different periods of time in their factor analyses and the ready interpretability of their findings. The studies of Bwy (1968b), the Feierabends (1966), Rummel (1963, 1966), and Tanter (1966) (all of which are printed together for some reason in Gillespie and Nesvold, 1970), and most later studies concur in finding that a number of forms of strife tend to co-occur. One factor is generally labelled 'turmoil' and features mass participation events such as general strikes, demonstrations and riots. Other indices, reflecting more clearly organised or co-ordinated activities such as guerilla warfare, purges and deaths in political violence are sometimes grouped into a single second factor (Tanter labels this 'internal war') or sometimes fall into several distinct groups. This latter finding is most common when a larger number of SIs is employed in the factor analysis.

Most of these studies have relied on a *post hoc* explanation of the clear distinctions between turmoil and other dimensions of internal conflict, for example relating these to mass movements and élite instability respectively. Sometimes evaluative and descriptive notions are mixed up here. Thus Bwy (1968b) describes the factor others label 'turmoil' as 'anomic violence' and it is often referred to as unorganised, although clearly strikes and demonstrations are rarely undirected and disorganised explosions of

171

frustration. (For research refuting the parallel notion that participants in civil strife are predominantly the poorly integrated, maladapted and anomic, see for example Caplan and Page, 1968; Eisinger, 1974.) Few authors have attempted to test theoretical conceptions of strife by factor analysis – exceptions include Schwartzmann (1968) and the more precise work of Morrison and Stevenson (1971). The latter study is based on a treatment of political conflict over values between élite, communal and mass groups. This study was influenced by the longitudinal work of Charles Tilly, to be touched on later; its authors choose their data base on theoretical considerations, and provide a cogent critique of early factor analytic studies.

As was remarked, the relatively atheoretical factor analytic studies were themselves influential on subsequent attempts to develop theoretical accounts of civil strife which could be validated against cross-sectional data. Authors have used indicators of national (or, in the case of Bwy, 1968a, provincial) levels of strife based on these factors as starting points for empirical analysis of differences between countries experiencing more or less conflict, and have sought to explain the distinct dynamics that must underlie uncorrelated dimensions of conflict. The most outstanding work in this tradition is that of Gurr (1968), who studied variations in the levels of occurence of variables designated turmoil, internal war, conspiracy and total magnitude of strife across 114 nations.

In common with several other prominent cross-sectional analyses of conflict (e.g. as represented in papers reprinted in Davies, 1972, Feierabend, Feierabend and Gurr, 1972, and Gillespie and Nesvold, 1970), Gurr tests out a theory based on pscyhological conceptions of aggression as a consequence of what may be termed frustration, or, in this case, relative deprivation. Mention was made in chapter 5 of his composite indices – suffice it here to remark that he collected data and developed elaborate measures to reflect long and short term economic and political forms of deprivation. Gurr then employed causal path analysis, within a conceptual framework in which aspects of social structure (such as government coercive ability and institutionalisation of opportunities to express discontent through labour unions and political parties) were expected to mediate the relationship between deprivation and strife, to develop an empirically based model accounting for differences in levels of strife between nations in the 1960s in terms of other national SIs.

Gurr's model accounted for about two-thirds of the variance in strife between the nations studied. The institutionalisation and coercive potential indices did not play an important role in the final model except in terms of their relationship with a third structural variable – facilitation.

(This was indexed in terms of external support for dissident parties, communist party strength and status, and a measure of physical accessibility. Gurr fully recognised the incomplete and inchoate nature of such a composite index, which limited its validity as a measure of the theoretical construct involved. In the absence of better data he still considered it worthwhile to attempt analysis.) Facilitation plays an important role in the 'explanation' of strife by mediating some of the impact of short term deprivation, which did, however, along with long term deprivation, retain a direct positive correlation with strife after other variables had been taken into account. A final variable, legitimacy (based upon measures of the duration and mode of establishment of the political regime), was negatively correlated with strife.

Gurr clearly considers his work relevant to forecasting political strife, as do other researchers in this field whose work is of less substantive interest. Thus his book *Why Men Rebel* (1970a) is described as being of value to both revolutionaries and holders of power. His paper on strife in Western societies is described as forming 'the basis for an explanatory and predictive categorization of the Western nations according to their structural, cultural and psychosocial potential for the several kinds of strife' (Gurr, 1970b, p.128) and invites readers to consider the applicability of the findings to the future (p.144). His more recent work 'can and should be used for policy evaluations' (Gurr and Duvall, 1973, p.160) although it neither predicts the occurrence nor the outcome of specific conflicts (p.159). The forecasts given by the models Gurr has developed are very short term compared to the interests of futures researchers: in general socio-economic conditions in one five-year period are employed to predict levels of strife in the following five years. Even so, the conclusions he reaches are cited in the forecasting and planning literature (e.g. Montgomery, 1974).

While the specific models developed by Gurr and similar theorists are thus apparently limited in forecasting capacity — although forecasts of strife alone could be made on the basis of assumptions about socio-economic conditions — they have been used as a starting point for more ambitious forecasting projects. For example, the work of Noton et al. (1974a, b), directed towards building a general computer simulation of intra-societal conflict that could be 'calibrated' to fit the cases of South Africa or Ulster, employs notions derived directly from this literature. It is interesting to note that this team has found it necessary to collect their own SI material to look at conflict between communities in a country more precisely, and also that the important variables of violence and frustration directed against member of one's own community and/or

173

oneself are bypassed (except as further indicators of relative deprivation) in such studies for the presumably more 'policy-relevant' variables of intergroup violence.

Other forecasts have made use of quantitative analyses of civil strife. For example, Wynn, Rubin and Franco (1973) present estimates of political violence and *coup* attempts in nations in the Indian Ocean area in the 1980s. Weil (1974) reports a study based on the same data bank but focused on Europe, in which turmoil and revolt were forecast for the 1971—1990 period by a simulation model based on twelve regression equations, derived from analyses of economic and military power and international relations. The long range forecast is that domestic unrest in these countries will decrease 'primarily because of better economic conditions and greater suppressive capabilities by the regimes in power' (Weil, 1974, p.483). Such formal models are fairly rare in social futures studies, but they have evident attractions for policy makers, and reflect the absorption of ideas from the social sciences into forecasting. It is notable that the selection of ideas from empirical political research is guided much more by pragmatic matters of data availability than by the overall models presented by writers like Gurr. There is also a rapidly expanding literature of 'counter insurgency'.

The psychologistic frustration—aggression theories of political violence can be criticised on several grounds which bear on their usefulness in forecasting. This is in addition to the general critique of cross-sectional analyses made earlier in this chapter and at other places in this book. For one thing, as with the studies of political structure reviewed in the previous section, there is a tendency to treat the dependent variable (in this case strife) as if it emerged within a single nation without any influence from the international system. This is clearly not so: not only is the observer confronted with, for example, the waves of student rebellion in the late 1960s, but in Sorokin's (1957) studies of long term social changes disturbances were found to be concentrated at particular periods. Second, these studies again treat politics as an output of socio-economic change, both in explicit theory and in the assumptions involved in statistical techniques, while in reality political variables (including strife) may exert influence over other factors.

Another line of criticism of such studies is advanced in a lengthy review by Nardin (1971), who questions the focus of the theories involved. He notes that aggression is called into play as an account of 'illicit' strife, that various forms of peaceful protest are included under the label of 'violence' (which is regularly interpreted as an expressive response to frustration), and that violence on the part of political authorities is virtually excluded from such an analysis, with the state seen as playing a conflict management role. This is despite the interaction of authorities and dissidents in, for example, riots, and despite the correlation of government actions with public protests, whereas intercorrelation between protests of different kinds justifies their being conceptualised as similar. The end of ideology thesis may be seen to underpin these perspectives. Civil strife is the act of dissidents rejecting an overall consensus, and the government is seen as managing conflict in a rational and benevolent way rather than itself responding to partisan interests; the political conclusions obtained are inevitably reformist. To forecast on the basis of such studies alone would be to accept a particular set of ideological premises which may not accord with one's aims. Noton's simulation follows this tradition by excluding the activities of the state from the analysis of intergroup conflict.

Perhaps the most concerted critique of such approaches to explaining and predicting collective violence has been made by Tilly, in his series of longitudinal studies. However, another pair of studies employing time series data will first be reviewed, since these follow more or less directly in the tradition of holonational analysis running from Rummel's factor analytic studies. Banks (1972b) carried out factor analyses of six sets of cross-sectional data on civil strife drawn from different years of this century and pertaining to fifty-one nations. He finds evidence for a changing factor structure over time. Before the Second World War 'turmoil' emerged as the dominant factor, but in more recent decades a factor labelled 'subversion' displaces it in ability to account for differences between nations in terms of strife. The work of Flanigan and Fogelman (1970) related national levels of internal violence (measured on a fairly limited unidimensional scale) to political indices, national economic development and to historical period, for sixty-five nations over a century and a half. Countries with sustained democratic institutions were likely to experience less overall violence, and successful democratisation was linked to both violence and social mobilisation. In general, during the course of socio-economic development, an early peak and subsequent decline in violence is noted; it appears that the later the onset of development, the greater levels of violence experienced at this peak. These two studies together point to the necessity of considering both the internal political context and the international situation in analysing civil strife. The moral for futures researachers in this is that it is inappropriate to forecast strife in a country on the basis of projections made for that country's economy in isolation from social, political and international considerations — especially with models based on cross-sectional analysis made at a particular historical instant.

The work of Charles Tilly and his associates has been based on historical data for European nations from the early nineteenth century onwards. He has been particularly critical of the frustration—aggression model of collective violence (Snyder and Tilly, 1974) and of notions of strife as stemming from modernisation (Tilly, 1973) or urbanisation (Lodhi and Tilly, 1973; Tilly, 1969a). For example, in a time series study of data relating to France (Snyder and Tilly, 1972), SIs reflecting hardship and wellbeing, such as prices of food and goods and industrial production were developed. Rising prices and declining production were employed as indices of relative deprivation. However, variations in these indices were not empirically related to measures of strife (e.g. levels of participation in disturbances), even after alternative procedures of time-lag regression and detrending had been applied to the data in order to investigate different possible forms of relationship.

Tilly believes that civil strife is best viewed as the result of struggles of social groups to exercise power. From historical studies, he has distinguished three modes of collective violence: primitive (feuds, religions, conflict, craft conflict, etc.), reactionary (against changes imposed by powerful groups which are seen as taking away rights, as in the case of the Luddite conflicts) and modern collective violence (e.g. demonstrations, strikes and guerilla conflicts involving specialised associations of people trying to achieve well-defined objectives) (Tilly, 1969b). Primitive modes have been becoming less frequent for several centuries; reactionary modes have led to the organisation of police forces and to some anti-poverty reforms; and modern collective violence, with its disturbances being of shorter duration but involving more participants, has led to the institutionalisation of the strike. The evolution of these forms of strife is related to the growth of central control during the course of political development. This nationalisation of politics was at first opposed, and was later met with by struggles for influence over the state. Futures researchers might ponder the implications of this analysis for studies of the consequences of such changes in the international system as the development of federations of states.

Tilly's perspective involves a focus on the political determinants of political unrest. He points out that such conflict is in fact a normal (although not necessarily desirable or inevitable) state of affairs from the viewpoint of historical statistics, and relates it to the struggle for roles in the structure of power rather than anomie and undirected expressive outbursts. Collective protest tends to accompany other attempts to gain given objectives by peaceful means, and its locus depends on features of the social and economic structure (e.g. urbanisation) which create, destroy or mobilise interest groups. Thus Snyder and Tilly (1972), after rejecting relative deprivation as an explanation for strife, find that, in their longitudinal French data, participation in disturbances can be closely related to power struggles as reflected by the occurrence of elections and the extent of repressive activities such as gaolings. Future studies from this team are expected to deal with possible feedbacks between strife and repression (Hudson, 1971, from a wider data base, has also presented work which begins to relate political changes to particular crises of strife).

The most obvious message such work bears for futures studies is that forecasters should not be seduced by the apparent parsimony of quantitative analyses which promise to predict strife or other political factors as passive outputs of socio-economic change, as merely responding to some evolutionary dynamic (and thus being 'progressive' or 'atavistic'). Political variables themselves play a causal role in directing paths of development and patterns of influence of international strains and stresses. An economic determinism in political forecasting is as short-sighted as a technological determinism in social forecasting. Political and social factors need to be treated in their own right whatever forecasting technique is employed, and the contributions that comparative political research may make to futures studies must be seen and subjected to critical appraisal in these terms.

8   Beyond Prediction

Earlier chapters raised a variety of criticisms concerning the stance of futures research and the image of the future dominating the social sciences. In this chapter these and the problems they raise are reviewed, and some ways in which these problems might be overcome are considered.

Three questions are taken up in some detail. First, the changing perspective and composition of futures studies and social sciences. Second, a number of challenges to the technocratic, historicist image of the future are outlined. Finally the possibility of public participation occupying an enlarged role in futures studies is seen to be an area where the social sciences may make useful contributions.

The future of the future

In the first chapter, reference was made to Goldthorpe's diagnosis of the futurological malady. Goldthorpe (1970) saw futures studies as having been overcome by crypto-historicism, and by a barely disguised reliance on assumptions of inexorable social evolution. One threatening effect of this might be the suppression of alternative images of the future which were not supported by the scientistic analyses of experts. How far is the diagnosis applicable to the interpenetration of futures studies and quantitative social science?

The areas where such interpenetration is taking place were reviewed in subsequent chapters and revealed common tendencies and themes which seem largely to confirm Goldthorpe's points. Furthermore, this analysis could be extended to the future orientations displayed in other areas of social science: applied research dealing with major problems such as inadequate nutrition and environmental damage, or with organisational problems in education, the workplace and social services. It is probable that quantitative social science is largely reinforcing rather than challenging an image of a future determined by economic and technological imperatives. Quantitative research can serve a mystifying function in that the high methodology of operational misdefinition and statistical alchemy, offered to computer oracles by a social science priesthood, can convey the impression that only the pronouncements and prescriptions of technical experts have any validity. Thus elaborate models of the future are often preferred to simple verbal conclusions based upon the same, often flimsy, data base.

Bodenheimer (1971) and Goldthorpe have both pointed to patterns of emphasis — Bodenheimer refers to a 'paradigm-surrogate' — which colour social scientists' approaches to the future. For one thing, the quantitative movement in the social sciences was itself fuelled to some extent by the 'value-free' position of postwar sociology and has largely taken over this standpoint. Social research is thereby seen as giving unbiased, disinterested technical analysis and advice. Those who dispute this are often condemned as irrational, or not distinguished from people who believe that scientific method is inherently flawed. Such condemnation is doubly acute if the heretics also doubt such canons as the technological imperative, the pioneering role of the knowledge élite, the subservience of the political to the economic, and the merely technical origin of social malaise.

The world view of the research reviewed here has often been historicist with an ahistorical and technocratic tinge. The ahistorical approach is explicit in the publication of analyses in which space is substituted for time. For example, the identification of disparities at one point in time between rich and poor individuals, social classes, or nations, with the growth of wealth over time, has been used as a method of estimating the future direction of change. An excessive focus is often turned onto a small set of indicators, such as those connected with 'economic development', and dynamic features of the environment and disparate initial conditions and histories are overlooked. The role of human choice enters such analyses as residual error. The technocratic elements of this world view are apparent in the identification of the 'knowledge class' as the cybernetic guide of post-industrial social change, in the belief that high technology can 'fix' social problems and underdevelopment if only the victims of such conditions had the right attitudes towards progress and authority.

Bound up with these technocratic views is the stress on expertise, which is the necessary ingredient for the solution of the technical problems of future society. With the end of ideology, a broad public consensus emerges which renders unnecessary extensive public debate on what values are to be manifest in policy. Some form of participation may be invoked to assure that the polity remains sensitive to changing public taste, but this should not involve too much public mobilisation. Pre-eminent are the values of stability and efficiency, which will rationally meet social demands. These demands (desires for increasing material consumption or, in more recent formulations, for technocratically defined 'quality of life'), along with continuing technological change, are taken to be the prime movers of future social evolution. The possibility of alternative directions of evolution in which different values are fulfilled is generally passed over, as are questions of the spiritual and cultural dimensions of the future.

To be sure the above is something of a caricature, or distillation of the worse elements of a diverse body of literature. To cite only one exception, Etzioni (1968) is clearly more concerned with an active citizenry than are other theorists of future society. But the prominence of the traits described above largely supports Goldthorpe's diagnosis; what then of his prognosis for futurology?

Goldthorpe sees these traits as threatening the development of futures studies. The cynicism and suspicion with which many people – not just academics – view expert pronouncements about the future may be strengthened by a view of the assumptions of futurology as being grounded in élite interests, manipulation and special pleading. If this were to happen, then futures studies might lose whatever constructive and critical potential they now display, and become simply instruments for what Ozbekhan (1968) terms operational and strategic planning rather than for goal-setting, normative planning. If any shreds of credibility were retained by the public, they might also serve a legitimising function.

The future of futures research need not be so gloomy. While much of this book has been critical of tendencies in research, it has also drawn on a lively body of criticism of the dominant assumptions and methods in use. In the following section some attempts to anticipate the form of the challenge to mainstream futurology will be reviewed. First, it is useful to consider factors that may be working in favour of futures studies. Several factors together should encourage a growth in informed criticism of such studies, as opposed to its outright rejection as inherently tainted with technocracy. These may be expected to encourage innovation and diffusion of futures research appropriate to a wider range of needs, values and social groups.

In chapter 2 current critiques of 'value-free' social science were briefly noted, and these critiques appear to be increasingly accepted within academia – related to this is turmoil in many areas of applied social research. Previous chapters have referred to attempts to reorient macro-sociological theory and development studies; movements for social responsibility in science may likewise be cited as signs of a growing appreciation of the significance of research in creating or reinforcing images of the future, that cannot be reduced to anti-scientific nihilism. Such developments should result in a greater awareness of the values served by particular research approaches on the part of both researchers and readers. As it is, detailed appraisals of forecasting exercises have been forthcoming from several futures research groups themselves (e.g. the Cole et al. (1973) critique of *The Limits to Growth*).

A further factor giving some grounds for optimism is the appearance of futures studies in educational curricula. Eldredge (1970) refers to several distinctive approaches found in a survey of futures courses in North America, ranging from technological forecasting to social criticism. The Open University course, which originated in the UK, and deriving from technological studies, should disseminate awareness of the controversial issues underlying futures research (see the reader edited by Cross, Elliot and Roy, 1974). Since such courses are engaging the interest of increasing numbers of social science students, the coming generation of social researchers may show more interest in constructing images of alternative futures than did their forbears, and may tackle the question of the relevance and actual role of these images in decision making in a systematic way.

Bell and Mau (1971) argued that a concern with social forecasting and with the functions of images of the future might provide a new organising paradigm for sociology as the structural—functional paradigm and the myth of value-freedom crumble. Whatever the merits of this view-point, which to date has evoked little noticeable response among either sociologists or futurologists (an exception here being Gastil, 1972), an involvement in futures studies will almost inevitably have one effect on the social scientist. When dealing with a complex problematique, disciplinary boundaries are rarely relevant. The researcher is thus faced with the necessity of crossing such boundaries and coming to terms with the insights and conflicts of widely different fields of knowledge. Several reports have consequently appeared dealing with matters arising in interdisciplinary teams (e.g. Etzioni, 1975; McEvoy, 1972).

Some of these developments will surely meet with opposition from within the futures movement. By a token admission of social and political constructs the central role of technological or economic factors in a forecast may be obscured; by elaborations of concepts and methodologies the value basis and meta-advocacy of studies may be made difficult to pinpoint, especially for those restricted to reading press releases and unable to scrutinise the separately published technical reports and appendices. There have also been signs of attempts to strengthen a futurological establishment. One noted observer, concerned by the presence of 'troubled young people without sufficient self-discipline' at futures conferences seeks some screening 'to avoid the futures movement from being ruined by dogmatists, self-appointed prophets and well-wishing bearded ignorants' (Dror, 1973, pp.110 and 112). But, even if the literature of futures research shows little sign of a wholesale change in orientation, the controversies and criticisms appearing in futures journals constitute a hopeful sign; reaction is relatively dormant.

Alternative images of the future

Two writers, Dator (1974) and Sklair (1973), have set out in a very similar way to assess different challenges to the mainstream futurological image of the future. Dator's analysis is set in the context of his critique of what he identifies as an orthodox notion of development as a model for the evolution of both industrial and developing countries. Dator takes the work of Rostow and similar authors as exemplifying this model of development. Sklair's target is 'techno-economism', the ideology which asserts that industrial and economic development along the lines historically taken by Western countries is the best way of meeting individual and societal needs.

These two authors are in essential agreement in identifying three main streams of thought posing challenges to the image of the future portrayed by 'development' and 'techno-economism', and in concluding that none of these currently offers a throughgoing reformulation of this image. For Dator these challenges are the ecology and counterculture world order, neo-nostalgia and Marxism; Sklair identifies the environment and resources lobby, primitivism amd Marxism. Dator also identifies an 'ethical critique' of development, which is one foundation of his model of a 'transformational society', while Sklair argues that 'correct' Marxism should provide a potent image of the future.

The ecological viewpoint challenges the assumption that unrestricted growth, at least insofar as this involves increasing consumption of energy and resources, is a feasible component of an image of the future. It takes as its starting point premises about the seriousness of environmental disruption, the depletion of natural resources, and the threat of pollution, that have inspired a host of gloomy forecasts and which have received extensive coverage in the media from the late 1960s onwards. There is clearly good reason to believe that growth in exploitation of natural resources cannot continue in its present form indefinitely. This has been accepted painlessly within the futures movement, since it leaves open the question of how soon and how rapidly growth will be restricted. Technological optimists have been able to point to failures on the part of environmentalists to take adequate account of substitution of materials and of untapped resources.

Both Dator and Sklair depict the ecological challenge as basically reformist, not substantially altering the image of future society. Although a number of revolutionaries and primitivists have adopted environmentalist perspectives, the general thrust of the admittedly wide spectrum of interests involved in environmentalism is towards a social order which is characterised by concerns for ecology, aesthetics and conservation, and which meets the concerns with better planning and more centralisation. A good example of the assimilation of environmentalist perspectives into forecasting is represented by the Ford Foundation report on future use of energy in the USA (*A Time to Choose,* 1974). This considers scenarios in which historical trends in energy use are simply continued, in which technological fixes are employed to reduce wastage, and in which growth is steadily reduced. This latter scenario is judged to be feasible and desirable after a study of the policy implications and consequences of each.

The ecological argument challenges the assumptions of unrestricted growth, but is rarely linked to any challenge of the basic social order of PIS; restrictions on growth are felt to be quite compatible with the established image of the future. (This interpretation certainly does violence to the ideas of some proponents of alternative technology, e.g. Dickson, 1974, but Dator and Sklair would probably and justly argue that the outline above represents the attitudes of the greater proportion of people associated with environmentalism.) What is seen to be needed is not so much major structural change in society as a turning away from values of materialism and conspicuous consumption. Existing structures may need regulation by national and even global institutions which could monitor technology's environmental impacts and the depletion of reserves, and perhaps society should aim at developing into a number of self-sufficient units. But the fundamental change advocated is a change in ecological consciousness, spearheaded by intellectual pressure groups, which regulates rather than transforms the image of the future.

The neo-nostalgic, primitivist challenge to futurology's image of the future is to some extent associated with the ecological position, although the two are conceptually, and often practically, distinct. The world view here is essentially anti-science, opposed to further innovative changes and the institutions — such as higher education — seen to produce them. A golden age society based on pre-industrial technology here forms an image of the future, and conservationist and humanist arguments may be used to support this position. Sklair does not credit this stance with political viability; on the other hand Dator sees the anti-intellectualism and apparent future shock of Nixon-era America as of sufficient significance to toy with a neo-nostalgic scenario for the West.

The primitivist perspective has rarely fared well within futures research circles, where a conscious return to a mythical golden age has been regarded as violating the realities of world poverty, inequality and conflict. It remains to be demonstrated that traditional agriculture could feed an expanding world population or that primitivists could escape the oppression of factions who retained high technology. The anti-intellectual and austere rhetoric with which primitivism is often associated makes it unlikely to have much impact on a futures movement which seeks academic acceptability and the recognition of élites.

Dator and Sklair reach similar conclusions about the Marxist challenge to the established image of the future. While he finds the Marxist critique of development theory (represented by Bodenheimer) very telling, Dator argues that it is directed at capitalist subversion of economic development in the Third World rather than at the notions of economic and industrial growth themselves. Sklair (1973, p.256) takes the view that Marxists have not risen to the challenge of techno-economism: 'Bureaucratic communists have become quite reformist in their concern that nothing should be allowed to interfere with economic growth; whereas libertarian radicals have become increasingly primitivist and anti-science and technology.' Marxist images of the future, then, envisage changing ownership of the means of production and an abolition of economic imperialism and the creation of dependency. However they share with the futurological image an emphasis on technology bordering on determinism (as in the acceptance of Western modes of production as the only way of meeting world needs) and a stress on expertise rather than on participation. (Sklair, 1973, p.241, excepts Chinese Marxism from this assessment.)

Dator outlines a further critique of 'development' based on the work of Goulet (1971). This 'ethical' perspective demands that images of the future be derived from the fundamental needs of all people for sustenance, esteem and freedom (in the sense of freedom for self-actualisation as well as freedom from oppression). At a minimum, future society should provide ample resources for these ends, support cultural diversity by a solidarity which minimises conflict, and allow people to participate effectively in choosing social goals. It is on such considerations that Dator develops his image of the 'transformational society' in which individual freedom is maximised with the aid of cybernation and decentralisation.

G2

185

Sklair only briefly sketches in the progressive Marxist image of the future. He argues that capitalism in inextricably bound to techno-economism. With 'correct' Marxism the notion of technological impera-tives is abandoned: technology is designed to be appropriate to human needs and may thus be intermediate or advanced as the situation demands. The relations between science and technology on the one hand, and industry and the economy on the other, would be transformed so as to make science policy a matter of participatory democracy. The scenario presented by Bodington (1973) may suggest some ways in which Sklair's image might be elaborated for industrial countries, at least. Bodington proposes that computer technology be applied to the co-ordination of relatively small self-managing communities, thus attaining a socialist society founded on direct democracy rather than centralised planning. While temporally unspecific, in terms of the criteria of chapter 3, Bodington's future makes a challenging image.

It is notable that these authors, despite their divergences, emphasise the need for greater public participation in the creation of future society as being one of the major elements of a coherent challenge to the 'development', 'techno-economist' image of the future. The very idea that an adequate image of the future might be defined and then turned over to experts to realise is suspect. Human goals are not fixed or static, but evolve in the course of intra-psychic and interpersonal conflict, of changing social relations, and not only a future but the route leading to it must be capable of reflecting emergent values. Simply to advocate greater participation in futures studies is insufficient, for social science may contribute to our knowledge of the benefits and limitations of different types of participation.

Public or publicised futures?

In chapters 3 and 5 futures studies and SI research were noted as generally lacking any participatory basis and being addressed to élites; this has often been criticised from within the ranks of futures researchers. In his review of social forecasting, Goldthorpe (1970) argued that futures studies should be rid of historicist and technocratic biases by an emphasis on social design, on action rather than on the passive forecasting of social processes, and by turning to an audience of pressure groups and activists rather than administration and technocrats. The role of the expert would be to test the soundness of alternative futures, to study consistencies and constraints rather than to legitimise slogans.

Similar suggestions have come from futurologists such as de Jouvenel and Jungk, who have advocated establishing public forums where images of the future may be shown and debated. Lasch (1970, chapter 6) proposes that futures, plans and options be propounded by groups of concerned citizens acting as alternatives to official planning agencies. The relationship between experts and the broader public is an important one which has been discussed in various terms and contexts relevant to the current discussion by many authors. (Examples of relevant writings include Aldous, 1972; Dickson, 1972; Jungk, 1969; Manheim, 1972; Mitchell, 1973; Sklair, 1973.) Proposals for enhancing communication include setting up of institutions which can serve the role of advocacy planners; public funding of community and consumer organisations; stimulation of diversity and public debate among forecasting teams; training people in skills and creating roles for interpretation and mediation between specialists and publics; developing novel communication systems which can serve as outlets and inputs for feedback about policy making and planning; and schooling and mass communications which could actually transmit the skills needed for assessing the goals of science and technology policy and the limits of social and environmental planning.

The social sciences could make an important contribution to futures studies by investigating the way in which such studies could be opened to a wider public — to active participations rather than just an audience. The existing social research into related issues is by no means systematic and, having concentrated on a limited number of isolated topics, displays large gaps. For example, a number of studies have been stimulated by community action projects and attempts to achieve decentralisation and local participation in administration in the wake of the 'Great Society' programmes in the USA. This research and discussion has focused on various issues arising out of this experience: the effects of participation on attitudes towards political institutions and policies, the co-opting or domination of community councils by representatives of élites, etc. (Examples of this literature include Kramer, 1969; Shingles, 1973; Vanecko, 1969; Yin and Lucas, 1973; the September/October 1971 issue of the *American Behavioural Scientist* was devoted to the topics of urban decentralisation and community participation, which have received much attention in planning and administration journals.) Forecasters and planners have been exposed to some of this literature through books and journals such as *Policy Sciences*. The extent to which the findings of this research are generalisable cannot be taken for granted one way or the other, however, and it is important that further studies should be set within a comparative framework. However, some conclusions may well be borne in mind by futures researchers. Resistance to effective sharing of power is an important factor to be reckoned with, and token participation is by no means guaranteed to produce public acceptance of policies or administration.

Other areas of social research may provide evidence bearing on the applicability and limitations of different approaches to participation where different issues are involved and different settings form the background. At present quantitative studies are often of tangential relevance and frequently impressionistic reports are of most value (e.g. Goodman, 1972, describes his experience with advocacy planning), although reviews of methodology are appearing (e.g. Fagence, 1974, reviews experience with designing questionnaires for participation in town planning). Two areas of empirical research which could make valuable contributions here may be mentioned.

One of these bodies of knowledge involves research dealing with how people perceive natural and man-made environments. Goodey (1973) has reviewed the literature in this field, and indicates that as yet it has offered little information about making preferences manifest in decision making. The work of Stringer (1973) suggests ways in which such research may be applied to issues in urban and environmental planning, as well as pointing to a large demand for more public involvement in local decisions (Taylor and Stringer, 1973). Stringer found that public evaluations and comparisons of different plans were affected by the types of maps used in presenting these plans. Clearly this finding is of significance to the forecaster who is concerned with communicating alternative images of the future, where a variety of different media and presentation styles might be used. Social scientists could help clarify what processes are involved in such situations, and perhaps point to modes of presentation that maximise people's use of information.

In the previous chapter we touched briefly on a second area of research which is related to these matters — studies into existing patterns of social and political participation. Such studies could be of use in a variety of ways. For example, it might be possible to investigate the skills which aid people in participating effectively, and to look at different ways in which such skills might be transmitted (e.g. Arnove, 1973; and Mathiason, 1972, on the potential of education and mass media in developing — or inhibiting — these skills). While many studies have pointed to class and sex biases in the distribution of existing political participation among populations, other demographic factors inhibiting or enhancing participation might fruitfully be studied (e.g. Nie, Verba and Kim, 1974 on the relation of participation to the lifecycle), and the effects of community

188

type and organisational size considered (e.g. Curtis, 1971). Costs and benefits of participation for the individual might be studied so as to determine favourable conditions for the formation of interest groups (e.g. J.Q. Wilson, 1973, on political organisations).

Participation of a wide public in creating desirable images of the future cannot solve basic problems overnight. 'Rules of the game' for political decision making depend on value commitments, and conflict rather than consensus may result from increased involvement in considering alternative options for social change. However, apart from its intrinsic worth and its being central component of a challenge to the technocratic historicist image of the future, participation may benefit futures studies in other ways. For example Richard Smith (1973) writes of the role of participation in planning in terms that may be applied to futures studies. He argues that participation can provide important information about local circumstances, particular interests, values and intentions from individuals and small groups that might otherwise go unheeded. It can help define community awareness and enhance solidarity in the process of democratic determination of ends and means. Finally it can help individuals develop social competence and knowledge of their environment. For forecasting to be based on such values as these would mean its becoming more like Maruyama's (1970) concept of 'human futuristics'. This envisages a role for futures studies which has more to do with learning than with conventional science and education. The aim of such studies would be to encourage the development of skills in design and experimentation in the social world.

In the futures field there have been a number of attempts to study means of involving citizen participation. These have often involved an emphasis upon 'futuristic' techniques such as computerised communications and Delphi-type aggregation of opinions and rounds of feedback. These techniques are advanced as being more flexible than conventional modes of participation, being responsive to individual requirements for information, feedback, time and timing, and anonymity.

Umpleby (1969) and Lamont (1973) have reported on the use of teaching computers for such purposes. Umpleby describes a man—machine game wherein the participant is invited to choose policies to follow and a scenario of the future emerging in consequence is eventually presented. The individual can compare this with his own ideals. Whether people would (or could justifiably) put faith in the programmer's choice of variables and model of society without some form of involvement in this choice is doubtful. Lamont describes a more strictly educational programme of information presentation in which individuals can follow up issues of particular interest when exploring a medium or long term planning question. Her pilot study met with favourable reactions from the participants, but the problems of selecting and ordering information remain political rather than technical. Theoretical and empirical studies of electronic group decision making conferences have been presented by, respectively, Etzioni (1972) and Remp (1974). These authors argue for the extension of these techniques to public planning. Turoff (1971) is more concerned with the combination of computers with Delphi techniques for the purposes of expert consultation in emergencies and extended dialogue between widely scattered and busy people than for mass participation, but again he foresees the use of such systems in planning and forecasting.

Reference was made in chapter 3 to the use of Delphi techniques, without electronic augmentation, in studies of participatory forecasting and policy assessment, and in chapter 5 Koelle's application of such techniques to the definition of SIs was touched on. As Delphi falls into disrepute as a forecasting technique, it seems set for a new career as a tool for participative policy definition. While some interesting pilot studies have appeared, none of those reported to date seems to have employed a true sample of citizens to appraise a major public decision. Schneider (1972) describes a 'policy Delphi' study in which 'expert' representatives of two adjacent cities evaluated a number of alternative policies (related to two future options for the relationship of the cities) and their possible consequences. Judd (1972) reviews application of Delphi in identifying policies, and planning, for institutions of higher education, reporting that problems in selecting panels were encountered in these studies. Skutsch and Shofer (1973) propose the use of Delphi in participative urban planning, but report studies within institutions in which considerable conflict of interests made the aim of establishing a hierarchy of goals impossible — although subsequent participation and organisational development are supposed to have improved. Their work also suggests that the consensus that Delphi studies often attain is influenced by pressures towards conformity, so that the question of whether Delphi is superior to face-to-face conferencing in this respect remains a matter for further research.

The Delphi procedure as normally constituted leaves a great deal of power in the hands of the technical experts involved. However, there are issues to be settled which are not merely technical. How shall groups be constituted, what goals should be selected for the initial round, when are options to be regarded as functionally equivalent, and what amount of feedback and inter-group communication should be encouraged? If forecasting and planning are to be truly participative, citizen involvement in such issues is needed. One way in which social scientists might contribute to such studies is in exploring the conceptual dimensions and practical issues involved here.

These participative studies often seem to have been motivated by an assumption that value-free techniques which impartially convey information, enhance communication, and aggregate preferences, will somehow hatch out optimum policy solutions that will upset nobody. Their results do not bear this out. The manner of constitution of participative forecasting and planning activies is a matter of political significance and choice. This said, there is good reason for social scientists to research into the processes and consequences of different participation modes. Comparative studies of the different modes described above in terms of several criteria would be valuable. Among the consequences of such participation could be studied the effects on individual feelings of competence, communication skills, and subsequent information seeking and action; the degree of polarisation and types of compromise emerging; the willingness of participants to question the conceptual bases of the techniques involved; and the nature of subsequent group coalescence and interaction.

Humanising the future

This book has contained much that is critical of the ways in which quantitative social science and futures studies have tended to reinforce each other, but I have also attempted to sketch out some grounds for optimism. Two significant roles for the social scientist have emerged from this analysis.

Social research may play a large role in the development of forecasts which satisfy criteria of quality such as those outlined in chapter 3. Since social and political factors are inextricably bound up with every issue of local or global significance with which futures studies deal, social scientists should be concerned to see that these studies take into account the conclusions and the conflicts of social research. Social scientists can foster awareness of unthinking historicism and simplistic determinisms in the assumptions of futures studies and, by making the relevance of their own work to social forecasting explicit (while admitting its qualifications and limitations), hopefully start a dialogue with futures researchers. It is important to expose the biases of futurology, but it is also important to recognise that work of value does exist, and that little purpose may be served by simply replacing a barren or inadequate image of the future with nihilism. Social research should thus be concerned with social design, and with addressing the question of whether piecemeal reform or thorough-going changes would be required for future society to be directed towards particular goals.

Social research may also contribute to experimentation with alternative participatory forms. Even if we are not undergoing a revolution in communications and in public demands for involvement in directing the course of social change, this would be an important role for the social scientist. While it is utopian to think that such experiments would be immediately influential on the selection of policies, or even on the practice of major futures research projects, the study of different approaches to participation in more localised planning (e.g. within institutions) and in existing or specially created futures groups could be a useful investment. Participants (including social scientists) could uncover salient constructs, relationships and policy options, share and develop skills of appraisal and communication in developing images of the future, recognise common interests and points of divergence, and provide evidence and practical experience concerning the viability of different modes of participation.

The above comments do not absolve the practising futurologist from responsibility. Futures researchers should themselves be concerned to establish dialogue with social scientists from various disciplines; and not only with those who already share their assumptions about the nature of social change and the desirability of a given social order. If, as will often be the case, the work of a project is already so urgent, abstract or global in its orientation as to make involvement of a wide public impractical, at least researchers would be concerned with addressing their reports to groups other than bureaucrats and administrators. Unions, pressure groups and the media, for example, should be kept informed of both the conclusions and the assumptions of research. Otherwise futures studies may continue, inadvertently or consciously, to celebrate a technocratic image of the future; and historicism cannot absolve the responsibility for translating that image into practice.

Bibliography

Abrams, Mark, 'Subjective Social Indicators' *Social Trends* no.4, 1973, HMSO, London.

Ackoff, Russell L., *Redesigning the Future,* Wiley-Interscience, New York, 1974.

Adelman, Irma, and Morris, Cynthia Taft, 'Economic Growth and Social Equity in Developing Countries' Stanford University Press, Stanford, 1973.

Aldous, Tony, *Battle for the Environment,* Fontana, London, 1972.

Alford, R.R. *Party and Society; The Anglo-American Democracies,* Rand-McNally, Chicago, 1963.

Allardt, Erik, 'About Dimensions of Welfare', University of Helsinki, Research Group for Comparative Sociology, Research Reports, no.1.

Allen, Francis R., *Socio-Cultural Dynamics,* Macmillan, New York, 1971.

Allen, Francis R. et al. *Technology and Social Change,* Appleton-Century Crofts, New York, 1957.

Allen, Philip J. (ed), *Pitirim A. Sorokin in Review,* Duke University Press, Durham, NC, 1963.

Almond, Gabriel, Political Development, Little, Brown & Co., Boston, 1970.

Almond, Gabriel, Flanagan, S.C., and Mundt, R.J. (eds), *Crisis, Choice and Change,* Little, Brown & Co., Boston, 1973.

Almond, Gabriel, and Verba, Sidney, *The Civic Culture,* Princeton University Press, Princeton, 1963.

Amara, Roy C., and Salancik, Gerald R., 'Forecasting: from Conjectural Art toward Science', *Technological Forecasting and Social Change,* vol. 3, 1972, pp.415–426.

Amara, Roy C., 'The Futures Field', *Futures,* vol. 6, 1974, pp.289–301.

Anderson, James G., 'Causal Models and Social Indicators', *American Sociological Review,* vol.38, 1973, pp.285–301.

Andrews, Frank M., and Withey, Stephen B., 'Developing Measures of Perceived Life Quality', *Social Indicators Research,* vol.1, 1974.

Appelbaum, Richard P., *Theories of Social Change,* Markham, Chicago, 1970.

Armistead, Nigel (ed), *Reconstructing Social Psychology,* Penguin Books, Harmondsworth, Middlesex, 1974.

Arnove, Robert F., 'Education and Political Participation in Rural Areas of Latin America', *Comparative Education Review,* vol.17, 1973, pp.198–215.

Banks, Arthur S., *Cross-Polity Time-Series Data,* MIT Press, Cambridge, Mass, 1971.

Banks, Arthur S., 'Correlates of Democratic Performance', *Comparative Politics,* vol.4, 1972, pp.217–230.

Banks, Arthur S., 'Patterns of Domestic Conflict: 1919–39 and 1946–66', *Journal of Conflict Resolution,* vol.16, 1972, pp.41–50.

Banks, Arthur S., and Gregg, Philip M., 'Grouping Political Systems: Q-factor analysis of "A Cross-Polity Survey" *American Behavioural Scientist,* vol.9, 1965, pp.3–6.

Banks, Arthur S., and Textor, Robert B., *A Cross-Polity Survey,* MIT Press, Cambridge, Mass, 1962.

Bannock, Graham, *The Juggernauts,* Weidenfeld and Nicholson, London, 1971.

Barrett, G.V., and Franke, R.H., '"Psychogenic" Death: a reappraisal', *Science,* vol.167, 1970, pp.304–306.

Bauer, Raymond A. (ed), *Social Indicators,* MIT Press, Cambridge, Mass, 1966.

Bauer, Raymond A., *Second-Order Consequences,* MIT Press, Cambridge, Mass, 1969.

Beer, Stafford, *Platform for Change,* Wiley, London and New York, 1975.

Bell, Daniel, *The End of Ideology*, Free Press, Glencoe, Ill, 1960.

Bell, Daniel, 'The Year 2000 – the trajectory of an idea' and 'A Summary by the Chairman', *Daedalus,* summer issue, vol.96, 1967.

Bell, Daniel, *The Coming of Post-Industrial Society,* Basic Books, New York and Heinemann, London, 1974.

Bell, Daniel, 'Religion and Post-Industrial Society', *The Listener,* vol.95, 1975, pp.336–337.

Bell, Wendell, and Mau, James A. (eds), *The Sociology of the Future,* Russell Sage Foundation, New York, 1971.

Bell, Wendell, et al, 'A Paradigm for the Analysis of Time Perspectives and Images of the Future', in Bell and Mau, 1971.

Beneveniste, Guy, *The Politics of Expertise,* Glendessary Press, Berkeley, and Croom Helm, London, 1972.

Bennis, Warren G., and Slater, Philip E., *The Temporary Society,* Harper and Row, New York, 1968.

Bensman, Joseph, and Vidich, Arthur J., *The New American Society,* Quadrangle Books, Chicago, 1971.

Bereiter, Carl, 'Multivariate Analyses of the Behavior and Structure of

Groups and Organizations' in Cattell, R.B., (ed). *A Handbook of Multivariate Experimental Psychology*, Rand-McNally, Chicago, 1966.

Berk, Richard J., and Aldrich, Howard E., 'Patterns of Vandalism during Civil Disorders as an Indicator of Selection of Targets', *American Sociological Review*, vol.37, 1972, pp.533–547.

Berry, Brian L.J., (ed), *City Classification Handbook*, Wiley-Interscience, New York, 1972.

Betz, Michael, 'Riots and Welfare: are they related?' *Social Problems*, vol.21, 1974, pp.345–355.

Bezdek, Roger H., and Getzel, Barry, 'Alternative Forecasts of the Job Contents and Skill Requirements of the American Economy in 1980', *Technological Forecasting and Social Change*, vol.5, 1973, pp.205–214.

Biderman, Albert D., 'Social Indicators and Goals', in Bauer, 1966.

Bill, James A., 'The Politics of Legislative Monarchy: the Iranian Majlis', in Hirsch, H., and Hancock, M.D. (eds), *Comparative Legislative Systems*, Free Press, New York, 1971.

Blackburn, Robin, *Ideology in Social Science*, Fontana, London, 1972(a).

Blackburn, Robin,(b) 'The New Capitalism', in Blackburn, 1972 (a).

Blalock, Herbert M., and Blalock, Ann B. (eds), *Methodology in Social Research*, McGraw-Hill, New York, 1968.

Bodenheimer, Susanne J., 'The Ideology of Developmentalism' *Sage Professional Papers in Comparative Politics*, vol.2, 1971, nos. 01–015.

Bodington, Stephen, *Computers and Socialism*, Spokesman Books, Nottingham, 1973.

Boguslaw, Robert, *The New Utopians*, Prentice-Hall, Englewood Cliffs, NJ, 1965.

Brandt, Richard M., *Studying Behavior in Natural Settings*, Holt, Rinehart and Winston Inc., New York, 1972.

Brass, W., 'On the Possibility of Population Prediction', in Freeman, Jahoda and Miles, 1975.

Brewer, Garry D., *Politicians, Bureaucrats, and the Consultant*, Basic Books, New York, 1973.

Bright, James R., and Schoeman, Milton E.F. (eds), *A Guide to Practical Technological Forecasting*, Prentice-Hall, Englewood Cliffs, NJ, 1973.

Bronfenbrenner, Uri, 'The Origins of Alienation', *Scientific American*, vol.231, 1974, pp.53–61.

Brown, Phil (ed), *Radical Psychology*, Harper Colophon, New York, 1973.

Buckley, Walter, *Sociology and Modern Systems Theory*, Prentice-Hall, Englewood Cliffs, NJ, 1967.

Burnham, James, *The Managerial Revolution,* University of Illinois Press, Urbana, 1940.

Burrowes, Robert, 'Theory Si, Data No! A Decade of Cross-National Political Research', *World Politics,* vol.25, 1972, pp.126–144.

Bwy, Douglas P., 'Dimensions of Social Conflict in Latin America', in Masotti, L.H., and Bowen, D.R. (eds), *Riots and Rebellion: Civil Violence in the Urban Community,* Sage Publications, Beverly Hills, 1968.

Bwy, Douglas P., 'Political Instability in Latin America: the Cross-Cultural Test of a Causal Model', *Latin American Research Review,* vol.3, 1968. pp.17–66.

Campbell, Angus, and Converse, Philip E. (eds), *The Human Meaning of Social Change,* Russell Sage Foundation, New York, 1972.

Campbell, Donald T., 'Definitional versus Multiple Operationalism', *Et Al,* vol.2, 1969, pp.14–17.

Campbell, Donald T., and Fiske, D.W., 'Convergent and Discriminant Validation by the Multitrait–Multimethod Matrix', *Psychological Bulletin,* vol.56, 1959, pp.81–105.

Campbell, Donald T., and Stanley, Julian C., *Experimental and Quasi-Experimental Designs for Research,* Rand-McNally, Chicago, 1966. Originally published in Gage, N.L. (ed), *Handbook of Research on Teaching,* Rand-McNally, Chicago, 1963.

Cantril, Hadley, *The Pattern of Human Concerns,* Rutgers University Press, New Brunswick, NJ, 1965.

Caparaso, James A., and Roos, Leslie L. Jr (eds), *Quasi-Experimental Methods: Testing Theory and Evaluating Policy,* Northwestern University Press, Evanston, Ill, 1973.

Caplin, Nathan S., and Paige, Jeffrey M., 'A Study of Ghetto Rioters', *Scientific American,* vol.219, 1968, pp.15–21.

Carey, James W., and Quirk, John J., 'The History of the Future', in Gerbner, G., Gross, L.P. and Melody W.A. (eds), *Communications Technology and Social Policy,* John Wiley, New York, 1973.

Carneiro, Robert L., 'Scale Analysis, Evolutionary Sequences and the Rating of Cultures', in Naroll and Cohen, (eds), 1970.

Cattel, Ramond B., 'The Principal Culture Patterns Discernable in the Syntal Dimensions of Existing Nations', *Journal of Social Psychology,* vol.32, 1950, pp.215–253.

Cetron, Marvin J., 'The Trimatrix – an Integration Technique for Technology Assessment', in Cetron, M.J. and Bartocha, B., (eds), *The Methodology of Technology Assessment,* Gordon and Breach, New York, 1972.

Chadwick, Bruce A., 'In Defense of Density: Its Relationship to Health and Social Disorganization', in Bahr, H.M., Chadwick, B.A. and Thomas D.C. (eds), *Population, Resources and the Future,* Brigham Young University Press, Provo, Utah, 1972.

Clark, Terry N., *Community Structure and Decision-Making: comparative analyses,* Chandler Publishing Corp, San Francisco, 1968.

Clark, Terry N., 'Urban Typologies and Political Outputs', *Social Science Information,* vol.9, 1970, pp.7–33.

Clark, Terry N., 'Citizen Values, Power and Policy Outputs' *Journal of Comparative Administration,* vol.4, 1973, pp.385–427.

Cnudde, Charles E., and Neubauer, Deane E. (eds), *Empirical Democratic Theory,* Markham, Chicago, 1969.

Coates, Joseph F., 'The Future of Crime in the United States from Now to the Year 2000', *Policy Sciences,* vol.3, 1972, pp.27–45.

Cockcroft, James D., Frank, André Gunder, and Johnson, Dale L., *Development and Underdevelopment: Latin America's Political Economy,* Doubleday Anchor, Garden City, NY, 1972.

Cohen, Percy S., *Modern Social Theory,* Heinemann, London, 1969.

Cole, H.S.D. et al (eds), *Thinking About The Future,* Chatto and Windus, London, 1973. Published in the USA, as *Models of Doom,* Universe Books, New York, 1973.

Coleman, James S., 'The Methods of Sociology', *American Academy of Political and Social Science, Monograph 9,* April 1969.

Coleman, James S., 'Social Inventions', *Social Forces,* vol.49, 1970, pp.163–173.

Colfax, J. David, and Roach, Jack L. (eds), *Radical Sociology,* Basic Books, New York, 1971.

Compton, D.G., *The Electric Crocodile,* Hodder and Stoughton, London, 1970.

Conger, D. Stuart, 'Social Inventions', *The Futurist,* vol.7, 1973, pp.149–158.

Conradt, David P., 'West Germany: A Remade Political Culture?' *Comparative Political Studies,* vol.7, 1974, pp.222–238.

Cook, Steven, 'Implications of Zero Growth', paper presented at the Fifth Joint Conference, Behavioral Sciences and Operational Research, London Graduate School of Business Studies, 19 December 1974.

Cortazzi, Diana, and Baquer, Ali, *Action Learning,* The Hospital Centre, King Edward's Hospital Fund, London, 1972.

Cross, Nigel, Elliot, David, and Roy, Robin, *Man-Made Futures,* Hutchinson, London, 1974.

Curtis, James, 'Voluntary Association Joining: A Cross-National Comparative Note', *American Sociological Review,* vol.36, 1971, pp.872—880.

Cutright, Phillips, 'National Political Development: measurement and analysis', *American Sociological Review,* vol.28, 1963, pp.253—264.

Cutright, Phillips, 'Political Structure, Economic Development and National Social Security Programs', *American Journal of Sociology,* vol.70, 1965, pp.537—551.

Cutright, Phillips, 'Income Redistribution: A Cross-National Analysis', *Social Forces,* vol.46, 1967, pp.180—196.

Cutright, Phillips, and Wiley, James A., 'Modernisation and Political Representation', *Studies in Comparative International Development,* vol.5, series no. 052, 1970.

Dahl, Robert A., *A Preface to Democratic Theory,* University of Chicago Press, Chicago, 1956.

Dahrendorf, Ralf, *Class and Class Conflict in Industrial Society,* Stanford University Press, Stanford, Calif., 1959.

Dator, Jim, 'Neither There Nor Then', in *Human Futures,* a *Futures* special publication, IPC Press, Guildford, Surrey, 1974.

Davies, Bleddyn, *Social Needs and Resources in Local Services,* Michael Joseph, London, 1968.

Davies, James C. (ed), *When Men Revolt — And Why,* Free Press, New York, 1972.

de Charms, R., and Moeller, C., 'Values Expressed in American Children's Readers: 1800—1950', *Journal of Abnormal and Social Psychology,* vol.64, 1962, pp.136—142.

de Houghton, Charles, Page, William, and Streatfeild, Guy, . . . And Now *The Future,* PEP London, broadsheet 529, vol.37, 1971.

de Jouvenel, Bertrand, *The Art of Conjecture,* Basis Books, New York, 1967.

Dickson, David, *Alternative Technology and the Politics of Technical Change,* Fontana, London, 1974.

Dickson, David, 'Science to help the people', *New Scientist,* vol.51, 1972, pp.277—278.

Dror, Yehezkel, 'A Third Look at Futures Studies', *Technological Forecasting and Social Change,* vol.5, 1973, pp.109—112.

Duncan, Otis Dudley (ed), *William F. Ogburn on Culture and Social Change,* University of Chicago Press, Chicago, 1964.

Duncan, Otis Dudley, 'Social Forecasting — the state of the art', *The Public Interest,* vol.17, 1969, pp.88—110.

Duncan, Otis Dudley, Schuman, Howard, and Duncan, Beverly, *Social Change in a Metropolitan Community*, Russell Sage Foundation, New York, 1973.

Durkheim, Emile, *The Division of Labour in Society*, 1893; translation Free Press, Glencoe, Ill., 1964.

Durkheim, Emile, *Suicide*, 1897; translation, Routledge and Kegan Paul, London, 1952.

Duvall, Raymond, and Welfling, Mary, 'Determinants of Political Institutionalization in Black Africa: a quasi-experimental analysis', *Comparative Political Studies*, vol.5, 1973, pp.387–417.

Easthope, Gary, *A History of Social Research Methods*, Longmans, Harlow, Essex, 1974.

Easton, David, *A Systems Analysis of Political Life*, Wiley, New York, 1965.

Easton, Loyd D., and Guddat, Kurt H. (eds), *Writings of the Young Marx on Philosophy and Society*, Doubleday Anchor, Garden City, NY, 1967.

Eisenstadt, S.N., and Rokkan, S., *Building States and Nations*, Sage Publications, Beverly Hills, 1973.

Eisinger, Peter K., 'Racial Differences in Protest Participation', *American Political Science Review*, vol.68, 1974, pp.592–606.

Eldredge, H. Wentworth, 'Education in Futurism', *The Futurist*, vol.4, 1970, pp.193–196.

Ellul, Jacques, *The Technological Society*, Cape, London, 1965, originally published in French, 1954.

Elsner, Henry, Jr, *The Technocrats*, Syracuse University Press, Syracuse, NY, 1967.

Emery, Fred, *Futures We're In*, Centre for Continuing Education, The Australian National University, Canberra, 1974.

Encel, Sol, Marstrand, Pauline, and Page, William (eds), *The Art of Anticipation*, Martin Robertson, London, 1975.

Environmental Protection Agency, *The Quality of Life Concept*, Environmental Protection Agency, Washington, DC, 1973.

Etzioni, Amitai, *The Active Society*, The Free Press, New York, 1968.

Etzioni, Amitai, 'MINERVA: An Electronic Town Hall', *Policy Sciences*, vol.3, 1972, pp.457–474.

Etzioni, Amitai, 'An Engineer–Social Science Team At Work', *Technology Review*, vol.77, 1975, pp.26–31.

Etzioni, Amitai, and Lehman, Edward W., 'Some Dangers in "Valid" Social Measurement', in Gross, 1969.

Fagence, Michael T., 'The Design and Use of Questionnaires for Participation Practices in Town Planning', *Policy Sciences*, vol.5, 1974, pp.297–308.

Feierabend, Ivo K., and Feierabend, Rosalind L., 'Aggressive Behaviors Within Politics, 1948–62: A Cross-National Study', *Journal of Conflict Resolution,* vol.10, 1966, pp.249–271.

Feierabend, I.K., Feierabend, R.L., and Gurr, T.R. (eds), *Anger, Violence and Politics,* Prentice-Hall, Englewood Cliffs, NJ, 1972.

Ferkiss, Victor, *Technological Man,* Heinemann, London, 1969.

Firestone, Joseph M., 'The Development of Social Indicators from Content Analysis of Social Documents', *Policy Sciences,* vol.3, 1972, pp.249–263.

Flanigan, William and Fogelman, Edwin, 'Patterns of Political Development and Democratization: a quantitative analysis', presented at annual meeting of American Political Science Association, 1967, reprinted in Gillespie and Nesvold, 1970.

Flanigan, William, and Fogelman, Edwin, 'Patterns of Democratic Development: a historical comparative analysis', presented at annual meeting of the American Political Science Association, 1968, reprinted in Gillespie and Nesvold, 1970.

Flanigan, William, and Fogelman, Edwin, 'Patterns of Political Violence in Comparative Historical Perspective', *Comparative Politics,* vol.3, 1970, pp.1–20.

Flora, Peter, 'Historical Processes of Social Mobilization: Urbanization and Literacy', in Eisenstadt and Rokkan, 1973.

Forbes, Hugh Donald, and Tufte, Edward R., 'A Note of Caution in Causal Modelling', *American Political Science Review,* vol.62, 1968, pp.1258–1264.

Ford Foundation, Energy Policy Project, *A Time to Choose,* Ballinger, Cambridge, Mass, 1974.

Fowles, Jib, 'Mass Advertising as a Social Forecast: a proposed method for futures research', *Futures,* vol.7, 1975, pp.107–118.

Fox, Thomas, and Miller, S.M., 'Occupational Stratification and Mobility', in Merrit, R.L., and Rokkan, S. (eds), *Comparing Nations,* Yale University Press, New Haven, 1966.

Freeman, Christopher, 'The Luxury of Despair', *Futures,* vol.6, 1974, pp.450–462.

Freeman, Christopher, et al, 'The Goals of R & D in the 1970's', *Science Studies,* vol.1, 1971, pp.357–406.

Freeman, Christopher, Jahoda, Marie, and Miles, Ian (eds), *Progress and Problems in Social Forecasting,* Cambridge University Press, London, 1975 (forthcoming).

Freeman, Michael, 'Sociology and Utopia: some reflections on the social philosophy of Karl Popper', *British Journal of Sociology,* vol.26, 1975, pp.26–34.

Frejka, Tomas, *The Future of Population Growth*, Wiley, New York, 1973.

Fried, Marc, 'Social Problems and Psychopathology', in Duhl, L.J., *Urban America and the Planning of Mental Health Services*, Group for the Advancement of Psychiatry, New York, 1964.

Friedrichs, Robert W., *A Sociology of Sociology*, The Free Press, New York and Collier-MacMillan, London, 1970.

Galbraith, John Kenneth, *The New Industrial State*, Hamish Hamilton, London, 1967.

Galtung, Johan, 'On the Future of the International System', in Jungk, R., and Galtung, J., *Mankind 2000*, Universitetforlaget, Oslo, and Allen and Unwin, London, 1969.

Gappert, Gary, 'Post-Affluence: the Turbulent Transition to a Post-Industrial Society', *The Futurist*, vol.8, 1974, pp.212–216.

Garaudy, Roger, *Karl Marx: the evolution of his thought*, International Publishers, New York, 1967.

Garfin, Susan Bettelheim, 'Comparative Studies: a selective, annotated bibliography', in Vallier, I., *Comparative Methods in Sociology*, University of California Press, Berkeley, 1971.

Gastil, R.D., 'A General Framework for Social Science', *Policy Sciences*, vol.3, 1972, pp.385–404.

Gerbner, George, et al, *Analysis of Communication Content*, John Wiley, New York, 1969.

Gerbner, George, 'Cultural Indicators: the case of violence in television drama', *Annals of the American Academy of Political and Social Science*, vol.388, 1970, pp.69–81.

Gerbner, George, 'Cultural Indicators: The Third Voice', in Gerbner, G., Gross, L.P., and Melody, W.A. (eds), *Communications Technology and Social Policy*, John Wiley, New York, 1973.

Gerbner, George, 'Teacher Image in Mass Culture: Symbolic Functions of the "hidden curriculum"', in Gerbner, G., Gross, L.P., and Melody, W.A. (eds), *Communications Technology and Social Policy*, John Wiley, New York, 1973.

Gerbner, George, Gross, Larry P., and Melody, William H., *Communications Technology and Social Policy*, John Wiley, New York, 1973.

Gillespie, John V., and Nesvold, Betty A., *Macro-Quantitative Analysis*, Sage Publications, Beverly Hills, 1970.

Glass, D.V., 'The History of Population Forecasting', in Freeman, C., Jahoda, M., and Miles, I., (eds), 1975.

Glenn, Norval D., 'Massification versus Differentiation: Some Trend Data from National Surveys', *Social Forces*, vol.46, 1967, pp.172–180.

Glenn, Norval D., 'Recent Trends in Intercategory Differences in Attitudes', *Social Forces,* vol.52, 1974, pp.395–401.

Goldthorpe, John H., 'Social Stratification in Industrial Society', in Bendix, R., and Lipset, S.M. (eds), *Class, Status and Power,* Routledge and Kegan Paul, London, 1967.

Goldthorpe, John H., 'Theories of Industrial Society: reflections on the recrudescence of historicism and the future of futurology', paper given to International Sociological Association, 7th World Congress of Sociology, Varna, Bulgaria, 1970. Later published in *Archives Européene de Sociologie,* vol.12, 1971, pp.263–288.

Goldthorpe, John, et al, *The Affluent Worker in the Class Structure,* Cambridge University Press, Cambridge, 1969.

Goldhammer, Herbert, and Marshall, A.W., *Psychosis and Civilisation: studies in the frequency of mental disease,* Free Press, Glencoe, Ill, 1953.

Golub, Robert, and Townsend, Joe, 'Malthus, Multinationals and the Club of Rome', unpublished paper, Science Policy Research Unit, University of Sussex, 1975.

Goodey, B., *Perception of the Environment: a guide to the literature,* Centre for Urban and Regional Studies, University of Birmingham, Birmingham, 1973.

Goodman, Robert, *After the Planners,* Penguin Books, Harmondsworth, Middlesex, 1972.

Gott, V.S., 'Neo-Positivist Scepticism versus Marxist Historism'. In Saifulin, M. (ed), *The Future of Society,* Progress Publishers, Moscow, 1973.

Gouldner, Alvin W., *The Coming Crisis of Western Sociology,* Basic Books, New York, 1970.

Goulet, Denis, *The Cruel Choice,* Atheneum Books, New York, 1971.

Gouré, Leon, Kohler, Foy D., Soll, Richard, and Stiefbold, Annette, *Convergence of Communism and Capitalism: The Soviet View,* Center For Advanced International Studies, University of Miami, Miami, 1973.

Graham, Hugh Davis, and Gurr, Ted Robert, (eds), *The History of Violence in America,* Praeger, New York, 1969.

Graham, William K., and Roberts, Karlene H. (eds), *Comparative Studies in Organizational Behavior,* Holt, Rinehart and Winston, New York, 1972.

Greenstein, Fred I., 'New Light on Changing American Values: a forgotten body of survey data', *Social Forces,* vol.42, 1964, pp.441–450.

Gregg, Phillip M., and Banks, Arthur S., 'Dimensions of Political Systems: factor analysis of "A Cross-Polity Survey" , *American Political Science Review,* vol.59, 1965, pp.602–614.

Grofman, Bernard N., and Muller, Edward N., 'The Strange Case of Relative Gratification and Potential for Political Violence: the V-curve hypothesis', *American Political Science Review,* vol.67, 1973, pp.514—539.

Gross, Bertram M., *The State of the Nation: Social Systems Accounting,* Tavistock Publications, London, 1966; also published in Bauer (ed), 1966.

Gross, Bertram M., *Social Intelligence for America's Future,* Allyn and Bacon, Boston, 1969.

Gross, Bertram M., 'Management Strategy for Economic and Social Development, 2', *Policy Sciences,* vol.3, 1972, pp.1—25.

Guetzkow, Harold, 'Simulations in the Consolidation and Utilization of Knowledge about International Relations', in Pruitt, D.G., and Snyder, R.C. (eds), *Theory and Research on the Causes of War,* Prentice-Hall, Englewood Cliffs, NJ, 1969.

Gurr, Ted Robert(a), 'A Causal Model of Civil Strife: a comparative analysis using new indices', *American Political Science Review,* vol.62, 1968, pp.1104—1124.

Gurr, Ted Robert,(b), *Why Men Rebel,* Princeton University Press, Princeton, 1970

Gurr, Ted Robert, 'Sources of Rebellion in Western Societies: some quantitative evidence', *Annals of the American Academy of Political and Social Science,* vol.391, 1970, pp.128—144.

Gurr, Ted Robert, and Duvall, Raymond, 'Civil Conflict in the 1960's', *Comparative Political Studies,* vol.6, 1973, pp.135—170.

Hakes, Jay E., 'Weak Parliaments and Military Coups in Africa: a study in regime instability', *Sage Research Papers in the Social Sciences,* (Comparative Legislative Studies Series), vol.1, no.90—004, 1973.

Hall, John, 'Measuring the Quality of Life Using Sample Surveys', in Stober, G.J., and Schumacher, D. (eds), 1973.

Hall, John, and Ring, James A., 'Indicators of Environmental Quality and Life-Satisfaction: a subjective approach', paper presented at International Sociological Association, 8th World Congress, Montreal, 1974.

Hamblin, Robert L., Jacobson, R. Brooke, and Miller, Jerry L.L., *A Mathematical Theory of Social Change,* Wiley-Interscience, New York, 1973.

Harbordt, Steffen C., *Linking Socio-Political Factors to the World Model,* Systems Dynamics Group, MIT Cambridge, Mass, 1971.

Harrington, Michael, *The Accidental Century,* Penguin Books, Harmondsworth, Middlesex, 1965.

Harrington, Michael,(a), 'A Subversive Version of the Great Society', in Stein, H.D., (ed), *Social Theory and Social Invention,* Press of Case Western University, Cleveland, 1968.

Harrington, Michael,(b), *Toward a Democratic Left,* MacMillan, New York, and Collier-Macmillan, London, 1968.

Harris, Louis, *The Anguish of Change,* W.W. Norton, New York, 1973.

Harp, John, and Gagan, Richard J., 'Scaling Voluntary Organizations as an Element of Community Structure', *Social Forces,* vol.49, 1971, pp.477–482.

Hayes, Margaret Daly, 'Policy Outputs in the Brazilian States, 1940–1960: political and economic correlates', *Sage Professional Papers in Comparative Politics,* vol.3, no.01-030, 1972.

Heilbroner, Robert L., *An Inquiry into the Human Prospect,* Norton, New York, 1974.

Hekhuis, Dale H., McClintock, Charles G., and Burns, Arthur L. (eds), *International Stability: military, economic and political dimensions,* John Wiley, New York, 1964.

Helmer, Olaf, *Social Technology,* Basic Books, New York, 1966.

Herriot, Robert E., and Hodgkins, Benjamin J., *The Environment of Schooling,* Prentice-Hall, Englewood Cliffs, NJ, 1973.

Hetman, François, *Society and the Assessment of Technology,* OECD, Paris, 1973.

Hickson, David J., Pugh, D.S., and Pheysey, Diana C., 'Operations Technology and Organization Structure: an empirical reappraisal', *Administrative Science Quarterly,* vol.14, 1969, pp.378–397.

Hindess, Barry, *The Use of Official Statistics in Sociology,* Macmillan, London, 1973.

Hofferbert, Richard I., 'State and Community Policy Studies: a review of comparative input-output analyses', in Robinson, J.B., (ed), *Political Science Annual, 3,* Bobbs-Merrill, Indianapolis, 1972.

Hogan, James Bennett, 'Social Structure and Public Policy: a longitudinal study of Mexico and Canada', *Comparative Politics,* vol.4, 1972, pp.477–510.

Hoos, Ida R., *Systems Analysis and Public Policy: A Critique,* University of California Press, Berkeley, 1972.

Hoos, Ida R., 'Criteria for "good" Futures Research', *Technological Forecasting and Social Change,* vol.6, 1974, pp.113–132.

Horowitz, Irving Louis, *Professing Sociology,* Aldine, Chicago, 1968.

Horowitz, Irving Louis, 'Social Science Mandarins: Policymaking as political formula', *Policy Sciences,* vol.1, 1970, pp.339–360.

Huber, Bettina J., 'Studies of the Future: a selected and annotated bibliography', in Bell, W., and Mau, J.A. (eds), 1971.

Hudson, Michael C., 'Political Protest and Power Transfers in Crisis Periods', *Comparative Political Studies,* vol.4, 1971, pp.259–294.

Hugger, Werner, and Maier, Helmut, 'Finding Invariant Structures in Forrester's World Dynamics', *Technological Forecasting and Social Change,* vol.5, 1973, pp.349–378.

Hulin, Charles C., 'Sources of Variation in Job and Life Satisfaction: the role of community and job-related variables', *Journal of Applied Psychology,* vol.53, 1969, pp.279–291.

Hyman, Herbert, *Secondary Analysis of Sample Surveys,* John Wiley, New York, 1972.

Hyman, Herbert, and Wright, Charles R., 'Trends in Voluntary Memberships of American Adults', *American Sociological Review,* vol.36, 1971, pp.191–206.

Inglehart, Ronald, 'The Silent Revolution in Europe: Intergenerational Change in Post-Industrial Societies', *American Political Science Review,* vol.65, 1971, pp.991–1017.

Inkeles, Alex, 'Continuity and Change in the Interaction of the Personal and the Sociocultural Systems', in Barber, B. and Inkeles, A. (eds), *Stability and Social Change,* Little, Brown and Co., Boston, 1971.

Inkeles, Alex, and Smith, David H., 'The Fate of Personal Adjustment in the Process of Modernization', *International Journal of Comparative Sociology,* vol.11, 1970, pp.81–114.

Institute for Social Research, *Study Abstracts Presented at the Second National Conference on Subjective Measures of the Quality of life,* Institute for Social Research, University of Michigan, Ann Arbor, 1974.

Jackman, Robert W., 'Political Democracy and Social Equality: a comparative analysis', *American Sociological Review,* vol.39, 1974, pp.29.

Janstch, Erich, *Technological Forecasting in Perspective,* OECD, Paris, 1967.

Jelin, Elizabeth, 'The Concept of Working-Class Embourgeoisement', *Studies in Comparative International Development,* vol.9, 1974, pp.1–19.

Jencks, Christopher, *Inequality: A Reassessment of the Effect of Family and Schooling in America,* Basic Books, New York, 1972.

Joes, Anthony James, 'Fascism: the past and the future', *Comparative Political Studies,* vol.7, 1974, pp.103–131.

Judd, Robert C., 'Use of Delphi Methods in Higher Education', *Technological Forecasting and Social Change,* vol.4, 1972, pp.173–186.

Jungk, Robert, 'Technological Forecasting as a tool of Social Strategy', in Arnfield, R.V. (ed), *Technological Forecasting,* Edinburgh University Press, Edinburgh, 1969.

Kahn, Alfred J., *Theory and Practice of Social Planning,* Russell Sage Foundation, New York, 1969.

Kahn, Herman, and Wiener, Anthony, *The Year 2000,* MacMillan, New York, 1967.

Kahn, Herman, and Bruce-Briggs, B., *Things to Come,* MacMillan, New York, 1972.

Kanter, Rosabeth Moss, *Commitment and Continuity: Communes and Utopias in Sociological Perspective,* MIT Press, Cambridge, Mass, 1972.

Kanter, Rosabeth Moss, *Communes: Creating and Managing the Collective Life,* Harper and Row, New York, 1973.

Katona, George, Strumpel, B., and Zahn, E., *Aspirations and Affluence,* McGraw—Hill, New York, 1971.

Kegley, Charles W., 'A General Empirical Typology of Foreign Policy Behavior', *Sage Professional Papers,* International Studies Series, vol.2, no.02—014, 1973.

Kelly, Kevin D., *Youth, Humanism and Technology,* Basic Books, New York, 1972.

Keniston, Kenneth, *Young Radicals,* Harcourt, Brace and World, New York, 1968.

Kerlinger, Fred N., *Foundations of Behavioral Research,* Holt, Rinehart and Winston, New York, 1964.

Kerr, Clark, et al, *Industrialism and Industrial Man,* Heinemann, London, 1962.

Kim, Chung Lim, 'Socio-Economic Development and Political Democracy in Japanese Prefectures', *American Political Science Review,* vol.65, 1971, pp.184—186.

Klages, Helmut, 'Assessment of An Attempt at a System of Social Indicators', *Policy Sciences,* vol.4, 1973, pp.249—261.

Klapp, Orwin E., *Collective Search for Identity,* Holt, Rinehart and Winston, New York, 1969.

Kleinberg, Benjamin S., *American Society in the Post-Industrial Age,* Charles E. Merril, Columbus, Ohio, 1973.

Knutson, Jeanne (ed), *Handbook of Political Psychology,* Jossey-Bass, San Francisco, 1973.

Koelle, H.H., 'An Experimental Study on the Determination of a Definition for the "Quality of Life"', *Regional Studies,* vol.8, 1974, pp.1—10.

Kornberg, Allan, Falcone, David J., and T.E. Mishler III, William 'Legislatures and Social Change: the case of Canada', *Sage Research Papers in the Social Sciences,* (Comparative Legislative Studies Series), vol.1, no.10—002, 1973.

Kramer, Ralph M., *Participation of the Poor,* Prentice-hall, Englewood Cliffs, NJ, 1969.

Kroeber, Alfred L., *Configurations of Culture growth*, University of California Press, Berkeley, 1944.

Kuhn, Thomas S., *The Structure of Scientific Revolutions*, University of Chicago Press, Chicago, 1962.

Kumar, Krishan, 'Inventing the Future, in spite of Futurology', *Futures*, vol.4, 1972, pp.369–374.

Laird, M.W., 'A Causal Model of American Political Value Change', in the *Proceedings* of the 1973 Summer Computer Simulation Conference, vol.2, Simulation Councils, Inc, La Jolla, California, 1973.

Lamont, Valerie, 'New Directions for the Teaching Computer: citizen participation in community planning', *Technological Forecasting and Social Change*, vol.5, 1973, pp.145–162.

Land, Kenneth C., 'Social Indicators' In Smith, R.B. (ed), *Social Science Methods*, Free Press, New York, 1970.

Land, Kenneth C., 'On the Definition of Social Indicators', *American Sociologist*, vol.6, 1971, pp.312–325.

Lane, Robert E., 'The Politics of Consensus in an Age of Affluence', *American Political Science Review*, vol.49, 1965, pp.874–895.

LaPiere, R.T., *Social Change*, McGraw-Hill, New York, 1965.

Lasch, Christopher, *The Agony of the American Left*, Andre Deutsch, London, 1970.

Lasch, Christopher, 'Take Me To Your Leader', *New York Review of Books*, vol.20, 1973, pp.63–66.

Laslett, Barbara, 'Mobility and Work satisfaction: a discussion of the use and interpretation of mobility models'. *American Journal of Sociology*, vol.77, 1971, pp.19–35.

Lazarsfeld, Paul F., Pasanella, Ann K., and Rosenberg, Morris, *Continuities in the Language of Social Research*, Free Press, New York, and Collier-Macmillan, London, 1972.

Leighton, Alexander H., 'A Comparative Study of Psychiatric Disorders in Nigeria and Rural North America', in Plog, S.C., and Edgerton, R.B. (eds), *Changing Perspectives on Mental Illness*, Holt, Rinehart and Winston, New York, 1969.

Lerner, Daniel, *The Passing of Traditional Society*, Free Press, Glencoe, Ill, 1958.

Levy, Sheldon G., 'A 150-year study of Political Violence in the United States', in Davis, H.G., and Gurr, T.R. (eds), 1969.

Lipset, Seymour Martin, 'Some Social Requisites of Democracy: Economic Development and Political Legitimacy', *American Political Science Review*, vol.53, 1959, pp.69–105.

Lipset, Seymour Martin, *Political Man,* Doubleday, Garden City, NY, 1963.

Lipset, Seymour Martin, and Ladd Jr, Everett Carl, 'College generations from the 1930's to the 1960's', *The Public Interest,* vol.25, 1971, pp.99–113.

Lodhi, Adbul Qaiyum, and Tilly, Charles, 'Urbanization, Crime and Collective Violence in 19th Century France', *American Journal of Sociology,* vol.79, 1973, pp.296–318.

Lorwin, Val R., and Price, Jacob M., *The Dimensions of the Past,* Yale University Press, New Haven, 1972.

Lynn, R., *Personality and National Character,* Pergamon Press, Oxford, 1971.

Manheim, Marvin L., 'Reaching Decisions about Technological Projects with Social Consequences: a normative model', Design Research Bag vol.2, 1972, reprinted in Cross, N., Elliot, D., and Roy, R. (eds), 1974.

Mann, Michael, 'The Social Cohesion of Liberal Democracy', *American Sociological Review,* vol.35, 1970, pp.423–439.

Mann, Michael, *Consciousness and Action among the Western Working Class,* Macmillan, London, 1973.

Marcuse, Herbert, *One-Dimensional Man,* Beacon Press, Boston, 1964.

Marien, Michael, 'Daniel Bell and the End of Normal Science' and 'Who Coined "Post-Industrial Society"', *The Futurist,* vol.7, 1973, pp.262–269.

Martino, Joseph P., 'Evaluating Forecast Validity', in Bright, J.R., and Schoeman, M.E.F. (eds), 1973.

Marx, Karl, *Capital,* originally published in Berlin, 1867 and Marx, Karl, and Engels, Friedrich, *The Communist Manifesto,* originally published in London; excerpts from the former and the complete latter reprinted in Feuer, L.S. (ed), *Marx and Engels: Basic Writings on Politics and Philosophy,* Fontana Books, London 1969.

Maruyama, Magoroh, 'Toward Human Futuristics', paper presented at meeting of American Anthropological Association, 1970, reprinted in *General Systems,* vol.2, 1972.

Maruyama, Magoroh, 'Cultural, Social and Psychological Considerations in the Planning of Public Works', *Technological Forecasting and Social Change,* vol.5, 1973, pp.135–143.

Maruyama, Magoroh, 'Endogenous Research versus "Experts" from Outside', *Futures,* vol.6, 1974, pp.389–394.

Maslow, Abraham H., *Motivation and Personality,* Harper and Row, New York, 1954.

Mathiason, John R. 'Patterns of Political Powerlessness among Urban

Poor: Toward the Use of Mass Communications for Rapid Social Change', *Studies in Comparative International Development,* vol.7, 1972, pp.64–84.

McClelland, Charles A., and Hoggard, G.D., 'Conflict Patterns in the Inter-actions among Nations', in Rosenau J.N. (ed), *International Politics and Foreign Policy,* Free Press, New York, 1969.

McClelland, David C., *The Achieving Society,* Free Press, New York, 1961.

McClelland, David C., and Winter, B.G., *Motivating Economic Achievement,* Free Press, New York, 1969.

McCoy, Charles A., and Playford, John, *Apolitical Politics,* Thomas Y. Crowell, New York, 1967.

McCrone, David J., and Cnudde, Charles F., 'Towards a Communications Theory of Political Development: a causal model', *American Political Science Review,* vol.61, 1967, pp.72–79.

Meadows, Dennis, Meadows, Donella, and Randers, Jørgen, *The Limits to Growth,* Universe Books, New York, 1972.

McEvoy III, James, 'Multi- and Interdisciplinary Research — problems of initiation, control, integration and reward', *Policy Sciences,* vol.3, 1972, pp.201–208.

Merton, Robert K., *Social Theory and Social Structure,* Free Press, Glencoe, Ill, 1957.

Miles, Ian, 'Social Forecasting: from impressions to investigation', *Futures,* vol.6, 1974, pp.240–252.

Mills, C. Wright, *The Power Elite,* Oxford University Press, New York, and London, 1956.

Mitchell, Jeremy, 'The Consumer Movement and Technological Change', *International Social Science Journal,* vol.25, 1973, pp.358–369.

Mitroff, Ian I., and Turoff, Murray, 'Technological Forecasting and Assessment: Science and/or Mythology?', *Technological Forecasting and Social Change,* vol.5, 1973, pp.113–134.

Montgomery, John D., *Technology and Civic Life,* MIT Press, Cambridge, Mass, 1974.

Morgan, William R., and Clark, Terry N., 'The Causes of Racial Disorder: a grievance-level explanation', *American Sociological Review,* vol.38, 1973, pp.611–624.

Morgenstern, Oskar, *The Accuracy of Economic Observations* (2nd ed), Princeton University Press, Princeton, NJ, 1963.

Morrison, Donald J., and Stevenson, Hugh Michael, 'Political Instability in Independent Black Africa', *Journal of Conflict Resolution,* vol.15, 1971, pp.347–368.

Moser, C.A., and Kalton, G., *Survey Methods in Social Investigation,* Heinemann, London, 1971.

Moul, William B., 'On Getting Something for Nothing: a note on causal models of political development', *Comparative Political Studies,* vol.7, 1974, pp.139–164.

Mueller, Eva, *Technological Advance in an Expanding Economy,* Survey Research Center, University of Michigan, Ann Arbor, 1967.

Muller, Edward N., 'Cross-National Dimensions of Political Competence', *American Political Science Review,* vol.64, 1970, pp.792–809.

Muller, Edward N., 'A Test of a Partial Theory of Political Violence', *American Political Science Review,* vol.66, 1972, pp.928–959.

Myrdal, Gunnar, *Challenge to Affluence,* Pantheon, New York, 1963.

Namenwirth, J. Zvi, 'Wheels of Time and the Interdependence of Value Change in America', *Journal of Interdisciplinary History,* vol.3, 1973, pp.649–683.

Nardin, Terry, 'Violence and the State: a critique of empirical political theory', *Sage Professional Papers in Comparative Politics,* vol.2, no.01–020, 1971.

Narrol, Raoul, 'A Holonational Bibliography', *Comparative Political Studies,* vol.5, 1972, pp.211–230.

Narrol, Raoul, and Cohen, Ronald, *A Handbook of Method in Cultural Anthropology,* Columbia University Press, New York, 1973.

National Commission on Technology, Automation and Economic Progress, *Technology and the American Economy,* Government Printing Office, Washington, DC, 1966.

National Resources Committee, Report of the Subcommittee on Technology, *Technological Trends and National Policy,* Government Printing Office, Washington, DC, 1937.

Neubauer, Deane E., 'Some Conditions of Democracy', *American Political Science Review,* vol.61, 1967, pp.1002–1009.

Nicolaus, Martin, 'The Unknown Marx', in Blackburn, R. (ed), 1972(a).

Nie, Norman H., Powell, G.B., and Prewitt, K., 'Social Structure and Political Participation: Developmental Relationships', *American Political Science Review,* vol.63, 1969, pp.361–378 and 808–832.

Nie, Norman H., Verba, Sidney, and Kim, Jae-On, 'Political Participation and the Life Cycle', *Comparative Politics,* vol.6, 1974, pp.319–340.

Nisbet, Robert, *The Sociological Tradition,* Basic Books, New York, 1966.

Nisbet, Robert, 'The Year 2000 and all that', *Commentary,* vol.45, 1968, pp.60–66.

Nisbet, Robert, 'Has Futurology a Future?', *Encounter,* vol.37, 1971, pp.19–28.

210

Nisbet, Robert, *Social Change and History,* Oxford University Press, New York, 1969.

Nissel, Muriel (ed), *Social Trends*, annual, HMSO, London, 1970 onwards.

Northrop, F.S.C., *The Logic of Science and the Humanities,* MacMillan, New York, 1947.

Noton, M., et al., 'A Dynamical Model of Conflict, part 1', unpublished paper, City University Department of Systems and Automation, London, 1974.

Noton, M., Mitchell, C.R., and Janes, F.R., 'The Systems Analysis of Conflict', *Futures,* vol.6, 1974, pp.114—132.

Ogburn, William F., *Social Change,* B.W. Huebsch, New York, 1922; 2nd edition, Viking Press, New York, 1950.

Ogburn, William F. (ed), *Recent Social Changes in the United States since the War and particularly in 1927,* University of Chicago Press, Chicago, 1929.

Ogburn, William F. (ed), *Social Changes in 1928 . . . 1932,* University of Chicago Press, Chicago, 1929—1933 annually.

Ogburn, William F. (ed), *Social Change and the New Deal,* University of Chicago Press, Chicago, 1934.

Ogburn, William F. (ed), *Social Changes During Depression and Recovery* University of Chicago Press, Chicago, 1935.

Ogburn, William F. (ed), 'Recent Social Changes', special edition of *American Journal of Sociology,* vol.17, May, 1942.

Ogburn, William F., *The Social Effects of Aviation,* Houghton Mifflin, Boston, 1946.

Ogburn, William F., (ed), *Technology and International Relations,* University of Chicago Press, Chicago, 1949.

Ogburn, William F., 'Technology and the Standard of Living', *American Journal of Sociology,* vol.60, 1955, pp.541-546, reprinted in Duncan, O.D. (ed), 1964.

Ogburn, William F., 'Cultural Lag as Theory', *Sociology and Social Research,* vol.41, 1957, pp.167—173, reprinted in Duncan, O.D., (ed), 1964.

Ogburn, William F., and Nimkoff, M.F., *Technology and the Changing Family,* Houghton Mifflin, Boston, 1955.

Olson, Mancur, Jr, 'Rapid Growth as a Destabilizing Force', *Journal of Economic History,* vol.23, 1963, pp.529—552.

Ozbekhan, Hasan, 'The Triumph of Technology — "can" implies "ought" , in Anderson, S. (ed), *Planning for Diversity and Choice,* MIT Press, Cambridge, Mass, 1968.

Ozbudon, Ergun, 'Party Cohesion in Western Democracies: A Causal

Analysis', *Sage Professional Papers in Comparative Politics,* vol.1, no.01–006. 1970.

Pahl, R.E., and Winkler, J.T., 'The Coming Corporatism', *New Society,* vol.30, 1974, pp.72–76.

Park, Tong-Whan, 'Peaceful Interactions in Asia: the delineation of nation groups', *Comparative Political Studies,* vol.5, 1973, pp.419–442.

Parsons, Talcott, *The Social System,* Free Press, Glencoe, Ill, 1951.

Parsons, Talcott, 'An Outline of the Social System' in Parsons, T. et al (eds), *Theories of Society,* Free Press, New York, 1961.

Parsons, Talcott, *Societies: Evolutionary and Comparative Perspectives,* Prentice-Hall, Englewood Cliffs, NJ, 1966.

Perkin, Harold, 'The History of Social Forecasting', in Freeman, C., Jahoda, M., and Miles, I. (eds), 1975.

Pill, Juri, 'The Delphi Method', *Socio-Economic Planning Science,* vol.5, 1971, pp.57–71.

Polsby, Nelson W., 'The Institutionalization of the U.S. House of Representatives', *American Political Science Review,* vol.62, 1968, pp.144–168.

Pool, Ithiel de Sola, 'Political Information Systems' in Jantsch, E., (ed), *Perspectives on Planning,* OECD, Paris, 1969.

Popper, Karl, *The Poverty of Historicism,* Routledge and Kegan Paul, London, 1957.

Price, Derek, *Science Since Babylon,* Yale University Press, New Haven, 1961.

Price, James L., *Handbook of Organizational Measurement,* D.C. Heath, Lexington, Mass., 1972.

Pride, Richard A., 'Origins of Democracy', *Sage Professional Papers in Comparative Politics,* vol.1, no.01–012, 1970.

Pride, Richard A., 'Pattern Analysis: an alternative approach to quantitative historical data', *Comparative Political Studies,* vol.4, 1971, pp.361–369.

Przeworski, Adam, and Teune, Henry, *The Logic of Comparative Social Inquiry,* Wiley-Interscience, New York, 1970.

Quinn, Robert P., Mangione, Thomas W., and Baldi de Manokovich, Martha S., 'Evaluating Working Conditions in America', *Monthly Labor Review,* vol.96, 1973, pp.32–41.

Rae, Donald W., and Taylor, M., *The Analysis of Political Cleavages,* Yale University Press, New Haven, 1970.

Rainwater, Lee, 'Post-1984 America', *Society,* vol.9, 1972, pp.18–28.

Reich, Charles A., *The Greening of America*, Random House, New York, 1970.

Remp, Richard, 'The Efficacy of Electronic Group Meetings', *Policy Sciences*, vol.5, 1974, pp.101–115.

Report of the President's Commission on National Goals, *Goals for Americans*, Prentice-Hall, Englewood Cliffs, NJ, 1960.

Report of the President's Research Committee on Social Trends, *Recent Social Trends in the United States*, McGraw-Hill, New York, 1933.

Reynolds, Ingrid, Ince, Roy, and Davies, David, 'The Quality of Local Housing Schemes', *The Architect's Journal*, vol.9, 1974, pp.451–460.

Riesman, David, *The Lonely Crowd*, Yale University Press, New Haven, 1950.

Robinson, John P., and Shaver, Phillip R., *Measures of Political Attitudes*, Survey Research Center, University of Michigan, Ann Arbor, 1969.

Robinson, John P., and Shaver, Phillip R., *Measures of Social Pscyhological Attitudes*, Survey Research Center, University of Michigan, Ann Arbor, 1969.

Rogers, Everett M, *Communication of Innovations*, Free Press, New York, 1971.

Rokeach, Milton, *The Nature of Human Values*, Free Press, New York, and Collier-Macmillan, London, 1973.

Rokeach, Milton, and Parker, Seymour, 'Values as Social Indicators Of Poverty and Race Relations in America', *Annals of the American Academy of Political and Social Science*, vol.388, 1970, pp.197–211.

Rosenau, James N., *Citizenship Between Elections*, Free Press, New York, and Collier-Macmillan, London, 1974.

Rossi, Peter H., Berk, Richard A., and Eidson, Bettye K., *The Roots of Urban Discontent*, Wiley-Interscience, New York, 1974.

Rossi, Peter H., and Williams, Walter, *Evaluating Social Programs*, Seminar Press, New York, 1972.

Rostow, Walt W., *The Stages of Economic Growth*, Cambridge University Press, London, 1960.

Rostow, Walt W., *Politics and the Stages of Economic Growth*, Cambridge University Press, London, 1971.

Rotter, Julian B., 'External Control and Internal Control' *Psychology Today*, vol.5, 1971, pp.37–42 and 58–59.

Rummel, Rudolph J. 'Dimensions of Conflict Behavior Within and Between Nations', *General Systems Yearbook*, vol.8, 1963, pp.1–50.

Rummel, Rudolph J., 'Dimensions of Conflict Behavior within Nations, 1946-59', *Journal of Conflict Resolution*, vol.10, 1966, pp.65–73.

Rummel, Rudolph J., 'Forecasting International Relations: a proposed investigation of three-mode factor analysis', *Technological Forecasting,* vol.1, 1969, pp.197–216.

Rummel, Rudolph J., *The Dimensions of Nations,* Sage Publications, Beverly Hills, 1972.

Russett, Bruce M., *World Handbook of Political and Social Indicators,* Yale University Press, New Haven, 1964.

Sachs, Ignacy, 'Marx and the Foundations of Socio-Economic Prevision', in International Social Science Research Council, *Marx and Contemporary Scientific Thought,* Mouton, The Hague, 1970.

Sackman, H., *Delphi Assessment: Expert Opinion, Forecasting and Group Process,* CA 90406, RAND Corp., Santa Monica, 1974.

Salancik, J.R., 'Assimilation of Aggregated Inputs into Delphi Forecasts: a regression analysis', *Technological Forecasting and Social Change,* vol.5, 1973, pp.243–247.

Sales, Stephen M., 'Economic Threat as a Factor in Authoritarianism: The case of the Great Depression', *Proceedings* of the 80th Annual Convention of the American Psychological Association, 1972, pp.249–250.

Schact, Richard, *Alienation,* George Allen and Unwin, London, 1971.

Schneider, Jerry B., 'The Policy Delphi: a regional planning application', *Technological Forecasting and Social Change,* vol.3, 1972, pp.481–497.

Schramm, Wilbur, and Roberts, Donald F., *The Process and Effects of Mass Communication* (rev. ed.), University of Illinois Press, Urbana, 1971.

Schulz, Ann, 'The Role of Legislatures and Comparative Research', *Journal of Comparative Administration,* vol.4, 1972, pp.117–124.

Schwartzmann, Simon, 'International System and International Tensions: a research report', *Bulletin Soziologisches Institut de Universität Zurich,* no.9, 1968.

Scolnik, Hugo, 'On a Methodological Criticism of the Meadows World 3 Model', unpublished paper, Department of Mathematics, Fundación Bariloche, San Carlos de Bariloche, Argentina, 1974.

Shapiro, Michael J., and Neubauer, Deane E., 'Meta-Advocacy in Comparative Political Analysis,' *Journal of Comparative Administration,* vol.5, 1973, pp.343–365.

Sharkansky, Ira, and Hofferbert, Richard I., 'Dimensions of State Politics, Economics and Public Policy', *American Political Science Review,* vol.63, 1969, pp.867–879.

Sheldon, Eleanor Bernert, and Freeman, Howard E., 'Notes on Social Indicators: Promise and Potential', *Policy Sciences,* vol.1, 1970, pp.97–111.

Sheldon, Eleanor Bernert, and Moore, Wilbert E., *Indicators of Social Change,* Russell Sage Foundation, New York, 1968.

Shingles, Richard D., 'Organizational Membership and Attitude Change', in Caparaso, J.A., and Roos, L.R. (eds), 1973.

Shonfield, Andrew, *Modern Capitalism,* (rev.ed.), Oxford University Press, London, 1969.

Shonfield, Andrew, 'Research and Public Policy. Lessons From Economics', in Cherns, A.B., Sinclair, R., and Jenkins, W.I. (eds), *Social Science and Government: Policies and Problems,* Tavistock Publications, London, 1972.

Sigelman, Lee, 'Modernization and the Political system: a critique and preliminary empirical analysis', *Sage Professional Papers in Comparative Politics,* vol.2, no.01–016, 1971.

Sigelman, Lee, and Narrol, Raoul, 'Holonational Bibliography: first supplement', *Comparative Political Studies,* vol.7, 1974, pp.357–382.

Simon, William, 'Reflections on the relationship between the individual and society', in *Human. Futures,* a *Futures* special publication, IPC Press, Guildford, Surrey, 1974.

Skjelsbaek, Kjell, 'Development of the Systems of International Organizations: a diachronic analysis', in *Proceedings* of the International Peace Research Association 3rd Conference, vol.2, Van Gorcum, Assen, Netherlands, 1970.

Sklair, Leslie, *The Sociology of Progress,* Routledge and Kegan Paul, London, 1970.

Sklair, Leslie, *Organized Knowledge,* Paladin Books, St Albans, 1973.

Skutsch, Margaret, and Schofer, J.G., 'Goals-Delphi for Urban Planning', *Socio-Economic Planning Science,* vol.7, 1973, pp.305–313.

Smith, A.K. Jr, 'Socioeconomic Development and Political Democracy: A causal analysis', *Midwest Journal of Political Science,* vol.30, 1969, pp.95–125.

Smith, Richard W., 'A Theoretical Basis for Participatory Planning', *Policy Sciences,* vol.4, 1973, pp.275–296.

Smith, Tom W. (compiler), *Social Change and the General Social Survey: an annotated bibliography,* National Opinion Research Center, Chicago, 1974.

Snow, Peter G., 'A Scalogram Analysis of Political Development', *American Behavioral Scientist,* vol.9, 1966, pp.33–36.

Snyder, David and Tilly, Charles, 'Hardship and Collective Violence in France, 1830–1960', *American Sociological Review,* vol.37, 1972, pp.520–532.

Snyder, David, and Tilly, Charles, 'On Debating and Falsifying Theories of

Collective Violence', *American Sociological Review,* vol.39, 1974, pp.607–611.

Sorokin, Pitirim A., *Society, Culture and Personality,* Harper and Bros. New York, 1947.

Sorokin, Pitirim A., *Social Philosophers in an Age of Crisis,* Beacon Press, Boston, 1950.

Sorokin, Pitirim A., *Social and Cultural Dynamics,* Porter Sargent, Boston, 1957.

Stauffer, Robert B., 'Great-Power Constraints on Political Development', *Studies in Comparative International Development,* vol.6, no.073, 1971.

Stefflre, Volney, 'Long-term Forecasting and the Problem of Large-Scale Wars', *Futures,* vol.6, 1974, pp.302–308.

Stober, G.J., and Schumacher, D., *Technology Assessment and Quality of Life,* Elsevier, Amsterdam, 1973.

Stone, Philip J., et al, *The General Inquirer: a computer approach to content analysis,* MIT Press, Cambridge, Mass, 1966.

Stringer, Peter, 'Individuals Evaluate Alternatives for a Shopping Centre Redevelopment', paper presented as seminar at University of Sussex on Retailing and Local Planning, PTRC/P/70, 1973.

Sunshine, Jonathan, 'Comparative Studies and Causal Analysis: a new approach', *Journal of Comparative Administration,* vol.5, 1973, pp.315–342.

Szalai, Alexander, *The Use of Time,* Mouton, The Hague and Paris, 1972.

Tanter, Raymond, 'Dimensions of Conflict Behavior within and between nations, 1958–60', *Journal of Conflict Resolution,* vol.10, 1966, pp.41–64.

Taylor, Charles L., and Hudson, Michael C., *World Handbook of Political and Social Indicators* (2nd ed), Yale University Press, New Haven, 1972.

Taylor, Maureen, and Stringer, Peter, 'Case Study 2: South London', *Journal of the Royal Town Planning Institute,* vol.29, 1973, pp.171–174.

Tilly, Charles, 'A Travers Le Chaos des Vivants Cités', in Meadows, P. and Mizruchi, E. (eds), *Urbanism, Urbanization and Change,* Addison-Wesley, Reading, Mass, 1969,(a).

Tilly, Charles, 'Collective Violence in European Perspective', in Graham, H.D., and Gurr, T.R. (eds), 1969,(b).

Tilly, Charles, 'Does Modernization breed Revolution?', *Comparative Politics,* vol.5, 1973, pp.425–447.

Toffler, Alvin, *Future Shock,* Bodley Head, London, 1970.

216

Touraine, Alain, *The Post-Industrial Society*, Random House, New York, 1971.

Triesman, David, 'The Radical Use of Official Data', in Armistead, N. (ed), *Reconstructing Social Psychology*, Penguin Books, Harmondsworth, Middlesex, 1974.

Trist, Eric, 'Structural Change in Post-Industrial Society', in Emery, F. and Trist, E. *Towards a Social Ecology*, Plenum Press, London, 1972, reprinted in Cross, N., Elliot, D., and Roy, R. (eds), 1974.

Tudor, Bill, 'A Specification of Relationships between Job Complexity and Powerlessness', *American Sociological Review*, vol.37, 1972, pp.596–604.

Tugendhat, Christopher, *The Multinationals*, Eyre and Spottiswoode, London, 1971.

Turner, Louis, *Multinationals and the Third World*, Allen Lane, London, 1974.

Turoff, Murray, 'The Delphi Conference', *The Futurist*, vol.5, 1971, pp.55–57.

Umpleby, Stuart, *The Delphi Exploration*, Computer-based Education Research Laboratory, University of Illinois (Social Implications of Science and Technology, report F1), Urbana, Ill, 1969.

Van Dusen, Roxann A., 'International Social Indicators', paper presented at Annual Convention of International Studies Association, St Louis, March 1974.

Vanecko, J.J., 'Community Mobilization and Institutional Change', *Social Science Quarterly*, vol.50, no.3, 1969.

Verba, Sidney, et al., 'The Modes of Participation: continuities in research', *Comparative Political Studies*, vol.6, 1973, pp.235–250.

Verba, Sidney, Nie, Norman H., and Kim, Jae-On, 'The Modes of Democratic Participation: a cross-national comparison', *Sage Professional Papers in Comparative Politics*, vol.2, no.01–013, 1971.

Wachs, Martin, and Kumagai, T. Gordon, 'Physical Accessibility as a Social Indicator' *Socio-Economic Planning Science*, vol.7, 1963, pp.436–456.

Waskow, Arthur I., 'The Historian's Role in Futures Research', *Futures*, vol.1, 1968, pp.117–124.

Waxman, Chaim I., (ed), *The End of Ideology Debate*, Simon and Schuster, New York, 1968.

Weaver, William Timothy, 'An Exploration into the Relationship between Conceptual Level and Forecasting Future Events', Ph.D. dissertation, Education, theory and practice, Syracuse University, 1969.

Webb, E.J., et al., *Unobtrusive Measures: Nonreactive research in the social sciences*, Rand-McNally, Chicago, 1966.

Weil, Herman M., 'Domestic and International Violence: a forecasting approach', *Futures*, vol.6, 1974, pp.477–485.

Weisskopf, Walter A., *Alienation and Economics*, E.P. Dutton, New York, 1971

Welfling, Mary, 'Political Institutionalization: Comparative Analyses of African Political Systems', *Sage Professional Papers in Comparative Politics*, vol.4, no.01–041, 1973.

Wertheim, W.F., *Evolution and Revolution*, Penguin Books, Harmondsworth, Middlesex, 1974.

Wilcox, Leslie, et al., *Social Indicators and Societal Monitoring*, Elsevier, Amsterdam, 1972.

Wilensky, Harold L., *Organizational Intelligence*, Basic Books, New York, 1967.

Willems, Edwin P., 'Behavioral Ecology and Experimental Analysis: Courtship is not Enough', in Nesselroude, J.R., and Reese, H.W. (eds), *Life-Span Developmental Psychology*, Academic Press, New York, 1973.

Willems, Edwin P., and Rausch, H.C. (eds), *Naturalistic Viewpoints in Psychological Research*, Holt, Rinehart and Winston, New York, 1969,

Williams, Robin M., Jr, 'A model of society – the American Case', in Gross, B.M. (ed), *A Great Society*, Basic Books, New York, 1968.

Wilson, A.G., 'On some problems in Urban and Regional Modelling', in Chisholm, M., Frey, A.E., and Haggett, P. (eds), *Regional Forecasting*, Butterworths, London, 1971.

Wilson, Andrew, *War Gaming*, Penguin Books, Harmondsworth, Middlesex, 1970.

Wilson, James Q., *Political Organizations*, Basic Books, New York, 1973.

Wilson, John Oliver, 'Qaulity of Life in the United States – an excursion into the new frontier of socioeconomic indicators', in Environmental Protection Agency, 1973.

Winham, Gilbert R., 'Political Development and Lerner's Theory: Further Test of a Causal Model', *American Political Science Review*, vol.68, 1970, pp.810–818.

Winthrop, Henry, 'The Sociologist and the Study of the Future', *American Sociologist*, vol.3, 1968, pp.136–145.

Wolfson, Robert J., 'In the Hawks Nest', *Society*, vol.9, 1972, pp.18–24 and 58–60.

Wynn, Mark, Rubin, Theodore, and Franco, G. Robert, 'Forecasting International Relations', *The Futurist*, vol.7, 1973, pp.244–249.

Wynne, Brian, 'At the Limits of Assessment', in Stober, G.J. and Schumacher, D. (eds), 1973.

Wynne, Brian, paper on technology assessment to appear in *Research Policy,* vol.3, 1975.

Yin, Robert K., and Lucas, William A., 'Decentralization and Alienation', *Policy Sciences,* vol.4, 1973, pp.327–336.

Young, Michael (ed), *Forecasting and the Social Sciences,* Heinemann, London, 1968.

Zeitlin, Maurice, 'Corporate Ownership and Control: the large corporation and the capitalist class', *American Journal of Sociology,* vol.79, 1974, pp.1073–1119.

Index

criticism and appraisal 91—5;
comprehensiveness critique 95—103;
as ideology 103—9; of psychological
states, research and analysis 109—21;
of political structure 153—61; *see
also* Political research; Social
indicators movement
Inference, *see* Objectivity, Inference and
Measurement in social
Inglehart (1971) 84, 138—9
Inkeles (1971) 117
Inkeles and Smith (1970) 142
Instability 170—7
Institute for the Future (1954) 59
Institute of Social Research (State of
Oregon, US), (1974) 96
Italy, political survey in 148

Jackman (1974) 159
Jantsch (1967) 41, 60
Japan, political survey in 149
Jelin (1974) 138
Jencks (1972) 34—5, 133—4
Joes (1974) 166
de Joevenel (1967) 6, 63, 187
Judd (1972) 190
Judgement forecasting 42, 46, 51, 54
Jungk (1969) 59—60, 187

Kahn, Herman 7, 39—40, 127
Kahn and Wiener (1967) 57, 66—7,
68, 152
Kanter (1972, 1973) 101
Katona, Strumpel and Zahn (1971) 139
Kegley (1973) 150
Kelly (1972) 138, 143
Keniston (1968) 138
Kerlinger (1964) 28
Kerr et al. (1962) 3, 6
Keynes, John M. 93, 104
Kim (1971) 159
Klage (1973) 95
Klapp (1969) 142
Kleinberg (1973) 128—33
Knutson (1973) 96
Koelle (1974) 62, 106, 190
Kornberg, Falcone and Mishler (1973)
100
Kramer (1969) 187
Kroeber (1944) 68, 94
Kuhm (1962) 94
Kumar (1972) 60, 126, 154, 156

Laird (1973) 120
Lamont (1973) 189
Land (1970, 1971) 88
Lane (1965) 136
LaPiere (1965) 66
Lasch (1970) 107, 130, 187; (1973)
127, 130
Laslett (1971) 102
Lazarsfeld, Pasanella and Rosenberg
(1972) 99
Leighton (1969) 143
Lerner (1958) 149, 162—3
Levy (1969) 143
Limits to Growth, The (Meadows) (1972)
53, 182
Lipset (1959) 162; (1963), 37, 125
134
Lodhi and Tilly (1973) 143, 176
Lynn (1971) 27

McClelland (1961) 116
McClelland and Winter (1969) 117, 150
McCoy and Playford (1967) 37
McCrone and Cnudde (1967) 162—4
McEvoy (1972) 182
McNamara, Robert 56, 130
Mainstream Futures Research 56, 183
Malthus, Thomas R. 2, 41
Manheim (1972) 187
Mankind 2000 Project 59, 63
Mann (1970) 119, 137; (1973) 138,
144
Marcuse (1964) 107—8, 125
Marien (1973) 123
Martino (1973) 49
Maruyama (1970) 189; (1973, 1974)
105
Marx, Karl 2, 14, 15, 40, 65, 66, 69, 127
Marx (1897) 69
Marx and Engels (1949) 69
Marxism 5—6, 9, 13—15, 45, 62, 126,
183, 185
Maslow (1954) 138
Mason's Dialectical Inquiring System 62
Mass observation project (Britain) 111
Mathiason (1972) 188
Meadow's World 3 Model 53
Measurement in social, *see* Objectivity,
inference and measurement in social
Merton (1957) 79
Mexico, political survey in 148
Miles (1974) 110, 136, 139, 142; (1975)
95

224

The Author

After a first degree in psychology Ian Miles joined the Science Policy Research Unit, the University of Sussex in 1972 and is now Research Fellow there.